In the Shadow of Angkor _____

MĀNOA 16:1   UNIVERSITY   HONOLULU
OF HAWAI'I
PRESS

In the Shadow of Angkor

CONTEMPORARY WRITING FROM CAMBODIA

Frank Stewart

EDITOR

Sharon May

FEATURE EDITOR

Centering, The Bayon,
Angkor Thom, 2002
Photograph by Richard Murai

Editor Frank Stewart

Managing Editor Pat Matsueda

Associate Editor Brent Fujinaka

Designer and Art Editor Barbara Pope

Typesetting Monkeypod Ink

Fiction Editor Ian MacMillan

Poetry and Nonfiction Editor Frank Stewart

Reviews Editor Leza Lowitz

Assistant Editors Georganne Nordstrom (managing),
Amber Stierli (editorial), Susan Bates (fiction)

Abernethy Fellow Leigh Saffold

Staff Jenny Ryun Foster, Lavonne Leong, Kathleen Matsueda,
Josh Morse, Lisa Ottiger, Michelle Pond, Shayne Takahashi

Corresponding Editors for North America
Fred Chappell, T. R. Hummer, Charles Johnson, Maxine Hong Kingston,
Michael Ondaatje, Alberto Ríos, Arthur Sze, Tobias Wolff

Corresponding Editors for Asia and the Pacific
CHINA   Howard Goldblatt, Ding Zuxin
HONG KONG   Shirley Geok-lin Lim
INDONESIA   John H. McGlynn
JAPAN   Masao Miyoshi, Leza Lowitz
KOREA   Kim Uchang, Bruce Fulton
NEW ZEALAND AND SOUTH PACIFIC   Vilsoni Hereniko
PACIFIC LATIN AMERICA   H. E. Francis, James Hoggard
PHILIPPINES   Alfred A. Yuson
WESTERN CANADA   Charlene Gilmore

Advisory Group Esther K. Arinaga, William H. Hamilton, Joseph O'Mealy,
Franklin S. Odo, Robert Shapard, Marjorie Sinclair

Founded in 1988 by Robert Shapard and Frank Stewart.

Permissions and acknowledgments can be found on page 216.

Mānoa is published twice a year. Subscriptions: U.S.A. and Canada—individuals $22 one year, $40 two years; institutions $40 one year, $72 two years. Subscriptions: other countries—individuals $25 one year, $45 two years; institutions $40 one year, $72 two years; air mail, add $24 a year. Single copies: U.S.A. and Canada—$20; other countries—$20. Call toll free 1-888-UHPRESS. We accept checks, money orders, VISA, or MasterCard, payable to University of Hawai'i Press, 2840 Kolowalu Street, Honolulu, HI 96822, U.S.A. Claims for issues not received will be honored until 180 days past the date of publication; thereafter, the single-copy rate will be charged.

Manuscripts may be sent to *Mānoa*, English Department, University of Hawai'i, Honolulu, HI 96822. Please include self-addressed, stamped envelope for return of manuscript or for our reply.

http://manoajournal.hawaii.edu/
http://www.uhpress.hawaii.edu/journals/manoa/

CONTENTS

⑥ Contemporary Writing from Cambodia

Avalokiteshvara (Compassionate Buddha),
The Bayon, Angkor Thom, 2002
Photograph by Richard Murai

Editor's Note

In the Shadow of Angkor marks the twenty-fifth anniversary of the defeat of the Khmer Rouge regime in Cambodia and celebrates the rise of a generation of writers and artists—the youngest of them born after the regime fell—who are actively restoring, wherever possible, what the Khmer Rouge destroyed: their country's physical and spiritual heritage, historical truth, literacy, and the freedom to create art of international importance in all its various forms of expression.

The obstacles to a renaissance in Cambodia's art and culture are significant, particularly in the area of literature. When Angkar, the "Organization" of the Communist Party of Kampuchea, set about eliminating real and imagined opponents to its authority, among the first to be killed were people who were educated or appeared to be educated, such as teachers, writers, artists, professionals, and civil servants—followed by those who happened to wear glasses or live in the cities, those who understood a foreign language, monks, nuns, and lay Buddhists.

The regime tried to destroy the country's libraries and with them the heritage of Cambodia's rich written and oral literature, as well as all traces of its excellent twentieth-century novelists and poets. Angkar's attempt to make the population illiterate almost succeeded. A February 2003 report by the Center for Khmer Studies, in Siem Reap, found that seventy percent of Cambodians over the age of fifteen are "not really literate." Access to books, whether through libraries or booksellers, continues to be extremely limited. Indeed, while gathering work for *In the Shadow of Angkor*, guest editor Sharon May came to know well the devastating effects of the last twenty-five years on literature and writers. At the same time, she was heartened by the efforts being exerted by Cambodians to renew their literature, promote publishing, and encourage reading. Some of those efforts are described in her interviews with Cambodian and Cambodian American writers.

Not only is there a shortage of printed books in Cambodia but a lack of Cambodian literature in translation, especially in the West. Here too, however, support for Khmer writers is growing. In her overview essay in this volume, May describes meeting French translator Christophe Macquet at a café in Phnom Penh. She and Macquet marveled at the coincidence that they were on similar quests at the same time: gathering and translating Cambodian literature for Western readers.

Writing about his research in the French journal *Europe,* Macquet rhetorically asks, "Who has ever had the occasion to read a Cambodian novel?" He replies, "No one, since there isn't a single title in French bookstores." However, Macquet points out, this absence of books does not mean that literature has not been and is not now being written in Cambodia:

> Since the 1950s, no less than 2,000 novels and collections of short stories have been published in Cambodia, which, considering the size of the country and the local publishing structures, is significant. The production is very diverse: sentimental novels, adventure novels, mysteries, spy novels, historical novels, comic novels, political, erotic, philosophical, etc. During more than half a century (an extremely short time if one thinks of the slow development of the European novel), Cambodian writers, often under difficult circumstances, invented the Khmer *pralamlok,* a new concept, a new object, a new way of narrating and listening to stories, a new form of writing, in prose, at the crossroads of Western and Asian influences....
>
> [There has been in those fifty years] the elaboration of a truly Khmer literature (in its themes, metaphors, grammar of silences, gazes, smiles) obsessed with modernity, with freedom (and the recurrent theme of imprisonment), with the loss of a greater time, of an original perfection, with an identity quest *(What is it to be Cambodian? What is the Khmer nation? What are today's people in comparison with the founders of Angkor?).* We see the growth of a literature orphaned of myth that begins to reflect on history, politics, the human condition, or the other way around, to try to mime a "lost paradise," a buried happiness, an old fossilized joy....
>
> The novel and the short story in Cambodia have followed the uneven contours of modernity, with numerous dazzling moments but also with frightening steps back (the worst of them: the Khmer Rouge horror, criminal crystallization of a fantasy of purity, of power and self-sufficiency, absolute hatred of modernity and subjectivity). Still, over the long run, one can distinguish a progressive evolution, marked by the political involvement of exceptional intellectuals and writers, punctuated by the appearance of new works, often remarkable in their composition and writing. [Translated by Daniela Hurezanu]

After meeting with May, Macquet generously offered *Mānoa* his French translations of five of Cambodia's most prominent writers whose careers began before the Khmer Rouge period: Khun Srun, Soth Polin, Hak Chhay Hok, Chuth Khay, and Kong Bunchhoeun. All were born between 1939 and 1945. We have translated them from French to English for this volume.

These five authors—two were killed by the Khmer Rouge and the rest forced into exile—are representative of the exceptional Cambodian writers whose contributions to the literature of the country were cut short by the Khmer Rouge regime's policies. Their work demonstrates their familiarity with modern Western literature and philosophy, particularly French, and the innovative ways in which they blended the new with the old and expressed a sensibility distinctly Khmer.

In the Shadow of Angkor also contains the work of Cambodian poet U Sam Oeur. Like the novelists of his generation, who began writing before 1975, U Sam Oeur is also an innovator, pushing the Khmer language to evolve and to absorb the best of modernity and internationalism. His work is presented here in the company of an innovative poet two generations younger. Born at the end of the Khmer Rouge regime and now residing in Long Beach, California, praCh uses the contemporary rhythms and rhymes of American rap and hip-hop music to create a bilingual, bicultural bridge between the past and the future, between two countries that are more closely linked than many Americans realize.

We're also fortunate to be able to publish the script of a documentary by the acclaimed Cambodian-French filmmaker Rithy Panh. His 1996 work, *Bophana: A Cambodian Tragedy,* shows in stark detail the courage of two lovers who defy totalitarianism. It also describes how, by means of writing, individuals are able to maintain their humanity and resist evil—and, therefore, why the freedom to write is always a threat to authoritarian regimes.

The stunning photographs of Richard Murai, most of which were taken at Angkor Wat, are an appropriate complement to the literature in this volume. In a sense, all of the works in this volume—whether rap lyrics, screenplay, folktales, memoirs, poetry, or supernatural tales—exist in the shadow of the great temple complex of Angkor Wat. Rising like a mysterious mountain filled with gods, Angkor Wat symbolizes Cambodia's past grandeur and its long tradition of spiritual contemplation. Its twelfth century architects created a structure that would be a harmonious reflection of the spiritual cosmos. On the temple's walls, in its galleries and courtyards, are carvings of the myriad demons, *asuras,* and the myriad beneficent gods, *devas,* who oppose their evil. As the struggle between demons and gods rages throughout eternity's long Brahmanic cycles, it is acted out in like manner in the light and shadows of Angkor Wat. Each great cycle ultimately ennobles life: over and over, the *asuras* are defeated by goodness, and the age of purity is restored—giving proof, as the great Buddhist teacher Maha Ghosananda writes at the end of this volume, that "peace is the strongest force in the world."

Smoking Man, Ta Som Temple,
Angkor Complex, 2002
Photograph by Richard Murai

Communicate, They Say

It lasted for months. For months. Like a huge whirlwind in my head. I was hunted, persecuted. Some images came back repeatedly, suffocating my soul in an obsessive spiral. I saw…I saw mountains, many mountains, then, like a jewel case, a dense forest, a long necklace of intense green…I saw water stream out of the summits only to plummet in a radiance of light…I saw thousands of sprays of foam shimmer in the sun: I saw white, pure white, gleaming. I saw blues, reds, and then yellows…I saw a whole fauna breathing simultaneously in small groups: tigers, rhinoceros, and herds of axis, gaur, and wild zebra…I saw myriad birds filling the air with their beating wings, an explosion of color and piercing cries…Finally— and this was the most penetrating image—I saw in the distance, along the gorges that cut the flank of the mountains…the Khmer empire…at the apex of its glory and power…I saw the temple at Angkor dominating in all its splendor the city of Siem Reap, the royal capital, where almost two million souls were living…I saw the intrepid Khmer army come out of the temple walls to fight the enemy…I saw warriors so numerous that they covered the earth and masked the spread of the sky…

There were still other images. Many others. So many that it is impossible for me to describe them all. It was a continual unfolding, a fountain of light: it rained diamonds inside my skull; the most brilliant gems sprayed out of my head.

These marvels I would have wanted to arrange at the bottom of my soul, a kind of intimate treasure, a personal reserve that I could comfortably draw on as I slept. But in spite of their value, they brought nothing to me: no joy, not one ounce of happiness. These images, these shining forms were rather the expression of a painful conflict, of a bitter battle between two opposing realities: on the one hand, powerlessness, mediocrity, lowliness, the debris of the visible; and on the other, like a mountain, the immensity and the grandeur, the power and force of the invisible.

I won't go into detail; suffice it to say that at that time, the visible was me. Quite simply me, a Little Phnom Penher, insignificant secretary, lost in a miniscule business, which was itself lost among hundreds of others. And the invisible, that was me too; it was this great treasure lodged in my very depths, this ideal in me that gave birth to fabulous visions.

The division was complete. Unfortunately. The energy that inhabited me—that extraordinary power—proved to be incapable of destroying my weakness. Eventually, I had to admit it. I was not its master but a kind of keeper. Nothing more. I guarded this treasure, and until my death, I would have neither right nor power to use it.

The day I understood I would never be anything but this absurd custodian, this useless concierge of a treasure hall, that I would always camp out in the antechamber of my ideal, the shock was terrible. Terrible. I collapsed within myself. All my hope vanished. I felt as if my legs had been cut off.

It was unbearable. So unbearable that one day, to console myself, I bared my soul to Sary, a colleague in my office, a pretty girl, approachable and smiling. I had always been a little in love with her. Of course, I didn't dare tell her about the images swirling in my head. I made her pity my fate, telling her of my anxiety, my sadness, my apathy, my sickening lack of decisiveness. I told her I was unhappy, rudderless, alone, much too alone and alienated from others.

She stared at me for a while. Intensely. Adorably. Then she said in a decisive tone, hammering every word, "You're suffering, sweet Vanna; but do you know why? I'll tell you why. You're suffering because you do not communicate!"

"What do you mean, Sary? I don't get it."

"We've been working together for two years and I've had time to observe you: you never talk; you never mix in with the others; you never make the least bit of effort; you're always in your corner, glum, invisible, indifferent to everything."

"I don't have anything to say to them, that's why…"

I tried to get off the hook, but Sary came back with another jab. "Why do you need something to say?! What's the need?! We communicate. That's all. We communicate!"

"I see. OK. But how do you do it?"

She took some chewing gum out of her purse, popped a piece of elastic confection in her mouth, and started to think. Then she continued, chewing. "It's natural, purely automatic. You communicate like you breathe, like you drink water. Listen. Tomorrow we're going to Kep with some of the office gang. There'll be two guys, Sothy and Sophan, and two girls, Bopha and Lina. They're good friends. If you want to learn, just come with us and do exactly what we do."

I accepted and followed her advice.

The next morning at eight o'clock, we left in a 404 Familiale—Sothy's car or, rather, Sothy's father's.

When we left the suburbs of Phnom Penh, I started dissecting my friends' behavior. I was in a laboratory. I regarded myself a great scholar, a great scientist analyzing a strange phenomenon, and I must say that the results were up to my expectations as well as my curiosity: from the evidence, the three women and two men who were with me in the car were communicating.

It was an incessant babble, a long verbal diarrhea, interspersed with jokes, laughs, and mild teasing. We had to forget the fatigue of a workweek; we couldn't touch on the intimate or anything profound. They shifted from one topic to another, going from sports cars to cigarettes, cowboy movies in which the hero shoots with deadly aim, and on to money and fashion. In short, they talked about everything, and their phrases, so peremptory, contained nothing new: no new idea, no original thought, just familiar territory that they had trampled many times before. After a while, there was such a clamor that no one listened to anyone else. Wanting to talk, everyone took his turn for all it was worth, the others tapping their feet for their turns to speak.

Sophan: "Did you see what they were showing at the Lux the other day? *Adieu l'ami!* Delon was fabulous in this film! Boy, is he good looking! And so well built, if you know what I mean!"

Sothy, connecting immediately: "Well, I prefer Charles Bronson. He's not as good looking as Delon, but does he have muscles. Wow! If he gave you a punch, you'd throw up your guts! If he kicked you, you'd piss in your pants! Let me tell you, someone who can fight like that, I'd give him my daughter sight unseen! I'm even training my sons to box like him. I tell them: Don't hesitate; if some punk tries to get you, just give it to him, right in the kisser."

Sary: "In *Adieu l'ami,* the actress is sexy, without a doubt!"

Lina: "Yeah, but not as much as Lili Hua or Cheng Pei-Pei. Those two really have curves. Aye, aye, aye. And their flesh! So fresh, the texture, the sweetness…"

Sary: "Lili Hua? She's not as great as Michele Mercier! She's the most sexy! You see a little stomach or belly button and you're gone!"

Sothy: "In any case, when it's one against a hundred, no one equals the old blind Ichi. He takes out his sword and *whack! whack!* At least five dead. Go on, find someone else who can do that!"

Sophan, in a woman's voice: "As for me, you know, the other night, I was on the way from Siem Reap to Phnom Penh when the motor broke down suddenly in the province of Kompong Thom. I was completely distracted when I saw these people coming from all over, headed for the governor's house. I followed them. Once there, I saw that they were playing *ayai.* Well, my friends, it was amazing. The *smien* Penh parodied a Vietnamese song! It was more real than nature! *Aem di dow doh-dey dam-dong dao-daw dom-dam dam-dah! Ha-ha! Hee-hee!* I'm still laughing and I'm not even telling you about Lak Seng Chuoy and Compère Poismanioc! That's talent in its purest state! From eight at night to three in the morning,

I stood there, hypnotized like a *sanday* fish, its mouth open from ear to ear! Pure genius!"

Sary, cutting him off: "Yeah…we were talking about movies, Sophan, and you bore us with talk about *ayai!* Me, the other day, I went to a sensational movie. *Le Serpent-calao!* It was funny, really funny and not at all stupid! You should have seen all the people! You couldn't find a seat at Compère Mandoline! And Sak Si Sbaong! What talent—really, what talent! You're not bored at all! She's so good, Sak Si Sbaong, when she plays the *chhantea!*"

Et cetera, et cetera, et cetera, et cetera.

Watch in hand, I verified that they had been talking for more than half an hour, going in all directions—from east to west, left to right, north to south—without making any connections. They had been yapping, yapping, yapping, and their excitement had made their mouths froth. If you had seen them, you would have thought that they were talking about some treasure sent to them by the gods or some terrible secret conferred on them by heaven. They were red in the face. Their eyes bubbled over with tears. It was unbearable.

Shit! I said to myself. *It's not possible! All they did was talk about Bronson, Delon, Lili Hua, and Cheng Pei-Pei, and look at them: all twisted and frenetic like fish smashed in the head with a Viet Cong chisel! Brilliant! Really brilliant!!!*

From time to time, I was seized by fear.

When we began driving again after a bit of noodle soup at Tram Khnar, I decided to join in the adventure of conversation. I, too, was going to learn to communicate so that Sary couldn't make fun of me any longer.

But first let me describe how we were seated. Bopha and Sary were in the front with Sothy, the driver, and Lina was seated in the back between Sophan and me. So I began by turning toward Lina.

"It's great to be driving in a 404 Familiale. Our backs are cool and we're going pretty fast. Phnom Penh to Kep is less than two hours and we're not even forcing it."

Right away Lina caught the ball in midair, just like a goalie. "Yeah," she said with a haughty pout that suddenly made two adorable dimples appear, "not bad for a 404…but it's not a Mercedes…With a Mercedes, you can go 120 without veering, there's not a hint of a vibration…you can hardly hear the engine…When you press the gas, it's a real blast!"

Sophan continued: "It's not like a DS! For curves, you can't be more confident than with the DS! You can drive as fast as you like and it'll hug the road. Steering is a cinch! And the shock absorbers! What a suspension! Super comfortable for the ass! It's not by chance that de Gaulle only drove a DS…"

I ventured my opinion: "The car is one thing, but there's also the road…"

Lina retorted: "The road to Kep is impeccable. You can drive as fast as 130 kilometers."

I swerved to avoid a collision with her: "The road to Kompong Cham is not bad either."

Lina counterattacked: "Yes, but you have to take the ferry."

Then Sothy, the driver, jumped into the conversation: "It's painful to wait for the ferry, it's true, but it's worse when you have to keep slowing down to pass a bicycle or a scooter or a car in tow or when you have to swerve to avoid a dog, a cow, or a pig crossing the road."

I objected: "That's true, but you could always drive at night. It's always calmer then, and cooler!"

Lina answered: "Yes, but driving at night is always more dangerous. It's cooler, for sure, but you can always fall asleep at the wheel."

And thus our conversation continued. Having exhausted the ins and outs of cars, driving, and the condition of the roads, I finally felt that I had communicated. Especially with Lina. There was velvet in her eyes. She slid against my shoulder and took my hand in hers. What a delicious sensation!

It was then that Sary abruptly turned toward us and looked at me as if I were an abject creature, as if she wanted to knock me out right there. In an awful, arrogant tone, she said ironically, "If it's a question of cars, nothing measures up to a Deux-chevaux, isn't that true? Isn't the Deux-chevaux [*seh-pi*] the car for everyone [*pi-seh*]?!"

Lina and I were horrified. Sary's voice, her eyes, her gestures were so evil that without saying anything we moved away from each other.

The 404 was really moving, and as we had planned, we arrived in Kep at ten sharp. The sky was bright, an extraordinary, intense blue. A lazy breeze caressed the surface of the sea rhythmically. Barely out of the car, the girls ran toward the beach, their things slung across their shoulders. In two shakes, they were in their bathing suits, ready to leap into the water. The guys had no great inclination to swim, but they followed the girls. Me, I was swept away by a sudden, irrepressible desire that led me to Sary. Unfortunately, she was talking to Lina, who had a cigarette stuck in her mouth and was spewing thick clouds of smoke. I approached and overheard their conversation.

Sary: "I smoke twenty cigarettes a day."

Lina: "Ten at the most."

"The ones I like are Salem. They're light and don't irritate your nose."

"For me, the best are 555, but if there aren't any, I'll take Winstons."

"American cigarettes smell better than French."

"Yes, but if you smoke too much, you'll get cancer."

"Really? They say that with filters, that's impossible."

"I have an older brother who smokes three packs a day."

"That's not much. My father smokes four and a half packs."

I was in despair. *So this is communicating?* I asked myself. *It's nothing! It's empty! You communicate to avoid communication?*

Sary looked at me and acted as if nothing was wrong. Aloof, distant, she headed for the water. Sophan, Sothy, and Bopha joined Lina, and together they started to blabber as before, going from west to east, east to west, talking about algae growing on the shore, sea cucumbers, swimsuits, bikinis, and slings. Tired of their talk, I dropped the clothes I was carrying and ran toward Sary. She was walking along the edge of the water, her knees cutting through the waves that broke on the shore and disappeared into the sand.

I caught up with her and forced her to turn toward me by pulling hard on her arm.

"Are you mad at me, Little Sister? Why? What did I do?"

She pulled away violently, giving me a dark look that lacked any trace of love.

I ignored it and continued. "What did I do? What? It's you who wanted me to communicate. I did exactly what you said I had to do. Didn't you see?"

"I saw, yes, I saw. Don't worry, Vanna, I saw very well!"

"Let me explain, Sary. Maybe Lina, maybe she misunderstood...my... she thought...I don't give a damn about Lina...I don't give a damn about their stupid conversations...It's you I love, Sary...You I want to talk to... talk...talk about this treasure...this ideal...in my heart...because there are mountains, Sary...in me...there is a virgin forest, a lush nature...animals...flocks of birds...and between each mountain...between each mountain, there is a kingdom...a kingdom, Little Sister...the Khmer kingdom of long ago...the royal Khmer kingdom of the time of empire...I see life swarming behind the enclosure of glorious Angkor...I see our great army marching against the enemy and making the skies tremble and shaking up the whole earth...Oh, my Sary...the visible is so sad...take the side of the invisible...touch its depths...everything hidden in me...all that can be...if you also loved me...reveal itself in the light...make sense..."

I couldn't go on. Sweat flowed from everywhere. It was the first time I had really spoken. It was the first time I had called forth everything in me so precisely, so honestly. My heart was suddenly full of hope! I swallowed my saliva in small portions; I stared at my Sary with imploring eyes.

Finally, she looked at me. She pouted indecisively, as if she were trying to judge me, to evaluate me. Then her mouth opened a little, and a derisive smile tightened her cheeks. She let go these piercing words: "Gibberish! Pure gibberish! I don't understand a thing you're saying."

In a flash I lost all my courage. I babbled, "But Sary...I—"

"I understand nothing," she interrupted, "and I don't want to understand more. I didn't see you communicate with anyone. Never! With me, let's not talk about it, you were even worse than with anyone else! Until

that instant…in the car…when I thought you weren't doing that badly…
You're not going to contradict me, are you? Go…go join your Lina…Go!
Hurry!"

"Sary, please, please, listen to me…"

"I don't know how to talk pretty, Vanna! Just go join them and stop
bothering me!"

All at once a frightening explosion echoed across the sky. I raised my
head and saw, right above us, two military jets flying like arrows toward
Phnom Penh, their contrails long and straight. A bright idea crossed my
mind, and I started to shout, "Looook! Looook! Jets…!"

Sary raised her pretty face to the sky and followed the planes as they cut
through the air with dizzying speed. "Good God! With such a fast plane,
we could be in Phnom Penh in the twinkling of an eye."

"You know, today they make planes that go faster than the speed of
sound. They'll soon be in operation. The French and the English are per-
fecting the Concorde. What a marvel of technology! The Russians, they've
just built the Tupolev. Imagine: Phnom Penh to Paris in six hours!"

"Yes, but the ticket will cost a fortune…"

"Maybe not…And then, when there are a lot of them, the price will go
down."

"They say that these planes make a hell of a lot of noise, especially on
takeoff and landing…Awful noise! A mechanical thunder that makes the
earth tremble."

"Yes, and traditional routes are too short for them…"

We talked about supersonic planes until we exhausted the subject. I had
communicated perfectly. I walked near Sary and took her hand, gently
squeezing it. She didn't resist a bit. She gave me her hand and a powerful
look, one so tender that my whole body shivered. A look full of love.

"Come, Older Brother," she said in a sweet voice, "let's go swimming
farther out, where the water is deeper."

"Yes, Little Sister. Let's go out where the water is deeper."

Our fingers entwined, we cut through the crest of the waves, together heading toward the deep.

*Translation from Khmer to French by Christophe Macquet and from French
to English by Jean Toyama*

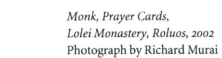

Monk, Prayer Cards,
Lolei Monastery, Roluos, 2002
Photograph by Richard Murai

Beyond Words:
An Interview with Soth Polin

Soth Polin was born in 1943 in Kompong Cham. He came from a middle-class, intellectual family, and grew up speaking both French and Khmer. Throughout his youth, he immersed himself in the classical literature of Cambodia and, at the same time, the literature and philosophy of the West. His first novel, *A Meaningless Life,* was strongly influenced by Nietzsche, Freud, and Sartre, as well as by Buddhism. It was an enormous success. Numerous novels, short stories, and philosophical tales followed, among them *The Adventurer, Whatever You Order Me...I Will Do It,* and *The Death of Love.*

Soth Polin was part of an active community of writers before the Khmer Rouge takeover. In the late 1960s, when he founded the newspaper and publishing house of Nokor Thom, he was a militant nationalist who was both anti-Sihanouk and anti-Communist. Through the publishing house, he supported the politics of Lon Nol before finally distancing himself and taking refuge in France in 1974. He worked in Paris as a taxi driver, published a French-Khmer dictionary, and published his novel *The Anarchist,* written in French. Later he and his two sons moved to America.

This interview was conducted by telephone in September 2003.

SM We've had so many interesting conversations before. You were telling me how you learned to read from your maternal great-grandfather, the poet Nou Kan. You were very young when he taught you Khmer...

SP I was four years old. He made me lift my arms up and around the top of my head. When each of my hands could reach the opposite ear, I was of the age of learning, and he began to teach me the Khmer alphabet: *ka, kha, ko, kho, ngo.* He thought I was intelligent; the other members of my family did not agree.

I was so young, but I remember when he left the province, moving from Kompong Cham to Phnom Penh. He became a member of Parliament. And so I began to write formal letters to him, helped by my mother. I was about five or six. I would write things like "From here, I sing to you over there." I would say that I missed him very much and ask that if something I wrote was not appropriate for a letter, to pardon me.

He was the patriarch of the family. We were living in his house in Kompong Cham. It was a very big house, near the pagoda, and all the family members lived there. He was educated in the Buddhist monastery. Later he became the mandarin of the king. He had the title Oknha Vibol Reach Sena [Servant of the King] Nou Kan.

SM He was a very well-known poet.

SP Yes, he was the national poet. In 1942, he received first prize for the *Teav Ek,* which is like the story of *Tum Teav.* He wrote it about thirty years after Som's *Tum Teav.*

I remember the flow of his poetry even now. What I read when I was a child was very powerful. I read his poems all day long. I loved very much the story *Inao Bosbar,* famous in Southeast Asia. I think he translated it from Thai, but he reinvented the story in his own style. I read that every day. I would sing his poems. For every one, I made a song. He was a great poet, you know. Even now, I am in love with his poems:

> *Anicha phka banan, klen khpong khpos*
> *Loeu tae chhmuos, lous tae chhmieng, tieng tot toan*
> *Sman bosbar, smeu bos bong, vong tevoan*
> *Sthet choan, sthan chuor, chhar kama.*

SM He was very prolific. He must have written every day.

SP My mother told me that after he retired from being a mandarin of the king, he wrote every night. He had passion—more than I do. Or maybe it was because he was richer. He could write without worrying about putting food on the table.

How do you say it in English: the fear of being unsuccessful? It is the sickness of every writer. But I think he had not this kind of sickness.

He was a translator and prose writer too. He translated the Chinese epic *Three Kingdoms,* and it was published by Som Mien, the paternal grandfather of Sam Rainsy. It was published bit by bit because it's a vast story. I remember reading it when I was very young. I would pass the morning reading it, separated from the world, separated from my brothers, my family.

I remember that when I was about four and a half, I wrote the word *changkran bay* [kitchen]. I was studying writing, trying to be like my great-grandfather. But I did not finish the word, writing only *changkran ba.* I left out the *yo* [the letter *y*]. My father said to me, "When you become a man, you will never finish your work."

I knew how to write that word, but I lacked the courage to finish it. I am so easily discouraged by my work. Now I have three or four unfinished novels, and I cannot forget what my father told me when I was young.

SM   Do you think that your love of writing began with your great-grand-father?

SP   Yes, with him. His books were the first ones I read. I was a shy boy. So I had his books as my world—like a spot in a garden, an Eden. When I read, nothing outside could affect me. Reading was my fortress, something that protected me, a fortress of the mind. I discovered everything in his books—not the real world, but the imaginary world.

It's true I've changed a lot since then. When I'm writing now, I have no ambition to succeed, so I have no fear either. Before, I wrote to imitate someone like my great-grandfather. I saw him as very big—a giant—so I feared him. When it was time to write by myself, I was scared I would not be able to reach him.

My great-grandfather wrote in many forms: seven-syllable, nine-syllable, four-syllable lines. In Khmer, when you recite poetry, you sing. What I sang to you earlier was in a nine-syllable form. Khmer poetry is very sophisticated in rhythm, rhyme, and alliteration, and each type of poem has a particular melody. You can improvise, though, if you know a lot about singing poems.

SM   So when you were very young, you were most influenced by Cambodian poetry.

SP   I learned to write in imitation of Cambodian poetry, but when I wrote on my own, it was in prose. There was a group of writers who wrote stories for *Reatrey Thngai Sau* [Saturday Night], which came out once a week. The magazine was very popular. I started reading it when I was about nine or ten years old. I became hooked on the stories that described the lives of couples who fell in love and got married and then suddenly were separated because the husbands disappeared in war.

I became obsessed with reading *Saturday Night*. My mother was not happy about that. She thought I had lost my mind. She felt I was a lost soul. I lived almost exclusively in literature. Later, when I became an adult, I lived in dreams and hid from reality. I had no courage to face life.

SM   Why didn't your mother want you to read?

SP   She thought I was too young for those stories. She subscribed to *Saturday Night* and kept the magazine in her room. The door was locked, so I had to climb through the window. I would read in her room and then put the magazines back exactly where I had found them and in the same order. If I heard her come home, I would jump out the window so she wouldn't know I had been in her room.

Once I was reading a shocking story about a wife who takes a lover; when the husband comes home, the lover hides in a clothes chest that is like a casket. While I was reading this story, my mother returned from the market. I heard her footsteps. I saw the same kind of chest in her room—a long chest made of wood—so I hid inside it like the character in the story and closed the lid like a casket. My mother didn't know I was in the room. I waited maybe fifteen minutes, but it felt like an eternity. When I was sure she had left, I came out.

SM What authors or novels did you read?

SP One of the first novels I read was by Madame Suy Hieng, *Stung Krohom* [The Red River]. I admired her very much. I stole that book from my mother—well, I did not steal, I read it without her consent.

It happened sometimes that I did steal money from my mother to buy novels, but just a little at a time so she wouldn't notice.

There is something I forgot to say. My mother told me that when my great-grandfather was young, he liked to write poems while sitting in the top of a sugar-palm tree. It was a way to hide himself from his mother in order to write.

SM Like you?

SP A little similar. But I am not able to climb like that. I fear the altitude.

SM You are known as a philosophical writer. How did you become interested in philosophy?

SP After Khmer high school, I had to choose a science: math or philosophy. I had no interest in math. So I chose philosophy. At that time, there was only one other Cambodian student in philosophy, so for my final year, they sent me to Lycée Descartes. That last year was taught in French.

Actually, it was a very difficult experience. When I first read Sartre, I didn't understand much, but I had no choice because I had abandoned math. So I studied hard. At the beginning, I didn't understand the reading fully, so to be successful, I tried to learn it by heart. I was reading Sartre, Nietzsche, Camus. I read certain books so many times that I memorized them. And when I wrote, their ideas came to me as if they were my own.

SM When did you write your first published novel?

SP I started writing it when I was nineteen, after I finished high school. I was reading Buddhist texts as well as Sartre, so the book was a mixture of philosophies. It's not true that I was influenced only by Occidental philosophers. I was also influenced by Buddha, by the Oriental philosophers and thinkers. My book, *Chivit at Ney* [A Meaningless Life], was influenced by Nietzsche, Sartre, and Buddha.

I published that first novel myself in 1965. I was twenty-two years old. I had sold a book of French composition essays that I wrote for high-school exams to a bookshop for twenty thousand *riels*. I used that money to publish *Chivit at Ney*. When I first wrote it, *A Meaningless Life* was not the title. It had a lot of titles. I started out with *Sophoan Sthet Khnong Duong Chet* [Charm Exists Only in the Heart], but decided that title was too sweet for me. The first run was fifteen hundred copies. It was later republished many times and was a great success. Even now, people still read it. *A Meaningless Life*. But I have changed. Back then, I thought life was meaningless, but now I see the world differently.

I had success very young, but I think that can spoil your thinking. Later, I had to leave my country. I had to know the distress of…When you lose your country, you lose everything. If you are a writer, you no longer have the echo of your readers. There is a Cambodian song I translated in West Berlin when I was homesick, *"Phot Chong Chroy"* [Missing the Cape]. There were no other Cambodians there besides my wife. The song compares Cambodia to the woman you love. In Khmer, the song is very erotic. The lyricist is saying, If I lose my country, I miss nothing, but if I lose a woman, I miss everything, I'm utterly desperate. In reality, the woman and the country are the same, and he misses it all. That song, I think, was written for a traveler.

That was 1968. I was working in West Berlin; I didn't see anything to remind me of home—no palms. I wanted to cry.

I lost my country once. And then I lost it a second time. The second time, it was permanent.

SM You also went to France in 1968.

SP Yes, I went in 1968. In 1969 I came back to Cambodia. At first I worked as an editor at my uncle's newspaper, *Khmer Ekkaraj* [Independent Khmer]. Then Prince Sihanouk threatened to put us in jail. So my uncle had to *suborder,* to kill his own paper, to save his life and mine. I had nothing to do, so I wrote *The Adventurer,* about my experiences in France, and *Whatever You Order Me…I Will Do It,* my short-story collection. At that time, I wrote the story that *Mānoa* is publishing.

A few months after that, I started *Nokor Thom* [Great Nation], but on my own. I was very young then, about twenty-seven.

SM   When did you leave Cambodia the second time?

SP   I left in 1974. In early June, my friend was assassinated. He was Thach Chea, the deputy minister of education. I think he was killed by the government, but they tried to pass it off as an assassination by the Khmer Rouge. I composed a vendetta and published it in *Nokor Thom*. It was a special edition of the newspaper that took three weeks to prepare. No one knew about it. *Nokor Thom* had been shut down and was not permitted to publish, so I had to prepare the vendetta in secret.

The title was "The Emperor Has No Clothes." Two or three hours after it was selling on the streets, I left for France. I was already at the airport with my wife and two sons. No one knew where I was. I escaped just in time.

People told me later that Phnom Penh was like a city struck by fire. A French diplomat wrote to me that the special edition was like a bomb. The military police confiscated it, then resold it to diplomats. Every copy sold out. The price went up fifty dollars a copy on the black market—that's what they told me. At the time, that was a lot of money. But I did not profit from it.

SM   You never went back to Cambodia.

SP   No, never went back. I spent ten years in France. Then I came to the United States.

SM   You wrote a novel in French, *L'Anarchiste* [The Anarchist].

SP   Yes, in 1980. The first part was a novel published in 1967 that I translated from Khmer and that was very controversial in Cambodia. It was very successful—maybe my most successful—because the government banned it. The Ministry of Information announced that anyone reading "that Soth Polin novel" risks going to jail. So I sold three or four editions on the black market, all of them gone after about a week. Because of the government, I became famous.

It was a daring novel. The title, *Chamtet Et Asor,* is ambiguous. *Chamtet* can mean "to make love" or "to provoke." *Et asor* means "without pity."

In the old Khmer folktales, there is the story of Thmenh Chey, who outwits the king. The king tells him, I don't want to see your face, so get lost! When the king passes by again, Thmenh Chey doesn't offer his face, but his backside. That book was like offering my backside to the king. I didn't write about Thmenh Chey, but I stole his style of being revolutionary, of indirectly criticizing the king. King Sihanouk had put to death many intellectuals. They were shot and hung upside down.

The word *chamtet* can also suggest absolute indifference to authority or government. Readers thought the title referred to making love, but the authorities knew that I was provoking them, so they banned the novel immediately after it was published.

SM   Your work is known for having a lot of sex.

SP   In the story *Mānoa* is publishing, there is no sex. That story was translated into Japanese. At the time, nobody liked it. You know, when I published that short-story collection [*Whatever You Order Me…I Will Do It*], nobody read it. I published it in 1969 after *The Adventurer*. I printed only two thousand copies, and they didn't sell. The short-story collection was completely, totally unsuccessful.

SM   Was *The Anarchist* popular in France?

SP   At the start, it was not. But when I came to the United States, there were no copies left. But they printed only five thousand. Now you can't find it. I have only one copy, which Tomoko Okada sent to me from Japan.

SM   What have you been writing recently?

SP   I have an unfinished novel, *Route á Palmier* [The Palm Road]. It's about a Cambodian intellectual who looks for fame in Paris, but is obliged to come home to the Palm Road. There he encounters the Khmer Rouge and is captured, along with a journalist, at the beginning of the war.

He has a diary. In it he writes about France and the Khmer Rouge, comparing life in Paris and life on the Palm Road—the killing road. After he disappears, they find only his diary. I wrote that novel in French, in Long Beach, but it's unfinished. I have no time to finish it.

I have another unfinished novel, *Angkor Princess*, a history from the Angkor times. It is also about a diary: the diary of Jayavarman VII, the greatest king of Cambodia. He writes about his first love in Angkor. I published it in French, serialized in the Long Beach newspaper *Sereipheap* [Freedom], but almost no one reads French here. Some readers wrote to ask, Is it true about the diary? Not true.

I have an unfinished dictionary too. So what my father told me—"you will never finish your work"—is like a prophecy. But the main reason, I think, is lack of money. I am not like my great-grandfather: he was the mandarin of the king. He was rich. He had a doorman, a huge house. He did not need to worry about money.

SM   What other kinds of jobs have you had?

SP   I have been driving a cab for four or five months now. I have written for newspapers. Sometimes I get royalties from France for my French-Khmer dictionary.

When I came to the United States, I was an illegal immigrant and had two kids to feed. Because I was illegal, it was hard to cope. Now I am legal, and at least I can be a cab driver. Before, I could only write for the Khmer newspapers to survive.

SM   When was the last time you published a novel?

SP   There was one published in Khmer, here in Long Beach around 1995, called *The Widow from L.A.* Other than that, since *The Anarchist,* I have published only novels serialized in the newspapers. There are not enough Cambodian readers abroad. And I haven't the means to publish in Cambodia. I have a lot of stories to tell, but don't have the opportunity. I hope I can escape my father's curse.

SM   After the war, so many writers were killed, and there has been so much destruction of culture.

SP   It is without words. It is beyond words.

SM   Do you think Cambodian literature can recover?

SP   I think it will recover. There are a lot of writers now. But it is not the same thing. What is lost is lost. There are young writers. But what we have lost will not come back.

SM   What advice do you have for young writers?

SP   That is difficult to answer. I cannot give advice to myself. How can I advise other people?

SM   What do you hope for?

SP   I hope our art continues. I think it will survive. I think Cambodia will survive. There will be another generation of writers. But right now, what we have lost is indescribable. Khun Srun, Hak Chhay Hok, Chou Thani, Kem Sat…They are gone. It is difficult now. What we have lost is not reconstructable. An epoch is finished. So when we have literature again, it will be a new literature.

Even if we had more writers of my generation, we could not succeed if we continued writing as we did. There is something that we cannot get past. It just kills the imagination. It is the atrocity of the Khmer Rouge.

Even if you are reaching in your imagination for a new destination, you cannot get past their cruelty. When you try to write something without mentioning the Khmer Rouge, you can't. The next generation will forgive that, they will forget, but for us, we cannot forgive it.

SM   You met Pol Pot.

SP   Yes, he was my teacher in a private school in 1957. At the time, his name was Saloth Sar. He was an obscure teacher, not known. He taught in a private school, not like his wife, who was famous and taught in the public schools. But I heard from my friends that he was a good French-literature teacher, so I took a special class from him for a month. It was one month only, but I cannot forget this man. He was so soft, so gentle, and people liked him as a teacher. I did not know that he was Communist. He never talked about Communism. He talked about nothing but the French poets.

I remember he loved Alfred de Vigny, the French poet who wrote "The Death of the Wolf." He talked about the stoicism of the wolf. Before dying, the wolf had bitten and killed the dogs that chased him. He admired how the wolf dies: *"Refermant ses grands yeux, meurt sans jeter un cri"* [Closing his great eyes, he dies without uttering a sound]. He admired the courage needed for that kind of death—the courage of dying without crying out.

SM   You wrote about Pol Pot in an article for *Le Monde*, *"La diabolique douceur de Pol Pot."*

SP   Yes, in 1980, when I published *The Anarchist*, I sent the article to *Le Monde*. It was also translated and published in a British literary journal and a German anthology. The article had a big impact. Not like *The Anarchist*. A lot of researchers asked me about Pol Pot. There was a journalist who came all the way from Australia to see me, and the historian David Chandler also read it and contacted me.

I still remember Pol Pot's voice, very melodious, very sweet. When I wrote about that, people hated me, especially the Cambodian intellectuals in France. When the article first came out, there was not much response, but after they read about it in Chandler's book [*Brother Number One*], they hated me. That was just a few years ago. They sent me letters and published articles saying that Pol Pot was not strong in the French language. They wanted to think he was stupid and mad and uneducated: their image of him.

SM   What was the reaction of the French intellectuals?

SP   The French didn't understand how a man who admired Verlaine or Vigny could become a monster. But they didn't hate me. I was only the messenger.

SM In 1980, when you wrote the article, did you know what had happened in Cambodia?

SP I knew it in 1975. By 1980, I knew I had lost my father and two brothers. One brother was killed in 1975 with his wife and his child while trying to escape to Thailand. My father and other brother were killed, I think, in 1978 in Kandal Province. It was not long before the end of the regime. At that time, I had a dream. In my dream, I cried. I dreamed I saw my father on the ferry that crosses the Mekong at Neak Luong. In real life, we had taken that ferry many times when we traveled by car from Phnom Penh to Prey Veng.

I dreamed that when I approached my father, he did not recognize me. "Who are you?" he asked. "Who are you?" I was so scared that my hair stood on end. He did not recognize his own son. Then I saw that his face was swollen. I asked him, "Did the Khmer Rouge do that to you?" He cried. That was in 1978, before I wrote *The Anarchist*. I think it was a presage.

I had another dream that same night. I dreamed I was walking on the street past my house in Prey Veng Province, where my father had been the chief of the veterinary agency. In my dream, I approached the house. I saw through the window that he was crying in pain, like a turtle on the fire, as we say in Khmer. It looked like he had been tortured. He was crying, but when he saw that I was watching him, he became silent. I asked him, "Father, what happened to you?" He said nothing. He was still. When I left the house, he began crying again. And then I cried.

When I wrote *The Anarchist,* I described that dream. So there is a bit of reality in that novel. But it is a shame that there is too much violence in it too. I think the book is too crude.

SM You put the violence in for readers.

SP That's what I thought in Phnom Penh. But it was a cycle I could not get out of. When you commit violence, even in fiction, you cannot get out of it.

SM When did you get the news of your father?

SP When the Vietnamese entered Phnom Penh, people were able to get in touch with their relatives. But I did not hear from my father. When you don't hear from your relatives, you have no hope. Before, you did not know if they were living or dead. But when you hear nothing, you know for sure that they are no longer of this world.

SM But your mother survived.

SP   Yes, my mother survived. She was near the Thai border. Because of the war, she had been trying to run a business there to survive. When the Khmer Rouge came, she escaped. My father was still in Phnom Penh.

SM   How did you find out about your brother who tried to cross the border in 1975?

SP   I have remorse about him. Before the fall of Phnom Penh, my brother sent me a letter asking me to take care of his son. He wanted to send his son by plane to Paris. It was just two months before the collapse of the Lon Nol government to the Khmer Rouge. But I could not do anything for him. I had no means to. I did not think then about the atrocities and cruelty of the Khmer Rouge. Nobody could foresee it. We thought that after the war, everything would be OK.

If I had taken in his son in Paris, I think he and his wife would have escaped the Khmer Rouge. But with a baby, they could not escape. It was too hard.

When I heard about my brother and his family, it was 1976. I was preparing a book about the Khmer Rouge with Bernard Hamel, a French journalist. I heard about my brother because I interviewed a lot of refugees—over one hundred people—who came to France. So I knew what had happened in Cambodia.

The book was *De sang et de larmes: La grande deportation du Cambodge* [Of blood and tears: The great deportation of Cambodia]. It was published around 1977 and was one of the first books about the Khmer Rouge. A lot of French intellectuals hated our work because at that time they were pro–Khmer Rouge. I was paid by the hour by an editor and named in the book as an assistant, but most of the work was done by me. I did not want to reveal my authorship at that time; I feared reprisals.

One of the refugees told me about my brother. I do not cry easily because I was educated that men don't cry. But when I was writing then— writing about refugees in Paris—and one of them told me my brother had been killed, I was speechless. I was crying without making a sound.

Later, when I knew about my father, it hurt even more because I feel I owe so much to him. When I left Cambodia, I promised myself I would do something for him, but I had no opportunity to.

Only to ruin him by publishing the special edition of *Nokor Thom*. After I left Phnom Penh for Paris in 1974, the government could not punish me, so they punished him. He had done nothing. He had not even known what I was doing. Not even my wife knew. When I heard two months later that my father had lost his job, it was a shock. I had vertigo. I wrote about that in *The Anarchist* too. There are a lot of things in it about my father—and a lot about myself.

When I learned later that he was no longer alive, I knew I had lost my chance to do something good for him, as I had promised when I was young. It is the feeling of all Cambodians who have lost a father or mother. It is the feeling of all Cambodians who lost their parents to the Khmer Rouge.

SM   So even though you were in France, far from Cambodia, you were affected in many ways.

SP   When I was in France, I was very affected. You miss your country, you miss your home. But you cannot go back—even if your father was killed. At that time, I abruptly lost all reason, all meaning. Maybe because of this, I became strange. My own wife could not understand me.

As I said before about the Khmer Rouge: you cannot get past it. You resuscitate a painful past, and you have to talk about it. You cannot pass over it. That is a lesson for humanity: not to let it happen again—that atrocity and that cruelty.

Maybe this is why I cannot finish my writing: because of this story. Because of this, I lost my inspiration. Because the reality surpasses the imagination.

The Diabolic Sweetness of Pol Pot

In the beginning was the Word/and the Word was with God/and the Word was God./All things were made by Him/and without Him nothing was made.   The Prologue of St. John

At the time that Pol Pot was teaching me Verlaine, I had not yet learned to distrust sweet things. In 1957, he was my French teacher, though later he claimed to have been a history teacher, in order not to appear to have been an advocate of the colonialists' culture. We knew him by the name of Saloth Sar, and nothing he said to us betrayed his engagement in politics—until the day in 1962 when he left for the resistance. I need to revise my memory of that school year: Pol Pot was not just the disciple of Verlaine who, as a good philologue, knew how to win over his students with his *explications de texte: "It rains in my heart as it rains on the city. From whence comes this languor that pierces my heart..."*

The consequences of the phantasmagoric catastrophe of human judgment that was the Khmer Rouge regime are now widely known, and it is time to take a closer look at the means by which they established themselves. Clearly, there were political and economic causes, but a cultural factor also played an important role, and until now it has been rather neglected: the use of the Cambodian language for propaganda, lie, and illusion. The word, particularly the spoken word, assumes great importance and prestige in countries with an oral tradition. In Cambodia, broadcasts by radio thus dominated the long workday. Before Phnom Penh fell, the radio transmitted Prince Sihanouk's interminable harangues; once the regime was installed, it broadcast the orders of the new masters, descriptions of an ideal society, and edifying biographies of the heroes of the revolution. Paradoxically, these broadcasts also found an avid audience over the border, in Bangkok, for they constituted the most reliable source of information about a country otherwise completely cut off from the world.

The method of the Khmer Rouge was to force together irreconcilable opposites. They presented rigidity as softness. They tangled sweetness and cruelty together until they could not be told apart. The verb *to request*, for example, became terrifying. You were never ordered, never forced to do

Grandmother and Granddaughter,
Preah Khan Temple, Angkor Thom, 2002
Photograph by Richard Murai

anything; you were *requested*…You were *requested* to give them your moped, you were *requested* to separate from your wife, you were *requested* to give yourself up to the *Organisation supérieure* [Angkar]. That is to say, you were *requested* to die…And Pol Pot, the bloody tyrant, soul of that regime, continued to present himself as a man so sociable and amiable he almost seemed naive. You could even be briefly annoyed with yourself for begrudging him his *request* for your self-genocide.

It was at the pagoda that Pol Pot learned the Khmer language. Just as Nietzsche drank deeply of Biblical poetry before doing away with God, so Pol Pot, a shaven-headed monk for many years, imbibed Buddhist poetry in the verses of religious literature and then executed Buddha. Realizing the power of language, Pol Pot kills, but he kills with poetry. His wife, Madame Khieu Ponnary, a high-born aristocrat who studied at both French and English universities, has proceeded to excite admiration by her lessons in Khmer philology. Did not Prince Sihanouk, in his *Chronicles of War and Hope,* praise her as "a woman of superior intelligence"?

It is difficult to render in translation the musicality of Cambodian verses and sayings. Yet I must try; for to do so is to realize how deeply the mass of Cambodian peasants (who knew nothing of Marxism-Leninism) responded to the poetry in the writing done by Pol Pot and Khieu Ponnary when they were in the Buddhist phase of their youth.

With his words, Pol Pot simplifies society. Everything is reduced to caricature, to extreme polarities, to a puerile Manicheanism swathed in the finery of well-turned phrases. This is what is now denounced about the old way of life: its nuances, its richness, its plurality. On the future, only one kind of new man shall impose himself, crushing all these elements in order to be no more than a sort of specimen from which one can draw millions of identical copies.

Twisted Innocence

So it is that the *petit-bourgeois* is called *sambo beb,* which literally translates as "an abundance of manners" or perhaps "a profusion of styles." Hence this nursery rhyme for grown-ups was composed:

> *Let us destroy monarchy, and establish Angkar;*
> *let us destroy taxes, and establish voluntary contributions;*
> *let us destroy the white, and glorify the black;*
> *let us dignify the unlettered, and eradicate the learned.*

Pin Yathay, in his book *Utopie Meurtrière* [published in English as *Stay Alive, My Son*], gives a characteristic example of the effect these sweetly seductive words can have on a simple soul. He describes a man dumping bundles of dollars into the Mekong, inflamed with hatred by the propaganda against the "profusion of styles."

Taken to its logical extreme, Pol Pot's reductive Manicheanism strips away all the layers of language and all the richness of traditional vocabulary. For example, there used to be a thousand and one ways to speak of eating or drinking or smoking, depending on one's social position, age, and degree of intimacy with one's interlocutor. These days, woe betide he who uses a forbidden word. Even denouncing yourself for having been "anti-revolutionary" would mark you for elimination.

The novelist Chuth Khay, who miraculously survived the regime, owed his survival only to a stratagem; for four years he passed himself off as a street vendor of bread who was almost deaf and hardly spoke. Others were betrayed by their skill with language, denounced for witchcraft by the children of the regime, and had their chests opened and their livers ripped out.

"The trees in the country, the fruit to the city." This Khmer Rouge refrain exploits the common sense of traditional maxims to generate resentment against city dwellers. Repeated a thousand times, it convinces peasants that eliminating those from cities is a right—even better, an imperative. Repeated a thousand times, this slogan has created an unquenchable hatred.

"To preserve you is no gain; to destroy you is no loss." A murderous distortion of the Buddhist proverb "Nothing is lost, only transformed." It is a slogan whose assonances and rhythm fall so perfectly in Khmer that it rings true without the slightest reflection. Taking possession of young girls whose naive smiles make them look as if they have hardly grown out of children's games, this incendiary phrase makes children into hardened killers confident of their righteousness. In a crowd, the individual's mentality is lost. Each person abandons his judgment to the group, to the party, to Angkar. Original faculties of reason and natural feeling dissolve under the influence of a language that acts like a drug.

I find this revolting. It is because they are more susceptible to the seductive powers of language that children and young women have become the most unflinching executioners out of all the murderers who have armed themselves and violated their consciences. Innumerable testimonies report they have killed without faltering, without blinking, as a smile played upon their lips. It is a perfect illustration of what words can do to innocence.

What is more, the blame is not on the individual, for it is the group that kills. And the more people one kills, the more merit one acquires in this new faith. Buddhists say, "The life of a man is a bowl of ashes." Buddhists cremate their dead, but under the Khmer Rouge, it is the living who are already ash. Death inscribes itself into all things; of their own accord, the coffinless dead melt indiscriminately into the material world. "To preserve a man is no gain; to destroy him is no loss."

The universe of the Khmer Rouge is the result of the most fearless trip to the limits of materialism. Man is a standardized robot; he has lost his soul. For the Khmer Rouge, what the Buddhists call soul becomes the "garden of the individual." Would illiterate peasants have invented so poetic a formula? This bourgeois garden is cluttered with undesirable plants and needs weeding. A little culture, a few diplomas—these must be thoroughly uprooted and cast far away, beyond even that glassy pond of being and nonbeing that is Nirvana. For the individual, there can be no secret garden, no memories, no compassion, no love. The soul must not be furnished in any fashion. The soul has entered the void; the body has only to follow.

And if the glamour of murder converts only some of the people, those latecomers to the collective madness end up carrying their own children to the row of victims awaiting the judgment of the butchers. For the Khmer Rouge do not want to let their newfound power slip from their grasp, and "it is better to make a mistake too early than to make it too late."

Never has the terrible weapon that is human language had such satanic efficiency. The words of the Khmer Rouge have created an apocalypse. From Buddha to Nietzsche, by way of Dostoyevsky, thinkers and poets have often toyed with words rank with nihilism…yet they always stopped short of the precipice. At the last moment, they diffused the spells they had uttered. But Pol Pot, the madman who takes himself for a vengeful god, has stepped over the edge. Life is worth nothing. A man is a louse to be crushed. And so a Cambodian prophecy is fulfilled: "The scholars go down into hell; the ignorant mount to Paradise."

Translation by Jeremy Colvin and Lavonne Leong

Caretaker, Entrance, The Bayon,
Angkor Thom, 2002
Photograph by Richard Murai

SHARON MAY

In the Shadow of Angkor:
A Search for Cambodian Literature

If its writing disappears, the nation vanishes.   Kambuja Surya, 1962

"You know, there is no tradition of the Western novel in Cambodia."

The man who declares this—an American journalist I have met my first morning back in Phnom Penh—speaks with such conviction that if I did not know better, I might believe him and be tempted to head right back to the United States. Instead, I stare at him in shock and a dizzy fatigue born of jet lag and the euphoria of being in Cambodia again. I haven't slept in seventy-two hours and can hardly speak, except to explain to him that I am looking for contemporary Cambodian writing, including novel excerpts, for a special issue of *Mānoa*, a journal published by the University of Hawai'i Press. He continues, "It's just not a very literate culture."

If I wasn't so tired, I would tell him that the modern novel appeared in Cambodia in the late 1930s and that over a thousand were published between 1950 and 1975, when the Khmer Rouge took over. I would say that you could ask almost any Cambodian educated before 1975 about the novels taught in school, and he or she would likely recall *The Rose of Pailan*, *The Waters of Tonle Sap*, *Sophat*, *The Wilted Flower*. I imagine they would name these books with a thinly disguised yearning and then laugh, saying they didn't have time to read anymore. If I wasn't so tired, I would ask the journalist if he knew the Khmer term for novel, *pralomlok*, and its literal meaning: a story that is written to seduce the hearts of human beings.

But I say nothing and continue to stare at him dumbfounded. As the journalist turns on the front steps to leave, I show him a copy of *Secret Places*, the issue of *Mānoa* with writing from Nepal.

"Well," he says, "I think the Cambodia book will be rather slimmer than that."

This trip, in December 2002, is my second to Cambodia in two years and is more than a search for Khmer literature. I first went to the Cambodian refugee camps in the mid-1980s, after the fall of the Khmer Rouge regime. I still don't have a good explanation of why I went.

I could say my journey began a couple of years before, with a photograph I saw in a magazine: three Cambodian women trudging up a charred hillside. Burnt rice stubble covered the ashen earth. The sky was drained of color, and the land desolate except for the three figures heading away from the camera. Only later would I wonder about the frames I couldn't see: the burning of the hillside that preceded that moment; the empty landscape after the women had passed. On the film's next frames, were there just two women? One? Did any of the three survive the Khmer Rouge?

At the time, I knew almost nothing about Cambodia. The instructor in my freshman writing course had asked us to describe a photograph, and I had quickly chosen this one from the magazines fanned out on the table. I was partly lured by the photograph's composition and color: the S-turn of the path, the symmetry of the three women, the shades of ash and sun-faded clothing. I imagined the women silent, wrapped in grief or exhaustion. I assumed they weren't speaking, that their world was devoid of life and sound.

Now I wonder why I didn't imagine that they might have been exchanging stories, singing, or perhaps even laughing over word play. It seemed nothing could survive in that landscape. Yet not only did the women exist, but they had passed often enough to trace a path through the jagged rice stubble.

Two years later, I found myself in the Cambodian refugee camps in Thailand. I arrived at the beginning of the monsoon season, armed with a camera, a press pass from the university weekly, about fifty rolls of bulk-loaded film, and several bottles of BullFrog mosquito repellent. What little I knew about Cambodia I had gleaned from watching the movie *The Killing Fields*.

My guide for the next three weeks was a priest who was working in Site Two, a camp located about half a mile from the heavily mined frontier at the base of the Dangrek Mountains. At that time, 140,000 people lived in Site Two, making it the third largest community of Cambodians in the world, the first two being Phnom Penh and Long Beach, California.

It was at Site Two that I first saw a performance of part of the Reamker, the Cambodian Ramayana. This epic narrative poem is one of the oldest and most famous pieces of literature to survive in Cambodia. Its stories have been carved into the stones of Angkor, performed in shadow plays, danced by the Royal Ballet and popular dance troupes, and sung by storytellers in performances that lasted for days.

I saw the Reamker danced on a square of blue U.N. tarp under a thatch roof. A large crowd had gathered to watch. In the back corner, old men played traditional instruments: flutes, hand drums, curved xylophones, and other instruments. A few feet away sat the singers, who were old women. In contrast, the dancers were young; many of them, I would learn, had been born in the border camps. The instructor was a former principal dancer with the Royal Ballet of Cambodia and one of the few performers who had survived the Khmer Rouge. She walked among the young dancers, raising an elbow, positioning a wrist, bending back curved fingers, adjusting the tilt of a head, the arch of a back. I was mesmerized by the beauty and precision of the dancers' movements, the music, the keening voices of the singers.

After the performance, the priest who was my guide told me that during the previous dry season, the camp had been attacked during a dance. As shells exploded, the dancers continued performing and the musicians playing. He couldn't believe it, he said. They continued until they finished the dance.

The day my three-week journalist's pass expired, the priest drove me out of the camp and through the seven military checkpoints on the way to Aranyaprathet, where the foreigners lived.

"So," he asked as we left the camp behind, "when are you coming back?"

"When are you getting me a job?" I replied, half in jest.

To my surprise, he did just that. I was soon back in Site Two, teaching English and learning Khmer. If why I came was unclear, why I stayed was not. In Khmer I would say *chap arom*. I've heard the phrase translated as *interesting*, but literally it means "to capture one's consciousness."

Now, more than fifteen years since my first trip, I am returning to Cambodia, to see old friends and continue a search for Cambodian literature that I had begun in the United States in 2001, when *Mānoa's* editor asked me to guest-edit this volume.

I hadn't found much Cambodian literature in English in the United States, so I should not have been shocked by the journalist's dismissive response the day I arrived. I'd heard similar remarks from international Cambodia experts. "Good luck," said the more generous ones when they heard what I was doing. Few could name any Cambodian literary writer in America except U Sam Oeur. In a *Phnom Penh Post* article published in April 2002 and bleakly titled "The Unlucrative State of the Khmer Novel," even the president of the Khmer Writers' Association, You Bo, stated flatly: "The works of Cambodian writers are dead."

Was it true? Did contemporary Cambodian literature not exist?

Given the circumstances, it should not. The losses from the war were staggering. Between 1975 and 1979, nearly two million people—out of a population of only seven million—died of torture, execution, starvation, and disease. About one in every four Cambodians perished.

According to one estimate, out of approximately thirty-eight thousand Cambodian intellectuals, only three hundred survived—less than one percent. Most reports estimate that during the war and its aftermath, eighty to ninety percent of artists died and eighty to ninety percent of all books and manuscripts were destroyed, lost, or scattered. During the Khmer Rouge period the National Library grounds were used to raise pigs, and Buddhist monasteries—the traditional repositories of literature—were ransacked or converted to prisons.

Laments traditional musician Sam-Ang Sam in his essay in *Cambodian Culture Since 1975: Homeland and Exile:*

> This slaughter has resulted in a severe shortage of artists and musicians, both as teachers and performers…We have lost so much. We have lost our most able musicians, artists who have devoted their entire lives to gaining knowledge and ability. Now they are gone.

The handful of artists and writers who survived found themselves in a shattered country. The nation's infrastructure had been destroyed, and the land seeded with mines and unexploded ordnance. There were widespread poverty and illiteracy and later, shortly after the arrival of foreign personnel, alarming increases in prostitution and AIDS. In addition, writers had to endure censorship and a lack of printing presses; spare parts, ink, even paper were hard to come by.

Considering all this, it is surprising that anyone wrote at all. But people did. Almost as soon as the Khmer Rouge regime ended, a new literature began to appear: novels were handwritten, often in pencil, on the cheap, graph-lined paper of student notebooks, then photocopied and rented out by the day at market stalls. Whether in serial form or their entirety, these books were sought by an eager public. Because the stories did not support the socialist government—many were about love—the books were often confiscated and pen names invented so that authors would not be arrested. In Phnom Penh, I meet two writers, Mao Somnang and Pal Vannariraks, who got their start secretly handwriting novels back in the 1980s. Today, they are among the few authors living in Cambodia who can support themselves by writing, although they must now supplement their book income by writing video scripts and song lyrics.

The negative Western perception of Cambodian writing dates to the nineteenth and early twentieth centuries, the time of the French Protectorate. While extolling the architecture of the ancient Angkor civilization, French scholars dismissed Khmer writing as inferior. This notion that Cambodians did not possess a sophisticated literature seems at odds with the richness of the Khmer language and the aesthetic complexity of its poetry. Soth Polin, a well-known fiction writer of the 1960s and 1970s, told me about his learning to read from his great-grandfather, the poet Nou Kan: "I remember the flow of his poetry even now. What I read when I was a child was very powerful." Soth later became obsessed with reading *Saturday Night,* the weekly Khmer-language literary supplement that was begun in 1935 and has been credited with giving birth to modern Cambodian literature. "I lived and dreamed literature," he has said.

Kim Hak, the author of *The Waters of Tonle Sap*, one of Cambodia's first novels, states in his 1939 introduction that he wrote the book partly to counter the foreign view of his country's literature. His novel was serialized in *Kambuja Surya* (Cambodian Sun), the first Khmer-language journal, launched in 1926 by the Buddhist Institute. Along with *Saturday Night*, the journal published some of the country's earliest modern fiction.

In the middle of the twentieth century came what literary scholars Jacques Nepote and Khing Hoc Dy describe as a renaissance in classical Cambodian literature. As the country was gaining its independence from France, education and publishing were expanding and classical works were being reproduced in books, filmstrips, radio broadcasts, and movies. A lively, sophisticated community of writers and intellectuals began to develop in Phnom Penh. Soth Polin would meet weekly with other writers, including some of the very authors who had inspired him a few years before.

In 1975, less than four decades after the publication of Cambodia's first novel, this flourishing of Khmer literature and scholarship was abruptly interrupted. The Khmer Rouge defeated the Lon Nol government and instituted the Democratic Kampuchea (DK) regime, which lasted till 1979. Revolutionary songs, printed in two booklets by the DK, are generally considered the only literature of the Khmer Rouge period. Writing of a personal nature was prohibited. Nonetheless, a few people wrote in spite of the danger. The eloquent and moving love letters of Hout Bophana and Ly Sitha, written at tremendous risk, are evidence of a concealed literature and the price paid for defying the Khmer Rouge: husband and wife were killed in the infamous Tuol Sleng prison.

In 1979, the Khmer Rouge were driven from power by the Vietnamese. Almost as soon as fleeing Cambodians arrived in the refugee camps on the Cambodia–Thai border, they began to write. At least forty novels, stories, and poetry collections were published in the camps. Inside Cambodia, state-sponsored novels began to be printed, and hand-written, illegally circulated novels became popular. In the United States, survivors began publishing novels in Khmer and memoirs of the Khmer Rouge period in English. In France, Cambodians continued to write while the war was being waged in their homeland, and in 1988 in Paris, Madame Pech Sangwawann founded the Association of Khmer Writers Abroad. In addition, some classical works, such as folktales and *chbap* (codes of conduct), were also printed in Cambodia and abroad.

Before I left for Cambodia to search for contemporary writing, Soth Polin sent me his story "Communicate, They Say," written in Khmer and translated into French, along with a letter from Christophe Macquet, the translator. The letter referred to "*un panel représentative de la littérature khmère en prose au xx siècle pour une revue littéraire française."* Soth told me that he had been impressed with the quality of the French translation, and the letter piqued my interest: could someone else be working on a similar project?

Soon after I arrive in Phnom Penh, I manage to contact Christophe, and we meet at a café on the banks of the Mekong. We have no trouble recognizing each other, but I don't speak French and he claims to speak little English. So we speak in our common language, Khmer, about the odd coincidences between our projects.

While I had been searching for two years for Cambodian literature, Christophe had been collecting and translating stories for an issue of the French journal *Europe*. His work had focused on five Cambodian authors: Soth Polin, Khun Srun, Kong Bunchhoeun, Hak Chhay Hok, and Chuth Khay. These were some of the same authors I had been trying to get translated into English.

"Cambodians can write," he tells me, emphatically contradicting the pronouncements of the American journalist I had met my first day in Phnom Penh. He then tells me about the works he has translated, describing philosophical stories, ghost tales, and a comedy. Laughing, he remarks on how strange it is for two foreigners to be communicating in Khmer, and to be pursuing a similar project on opposite sides of the world.

When I had begun my search, I had assumed there would be an abundance of Khmer literature in France, where many Cambodians found refuge before and after the war. But Christophe tells me Cambodian writing has been ignored there just as it has been in the United States. The French, he says, only cared about Angkor Wat. "But Cambodia," he stresses, "is not just old stones—it's people."

In 2000, during my last trip to Angkor Wat, both my cameras failed while I was on the upper level of the Bayon, the temple famous for its fifty-four towers, each constructed with faces that look in the four cardinal directions. I put the equipment away and talked with the boys I had been photographing, thinking of the children in the camps. I'd heard that most had been sent back to Cambodia when Site Two was closed in 1993.

While at the Bayon on this same trip, I met a Cambodian man working as a tour guide who recognized me from the border. He talked about the closure of the camps, the forced relocation to Cambodia, the difficulties of trying to start again, then he noticed his two American clients becoming restless. I wanted to explain to them how strange it was to meet him here, in the Bayon, at the center of the ancient city of Angkor Thom, among the stone faces the artists in the camp used to paint so vividly. Standing there, at that moment, the past and present seemed to overlap in indecipherable layers.

On this latest trip, I again return to the Bayon at different times of day: morning, noon, twilight. I talk to the caretaker of one of the shrines in the central structure, whom I remember from previous trips, and pay my respects. I ask her if many tourists stop to worship here. Mostly older Cambodians, she says.

Late one afternoon, I listen to two young women dressed in the light-blue uniforms of temple staff workers. They are singing softly in a stone doorway. The upper level is nearly deserted, and the women's melody is disarmingly beautiful. They sing in unison, leaning into each other, reading the lyrics from a songbook they are sharing. The book is smaller than the span of their hands.

Music is so entwined with Cambodian literature that it is difficult to separate the two. When Soth Polin recites examples of Cambodian poetry, he sings them in captivating melodies, supporting the alliteration and assonance of the Khmer phrases. U Sam Oeur—the first prominent Cambodian poet to break from the complex, rigid structures of traditional Khmer poetry in order to experiment with free verse—performs his Khmer work in moving arias. He has written an operetta based on his poem "The Krasang Tree," and traditional musician Chinary Ung plans to create a chamber opera from U Sam Oeur's poetry.

It might not seem so surprising then that one of the few Cambodian artists who have managed to connect young and old generations, Americans and Cambodians, English and Khmer, written and oral literature is a musician and poet: rap artist praCh, of Long Beach, California. His first CD became the top album in Cambodia without his knowledge; he heard about it only when an *Asiaweek* reporter tracked him down to ask him about it. praCh's music skillfully combines the rhyme and rhythm of rap with traditional Cambodian instrumentation and musical forms.

Near the end of my trip I stand on the steps of the library of Wat Damnak, at the Center for Khmer Studies in Siem Reap, near Angkor Wat. I am speaking with a young poet who teaches Pali and Sanskrit. When I ask him about the situation of Cambodian writers like himself, he tells me that he cannot make a living by writing or even teaching Pali and Sanskrit, so he has also begun teaching Khmer to foreigners.

We stand in the sun at the top of the stairs, and he shows me a small volume of his poems. Made of A4-sized sheets photocopied, folded in half, and stapled at the spine, it is similar to the books I have seen at market stalls in Phnom Penh. On the cover is a drawing: one of the Bayon faces overlooks a man plowing a rice field. On the back is an image of a stone Buddha statue, arms broken off just below the shoulders.

"I am a Khmer writer," the poet tells me, as if that explains everything. "I don't have much experience. But in my heart, I feel addicted to writing."

On one of my last evenings in Angkor Wat, I return to the Bayon. Here, there is no astonishing view of the sunset, as there is from the top of

Phnom Bakheng, but neither are there crowds pouring from tour buses. All the tourists have left. In the fading light, I meet two young monks. I greet them and apologize for not knowing the language that should be used when speaking to monks. They tell me not to worry.

Like the two young women I heard singing here, they were born after the fall of the Khmer Rouge. They are from a monastery on the outskirts of Siem Reap and occasionally visit the Bayon. They ask about my background, and I ask how they became monks. One says he was a farmer's son who had to work in the fields. Too poor to go to school, he became a monk in order to learn to read and write. The other was also born into poverty and a difficult family life and fled to the monastery for refuge and an education. Their stories are reminiscent of the Cambodia of long ago, when the monastery was one of the main sources of learning and literature and the only way for the poor to obtain an education.

As we talk, a chittering sound—like the rise and fall of musical notes—seems to be coming from inside one of the towers. It creates the illusion that the stone faces might be thinking out loud, and I start to laugh. One of the monks smiles. "It's the bats," he explains. "They live in crevices in the stone."

On the day I leave Phnom Penh, I speak to a young woman at the coffee counter inside Pochentong Airport. It turns out she was a child in Site Two at the time I was working there. She might have been one of the children I photographed. We talk until I hear the last call to board the plane.

After a nearly sleepless night in the Bangkok airport, I start on the next leg to Tokyo. I scan the cabin for Khmer faces but see none. My seat mate, who looks Japanese, seems equally fatigued. My carry-on luggage—full of books and stone sculpture—is too heavy to lift into the overhead compartment, so I put it under the seats, where it takes up all the space. As she puts on her Walkman headphones and sifts through her papers, I catch a glimpse of Khmer script. Cautiously, I ask where she came from. Cambodia, she says. I'm not sure if she means she was on vacation, so I ask if she is Cambodian. Yes, she answers, and we switch to Khmer. I tell her I thought she was Japanese, and she laughs, saying that even in Cambodia they don't know she's Khmer. Soon we are both apologizing for being grumpy. She explains she is stopping in Tokyo to see friends before returning to her family and computer job in California. By coincidence, she lives not far from where I do. I ask her, "Do you know Thida Butt Mam?"

She laughs and says, "I am Thida."

Thida Butt Mam's book, *To Destroy You Is No Loss,* written with Joan Criddle, was one of the first about the Khmer Rouge period to be published in the United States. I tell her I remember reading it when it came out in 1987, soon after I returned to the States from the camps. We talk for the next five hours, until we reach Tokyo. I tell her about my trip and this project. She tells me this is the first time she's been back to the village where she'd lived during the Khmer Rouge years. And we both wonder at this unlikely circumstance, the seeming impossibility of the two of us meeting here, at this place, in this way.

By the time this volume comes out, I will have contacted writers and translators in nine countries: Cambodia, United States, France, Australia, Canada, Mexico, Laos, Thailand, and Japan. There have been so many coincidences and fortuitous meetings like this one with Thida that I wonder where this project will take me next. But for now, this part of my journey is over.

The Origin of the Kounlok Bird

The bird known as the *kounlok* has an appearance resembling the *krolung krolong* bird's, but it is slightly larger and colored gray and has red speckles. It can mostly be found on wooded hills or in light forests. Elderly people in Cambodia tell a story about its origins that goes like this.

Long ago, two poor farmers, a man and his wife, had three little girls. The eldest girl knew how to draw water and cook, the second knew how to look after her little sister, and the third knew how to run around and play.

The husband died, and his young wife was left a widow with three little girls. Every day, she cut wood and gathered vegetables to take to the market to sell.

One day at the market, she met a good-for-nothing man who had plenty of money because he robbed the people who came to the market. When he saw the young widow, he pretended to be a decent, well-behaved person and asked her ever so politely, "Young woman, what village are you from? Is it near or faraway? Why don't you have a husband to help you with your heavy shoulder pole? Why do you carry so much by yourself?"

The young woman answered in a straightforward manner. "I'm a widow," she said. "My husband died. I'm very poor. I gather vegetables to sell for a little money so that I can buy food for my three little girls."

The good-for-nothing man was delighted by her reply and thought to himself, *This young woman's a widow. She has a pleasing appearance. If I follow her home and talk to her, I might be able to take her as my wife.* He said to her, "Young lady, I feel very sorry for you. Here, I beg you to take these ten coins as a gift: buy something for your children." Greatly pleased, the young widow hastily accepted the money, and when she had sold her wood and vegetables, she headed home. The good-for-nothing man followed her from a distance so as to find out where she lived, and when it was dark, he visited her. They talked sweetly for a while, and soon thereafter, they began to live as man and wife.

From that day on, the good-for-nothing man would leave to rob people in faraway places. Sometimes he'd be gone for three or four days and sometimes for half a month. His wife now had plenty of gold and silver to spend.

She wore only the most beautiful clothes. She became haughty, and when her husband was home, she'd go off with him to eat and drink at the market.

She neglected her poor children. At first, she was annoyed by them. Then she came to hate them. Whenever she saw their faces, she wanted to grab a knife and kill them. When she made soup, she cooked only enough for her husband and herself. If there was a little rice left in the bottom of the pot, the girls would try to scrape it out for their food. Sometimes they'd sleep near the fireplace, and sometimes they'd sleep in a lean-to, suffering mosquito and midge bites. In the mornings, their mother would go off to the market to eat and drink with her husband, the good-for-nothing man.

One day, the good-for-nothing man said to her, "I'm ashamed by all your devotion and by the way you follow me around when I go to the market. I beg you, please, stay at home and take care of your three little girls."

Hearing her husband talk like this, the widow thought to herself, *My husband is a terrible show-off. The bad women in the market know him well. If I obey him, he will abandon me. I need to find a way to kill my three little girls. Then he can't make me stay home on account of my children.*

In April, when the rains began, the widow called out to her children, "My beloved daughters! When your father was alive, he would take me to the forest to sow rice in a shallow pond at the foot of a mountain. Tomorrow, I'll take some seed there, and you children will see to it that the sparrows, doves, and pigeons don't eat the rice. There's an open hut nearby where you can wait while the rice is growing."

The next morning, the young widow led her children to a pond in a deserted part of a forest at the foot of a mountain. She brought some rice seed to scatter in the pond, and she told her children, "Now listen, all of you! You must wait for the rice to grow. Don't go far away, and don't come home. If you do, I'll beat you all to death."

After she'd spoken, she left portions of cooked rice for them, three plates of uncooked rice, fourteen kernels of corn, and a small earthenware pot with some fish paste and salt. She thought, *A tiger will come tonight and eat them up. If they don't die from that, they'll starve to death, for certain.*

She went back home and lay down, waiting for her husband to return from work. When he got home, he asked her, "Where have the three girls gone? I don't see them in the house."

She answered, "I sent them to watch the rice fields with some older people. They'll be back when the rice is ripe."

In the meantime, the three little girls buried the kernels of corn along the sides of the pond and went to sleep in the open hut. All night, they heard the cries of elephants, jackals, wild dogs, and monkeys in the haunted forest. The eldest daughter was frightened. Her body shuddered like a baby animal's. She almost lost consciousness, and she urged her sisters not to cry, fearing that wild beasts would find them if they heard them.

Nearby lived a guardian spirit. He said to himself, *Why did that young mother bring her three little girls to such an isolated place? If I don't help them, the wicked wild animals will eat them up. I'll protect them through the night, and then I'll talk to Indra, the king of the gods, about them.* The guardian spirit shouted ferociously, frightening the wild animals and scattering them.

When morning came, the guardian spirit went to see the god Varuna, in the northeast, to ask him to tell Indra, the king of the gods, about the three little girls.

Varuna said, "This isn't important enough to bother Indra, the king of the gods, about. The girls will turn into birds before long." He added, "You must protect them and keep wild beasts from harassing them. If they are ever hungry when they have turned into birds, you must put *krim* fish, rabbit fish, and freshwater clams and snails into the pond for them to eat." The guardian spirit returned to his lair and did as Varuna commanded.

After the girls waited three nights for the rice to grow, the cooked rice that their mother had left for them was gone. The young ones cried, wanting more rice to eat. The eldest gathered some sour *thnung* leaves, reached into puddles to pinch the buds off *trokuon* plants, and gathered leaves from a wild sugar-palm tree. She brought these back to her sisters to share, but the younger ones kept crying. Finally, their sister went to the pond and caught some *krim* fish and a large rabbit fish. She planned to cook the fish, but the burning stick that her mother had left behind had gone out. The girls tore at the fish and ate them raw. The younger ones kept weeping and whining to go home, but their older sister didn't dare return. She was afraid that their mother would beat them. The little ones continued crying, though. Unable to stand it any longer, she led them back.

When their mother saw them approaching, she was furious and cried out, "Disgraceful children! I thought you would die when I abandoned you, and here you are, coming home, not dead at all! I'll beat you! I won't let you come into my house!"

The eldest girl beseeched her, "Mother, please! Pity your children! The two little ones can't stop crying from hunger. For the last few days, they've eaten leaves instead of rice, and our firestick has gone out. If you won't let us stay, Mother, please give us a little uncooked rice and another firestick and we'll go back to the pond. Oh Mother, please don't mistreat your children! We ask for your mercy."

The youngest girl said, "Ma! Oldest Sister caught a 'bit and we ate some pieces."

But the mother thought she said, "We caught a rabbit and we ate till we were full." Angrier than ever, she cursed the little girls. "Disgraceful children!" she cried. "You caught a *rabbit*? Why didn't you bring me some?"

She beat, kicked, pummeled, and pinched the children and gave them nothing to eat. She hoped to drive them back into the forest to die.

She should have pitied the girls, but instead she beat them until they bled. She couldn't stop them from crying "Ma!" and they couldn't believe that their own mother wanted to kill them. The youngest one kept saying, "We caught a 'bit, ate some pieces." However, her mother heard incorrectly each time, and she beat the three little girls more fiercely.

Eventually, the eldest girl dragged the younger ones away. She knew that if they stayed, their mother would kill them. She took them back to the open hut, where they lost consciousness because of their injuries.

When the guardian spirit saw the three little girls, he brought some magic water to heal and revive them. When the girls woke up, they began to moan and cry. The oldest one went off to catch some *krim* fish, a rabbit fish, and some clams and snails.

She divided this food among her sisters. From then on, they ate their food raw. There were always plenty of fish, clams, and snails for them to eat. The guardian spirit saw to that. When the sun was nice and hot, they left the fish out in the open to dry. Then they divided it up and ate it.

One day, the eldest girl embraced her sisters and said, "Beloved younger sisters! The three of us will never see our mother again. She has a new husband. She hates us and wants to kill us. We can't hope to have any life after this. Each of us has only a single length of cloth to cover her body with, and these are wearing out. Soon we'll hug our ribs from the cold, and our bodies will be as naked as those of wild animals."

After three months, the corn that the girls had buried around the pond ripened. Wild pigs, geese, monkeys, and squirrels didn't dare eat it because the guardian spirit watched over the area. The eldest girl gathered up the corn to eat with *krim* fish, rabbit fish, clams, and snails.

After six months, the girls gradually began to grow downy feathers on their bodies. Their arms turned into wings. They began to fly up to treetops, where they plucked fruit, though they couldn't fly far.

Their lips narrowed into beaks. They couldn't speak like human beings anymore, though they knew that they were human. They made noises that sounded to human beings like *yuu yuu*. If people spoke to them, though, they understood. Slowly, they learned to fly a little farther.

Meanwhile, their mother's second husband, the good-for-nothing man, went on robbing until someone told government officials about him. He was arrested and put in prison for the rest of his life.

The girls' mother became very sad. She missed her three children.

She went into the forest and saw them huddled together in the open hut. Because they still had human form, she knew that they were her children, though they now had wings like birds.

"Oh my beloved children!" she cried. "I've come to take you back. I won't make you stay in the forest anymore."

The girls heard what the woman said, and they knew she was their mother. They thought, *Our mother has come to kill us; we can't let her do that. It's better to fly away.* They flew off slowly and perched on top of a tree. The words that they tried to speak to their mother weren't clear at all. They wanted to say, "We're no longer human beings [*kounlok*]. We've turned into birds, and it's better this way. Don't come near us!" But the words they tried to say were not like human words, and all their mother heard was "*kounlok.*"

When their mother drew near, they flew to another tree, crying, "*Kounlok, kounlok!*"

Their mother kept walking and calling out for them until she lost her strength and could go no further. Without any food to eat, she fell on the ground and died.

In Cambodia today, the *kounlok* bird gathers clams and snails in fields at the foot of hills or in lightly wooded areas. Whenever it is surprised by a person or another animal, it flies off, crying, "*Kounlok, kounlok!*" And in the still of the night, its cries fill us with unspeakable sadness.

Translation by David Chandler

Sokha and Apopeal

When Sokha was six years old, his father gave him a mother cow to take care of. This cow's name was Chompa. She had colored patches of yellow and brown and two tiny horns.

Every day after school, Sokha took Chompa to graze in the clover fields and along the rice paddies. And before nightfall, he would lead Chompa back to the stable. Then he would wash up. He would clean his hands and feet, put on fresh clothes, and eat with the rest of the family.

One day when Sokha came back home from school, he discovered that Chompa had given birth to a boy calf. He gave it the name Apopeal because it was covered with brown and white patches. He was very happy that Apopeal had joined them. Apopeal couldn't walk far because he was still small.

A month later, Apopeal could walk beautifully, just as well as his mother, Chompa. She still suckled him. When Sokha went to school, he let Chompa and Apopeal out to graze with the other cows. When he got back from school in the evening, he led the two of them to the clover fields. There in the clover field, Apopeal liked to sleep next to Sokha, and Sokha would stroke the calf's head, neck, back, and tail. Chompa ate a lot of clover so that she'd have enough milk for Apopeal.

Once after Apopeal had been sleeping for a long time and resting under Sokha's gentle caresses, his mother wandered far away to look for clover. Waking, Apopeal got up to look for his mother, and when he didn't see her, he cried, *"Moo! Moo! Moo!"* When Apopeal's mother heard his distant cry, she quickly returned to him. And when he saw her, he ran to her and started nursing. Before sunset, Sokha always led Chompa and Apopeal back to the house.

One Sunday, Chompa was stricken by a serious illness. Since it was not possible for Sokha's family to get the medicine she needed, she died. The next morning, Apopeal did not see his mother, so he got up to go to the field. When he finally found her, he cried, *"Moo! Moo! Moo!"* His mother did not stir at all. Sokha's father told him to take Apopeal far away from his mother. Sokha saw tears flowing from Apopeal's eyes and cried hard, too.

Lotus Field, Tonle Sap Delta,
Siem Reap, 2002
Photograph by Richard Murai

From that time on, Apopeal could not nurse as he had before. When his mother died, he was only five months old. Sokha's father bought milk so they could feed Apopeal by hand. Apopeal would not live long if he didn't have milk to drink.

Every morning, Sokha got up early to give Apopeal milk. Then he fed him a little straw. And every afternoon, he led Apopeal to the clover fields where he used to take him and his mother. He stroked Apopeal's head tenderly and fed him fresh clover by hand.

Apopeal was now a year old. He no longer needed milk and could eat hay as his mother had. He was still small, however, so Sokha's father did not let him wander very far. In the late afternoon, Apopeal would stand by the fence, waiting for Sokha to come back from school and lead him to the clover field. In the field, Apopeal was very happy because he could run, jump, and wander. When he got tired, he would return and sleep next to Sokha, who would stroke him.

They were good friends.

When Apopeal was five years old, he was full grown. His horns spread out on each side of his head, and his legs were heavy and strong, so he could run very fast. Every morning, Sokha tied Apopeal near the school and let him graze. And after school, Sokha would ride home on Apopeal's back.

In the hot season, Sokha took Apopeal to bathe in the river. In the rainy season, he tended a small fire in the stable, using the smoke to keep the mosquitoes from biting Apopeal. He loved Apopeal very much. The other children in the village loved him, too, because he was always clean and well behaved around them.

In May 1975, the Khmer Rouge made all the people leave the towns and go live in the countryside. All the schools closed their doors. All property and farm animals were taken away: cows, water buffaloes, pigs, chickens, and ducks were made collective property. This included Apopeal.

Sokha felt terrible when the men took Apopeal away. The people in charge of the village made Apopeal pull a cart because they could see he was very strong.

At that time, there was a great deal of hunger in the country. People received so little food that it was extremely difficult to live. They had to work long and hard and were not given time to rest.

One day, Sokha saw the village leaders with Apopeal, who was straining to pull a cart across a high bridge. Apopeal was unhappy. Refusing to go further, he began to buck. As the cart was about to fall in the river, Sokha grabbed it and yelled, "Whoa! Whoa, Apopeal! Whoa!" Apopeal recognized his master and stood still. Sokha stroked Apopeal's tail and helped guide the cart over the bridge.

The cart driver didn't forget Sokha's kindness. He gave him a large parcel of rice, then left. Taking it gratefully, Sokha ran home and gave it to his father.

The time of hunger grew worse and worse. One day, Sokha was so tired and hungry from the hard work that he decided to pick a few oranges from one of the orchards. He had only picked one when he heard the village chief cry, "Thief! Thief! Thief!" Terrified, Sokha dashed toward the rice fields but stumbled over some shrubbery and fell. The village chief caught him and was about to hit him with a cane. Apopeal—where did he come from?!—suddenly appeared behind the village chief and knocked him to the ground. Sokha, relieved, ran away. And Apopeal disappeared into a herd of cows.

In those days, there were no proper schools. Children had to work as if they were adults. Every day, Sokha had to carry heavy sheaves of rice suspended from a shoulder piece. One day, he was doing this when he heard *"Moo! Moo! Moo!"* in the distance. An old man was leading Apopeal to Sokha. The old man said to him, "You can put those sheaves on the cow's back, son."

"Thank you!" Sokha said.

Sokha saw that Apopeal's body was soiled with mud. Gently, he stroked Apopeal's head. In return, Apopeal licked his hand.

"Apopeal! I have missed you so much. I can see you've had trouble working hard, just like I have."

Having been brought together again, Sokha and Apopeal forgot how tired and hungry they were. They felt happier than you could imagine. No matter how hard their lives had been, they were overjoyed to be together.

Because there wasn't enough food to eat, Sokha became very sick. But even though he was sick, he was forced to work. One day, it was raining very hard, and Sokha was soaked. He suddenly felt very hot. The overseers let him rest under a nearby tree. He had a high fever and began to cry and groan.

On the road, the village chief was riding on Apopeal's back. When they came to the place where Sokha was crying, Apopeal stopped walking.

The village chief raised his stick and hit Apopeal, but he refused to move. Sokha, straining to see over the tips of his toes, saw Apopeal buck up and down until the village chief fell into the water of the rice field.

When the village chief got up, he aimed his gun at Apopeal. Seeing this, Sokha jumped up and climbed onto Apopeal's back. Knowing that it was Sokha, Apopeal started to run. Sokha was so tired and weak that he knew he would not be able to keep himself from falling off Apopeal's back. He pulled his *krama* off and tied himself on. Then he reclined on Apopeal's back and fell asleep.

When Sokha woke up, he found himself far from the village. Nearby was a hut with a pan full of rice and a grill with fish on it. He was so hungry that he ate some of the rice and fish.

He heard a voice crying from a distance, "Thief! Thief! Thief stealing my rice!"

Sokha grabbed the pan of rice and jumped on Apopeal's back, and Apopeal charged through the fields and into the forest, deeper and deeper, until he reached a place he had never been before.

That evening, at an hour when Sokha could see the sun slowly setting through the trees, Apopeal led him to a large lake covered with lotus flowers, many in full bloom and countless more still in the bud. The lake was surrounded by a field of grass, fresh and green.

As night fell and the air cooled, dew formed on the grass. Sokha began to feel cold. "Gee, I'm cold, Apopeal!" he cried.

Sokha regretted not having any way to fight off the cold. He wistfully imagined a nice fire, a blanket covering him, and a shirt that would keep him warm. He thought about his grandmother, who started the fire every morning.

"Apopeal, I have it!" he cried joyfully. "If we strike two pieces of iron together, we will certainly have a fire." But looking around him, he found nothing but trees and grass.

He gave up trying to find iron. Hugging Apopeal's neck in order to fight the cold, he felt an oval-shaped object on his arm. He jumped up quickly.

"I found iron after all, Apopeal!" He untied the bells from Apopeal's neck, took out the clappers, and began striking the iron pieces against each other. Little flowers of flame shot out.

Then Sokha looked for loose grass, broke up wood for kindling, and gathered them together. He struck the pieces of iron again. Sparks fell onto the pile of kindling, and a tongue of fire appeared. He went to find more pieces of wood to stack on the fire so it would burn for a long time. Once they had the warmth of the fire, Sokha and Apopeal fell into a deep, satisfied sleep.

The morning sun rose through the trees. Not very far from Sokha and Apopeal was a sound like that of an animal playing in the water. *Kweek, kweek, kweek!* Sokha woke up and made a small opening in the grass, crawling toward the strange sound. He saw a pair of otters catching fish by a clump of lotus plants and putting the fish on the grass. Then the otters ate the ones they had caught. A couple were left on the grass, so Sokha took them and cooked them over the fire.

Sokha and Apopeal lived peacefully by the lake full of lotus. Each day, Sokha would pick lotus, boil the root stalk, and fry fish. As for Apopeal, he had enough fresh green grass to eat. They did not worry that someone would hurt them the way they had been hurt before.

One day Sokha was picking lotus when he suddenly heard a cry of pain. Looking about, he saw a rabbit with a broken leg darting back and forth to avoid a snake that was pursuing it.

Sokha tried to chase the snake away. It wasn't afraid of him at all, so he wrapped a *krama* around his face. The snake leaped at his face to bite him, but it just bit into the scarf. Giving up, it slithered away.

Sokha reached down, picked up the rabbit, and said, "Oh, little bunny, your foot is broken! Come, let me bandage it for you!" He lifted the rabbit gently and took it home. Then he bandaged the rabbit's leg with grass, and the next few mornings, he massaged it with dew.

Sokha's small community now had three members. A few days later, the rabbit could hop around as easily as before. At night, the three of them sat together by the fire.

A year went by quickly. Sokha had eaten all the lotus on one side of the lake. "Apopeal, I have eaten all the lotus! We'll have to move to the north side of the lake!"

So Sokha arranged a new living place on the north shore. They found plenty of grass and lotus flowers, and the grass there was just as fresh as it had been in their former home.

One day while Sokha was picking lotus to eat, he saw a baby monkey in the lake, struggling to keep from drowning. He pulled it out and took it to its mother, who was crying on the shore. The baby was overjoyed to see its mother, and the mother jumped up and down with gratitude to Sokha. From that time on, all the monkeys in the forest thought of him as their friend.

Not long after, the two otters came to live with Sokha, too.

"Brother otters, I won't take your fish anymore. I've figured out how to catch fish myself," he said.

Sokha began digging a hole in the lake mud about a half meter wide at the top and as deep as your knee. After scooping out the water in the hole and smoothing the sides, he put grass around it. When the fish swam through the grass, they fell into the hole one at a time. In the morning, Sokha found he had caught fish of all kinds: catfish, perch, *roh*. He was very happy. His life was getting better and better.

The third year, Sokha moved to the west side of the lake. One morning when he woke up, he couldn't find Apopeal or the rabbit.

"Apopeal! Rabbit! Where have you gone?!" Sokha cried out.

Soon he saw Apopeal in the distance, running toward him as though to tell him something important. "Apopeal, what is it?" he asked, surprised.

He jumped on Apopeal's back, and Apopeal took him to a place in the forest some distance from where they lived. From afar, he could see many monkeys gathered around two men.

"How strange! For two or three years I have lived here and never seen anyone else at all," he muttered to himself.

The monkeys jumped up and down as though they were trying to keep the men from going any further. Gazing at them, Sokha yelled, "Father! Father! Brother!"

The three of them hugged each other and cried. When the monkeys saw this, they retreated to the forest.

"How did you find me?" Sokha asked his father and older brother.

"After we discovered that you and Apopeal had run away from the village, I assumed that Apopeal would bring you here because he used to come here with his mother. Now, everything is fine again in our country. You can come back home without any danger."

Sokha, Apopeal, the rabbit, and Sokha's father and brother all went back to his village. He returned to school, joining the other children. Every day, he rode Apopeal to school, the rabbit sitting on Apopeal's head.

From then on, Sokha and his family lived peacefully in their village.

Translation by John Marston

Window, Killing Fields
Memorial Stupa, Siem Reap, 2002
Photograph by Richard Murai

Surviving the Peace:
An Interview with Loung Ung ⎯⎯⎯⎯⎯⎯⎯⎯⎯⎯

Loung Ung was born in 1970 into a middle-class family in Phnom Penh. Five years later, her family was forced out of the city by the Khmer Rouge in the mass evacuation to the countryside. By 1978, the Khmer Rouge had killed Ung's parents and two of her siblings, and she was forced to train as a child soldier. In 1980, she and her older brother escaped by boat to Thailand, where they spent five months in a refugee camp. They then relocated to Vermont.

Ung's memoir, *First They Killed My Father: A Daughter of Cambodia Remembers,* was published by HarperCollins in 2000, becoming a national bestseller and receiving the 2001 Asian/Pacific American Librarians' Association award for excellence in adult nonfiction. The book has been published in eleven countries and translated into more than a dozen languages, including German, French, Spanish, Italian, Japanese, and Khmer.

Today, Ung is sought after as a speaker on Cambodia, child soldiers, women in wartime, refugee issues, domestic violence, and land mines. From 1997 to 2003, she worked for the Vietnam Veterans of America Foundation's campaign for a land-mine-free world. Before that, she was a community educator for the Abused Women's Advocacy Project of the Maine Coalition Against Domestic Violence. She continues to serve as a national spokesperson for the campaign to ban land mines.

This interview was conducted by telephone in August 2003.

SM   How did you come to write *First They Killed My Father?*

LU   I decided to publish the book for one main reason: I'm an activist. I wanted to talk about land mines. I wanted to talk about child soldiers. I wanted to talk about poverty and AIDS issues and child prostitution—all the problems in Cambodia I learned about when I went back in 1995.

But when I returned to the U.S., I just couldn't get anybody interested in these issues. I realized that I would have more credibility if I was a published writer. Publishing this book was a vehicle for my activism.

SM How difficult was it for you to relive the war, and talk about the horrors left over from the war?

LU It was really difficult. I had to imagine my sister's last day before she died, her physical suffering, and her deterioration.

And going back to Cambodia was scary. I left when I was ten years old, and the images I had of Cambodia were ones of blood and wounded people and war and pain and hunger. And even though I was going back as a twenty-five-year-old adult, I still had dreams of getting off the plane and being a child again—of being lost, extending my hand and having no one there to grab it. It was really painful. But when I arrived, I saw my brothers and sisters, and it was a great reunion.

Then I got out in the country and saw the amputees, the poverty, the red-light districts where young girls are selling their bodies, and I realized how really blessed I am, how lucky, how much I have. Of course, a lot of guilt comes with that. I think that for the last eight years, since 1995, I've been trying to do good work to make sure that those left behind are not forgotten.

SM Is that how you got involved with the campaign for a land-mine-free world?

LU I always knew a little about land mines, but it wasn't until I went back to Cambodia in 1995 that I decided to get more involved. It made me so mad when I learned the story of how people fought to survive. Five million Cambodians survived the war. Now, years later, they are having a hard time surviving the peace—because of land mines.

I remember I was walking in the street and I met a young girl. This was my third day in Cambodia. Up to that time, I had seen adult amputees, of course. But I had kept my sunglasses and my Walkman on, and I was going around the country like a tourist. I didn't want to see or hear. And I didn't want them to see me. Once you make eye contact, they talk to you, so I wore sunglasses. But it was night when the girl approached me, and she wasn't an amputee herself. She came up to me to ask for money. She was really poor and carried a little baby with a bloated body and tiny arms. The baby was sleeping. The girl herself looked about seven or eight years old. She was dressed in rags, and the baby was just torso and limbs. She said her father had stepped on a mine, and now she needed money to feed her family, her baby sister, and her mother. I gave her some money, but I didn't have enough. I told her to wait while I got more money. And she kind of stood there, as if she wasn't sure whether or not to believe me. I went up to my room, and when I came back, she was gone. I walked up and down the streets a few times, trying to find her to give her the money. But the hotel people hadn't wanted her loitering in front, so they'd chased her away. I kept thinking, *Where did she go?*

For whatever reason, she reminded me a lot of myself in 1979, after the Vietnamese came and I was living on the street and eating out of garbage cans. People didn't want to see me either and would chase me away. I knew how she felt. Since then, I've been trying to help many others like her. I still think about her. I wonder where she is. I don't know why, but I really *saw* her. And now I see her everywhere.

SM Cambodia is one of the most heavily mined countries in the world. I have read that nearly half of all villages in Cambodia are either known or suspected to be contaminated by mines or unexploded ordnance (UXO). Land mines have injured more than 41,000 people since 1979, when the Khmer Rouge were driven from power. There are 68 new land-mine and UXO victims each month; 95 percent are civilians, and almost 30 percent are children.

LU Yes, there are an estimated 4 to 6 million land mines in Cambodia right now, and it has one of the highest percentages of land-mine victims anywhere in the world. About 1 out of 242 Cambodians is an amputee. Children are often the ones who have to graze the cows and wander the fields to find firewood. For very young children, their curiosity can get them killed. They are the ones who will pick flowers or chase butterflies, or pick up a mine named the Butterfly because it's shaped like one. But this thing has a detonator in the middle of it.

Land-mine mutilation is the second most painful injury, burns being the first. Psychologically, physically, it's very destructive to human beings. Socially, culturally, economically, and religiously, it's disrupted the whole society. We're Buddhist people and so our deities tend to be based in the rivers and the earth. Now that the land is mined, where do you go to find spiritual sanctuary?

For tourists—people like you and me—we can go to Cambodia and it's quite safe. If I'm hungry, I can buy food. If I'm cold, I can go to my hotel. If I need a shower, I can just turn on the faucet and there's water. But 85 percent of the people live in the countryside and are farmers. They have to work in the fields; their children have to walk to school. And there are land mines everywhere.

SM Despite all of this, you've said that Cambodia is still a beautiful country; it's not only the land of genocide and war.

LU I love going back. Cambodians are incredibly resilient, incredibly strong, incredibly soulful. Cambodians are such fighters, and we've got a two-thousand-year-old history of culture. The land itself is stunning: all the red rooftops and the orange temples and the palm trees and the many shades of green dotting the landscape.

In America, everything is so big that you don't celebrate small things. For example, you don't celebrate when it rains. I've never seen people so happy as the villagers in Cambodia when it rains. They scurry outside. The kids are playing and the adults running around with plastic containers and metal pots and lining them up to collect the rainwater from the thatched roofs. Everyone is dancing and celebrating, and I'm thinking, *It's free rain.* When was the last time you saw someone in America so happy because the sky was pouring free water?

SM Given all the cultural differences between Cambodia and America, what was it like when you arrived in Vermont at age ten?

LU I grew up wanting to be American more than I wanted to be Cambodian. I wanted to fit in. I wanted to be popular.

But I think the first time I ever felt completely at home after the war was when I went to the U.N. World Conference of Women, held in Beijing in 1995. In that community of forty thousand—from all different countries, speaking different languages, with different skin colors—I had never felt so comfortable and so completely at home.

SM Are you optimistic or pessimistic about the future of Cambodian writing?

LU I'm very optimistic. Right after the war, the priority was to survive. Those in Cambodia did not really have the opportunity or the luxury to continue with the arts. And those of us who left the country had to survive too: by getting an education, learning about ourselves, our new country and new culture. Now that we are of age and the country is stable enough, we are putting more and more energy into creating a better Cambodia for all of us. There is a resurgence in the arts from dance to music to poetry—everything.

I was just reading on the internet about Koun Khmer Amatac Productions, a Cambodian student theater organization based in Seattle, Washington. My friend Ang Chorn Pond, a member of the Cambodian Master Performers Program—featured in the documentary *The Flute Player*—searches for surviving Khmer master musicians and takes them to a camp where they train young musicians. And Youk Chhang, director of the Documentation Center of Cambodia, is helping with biography and memoir writing by compiling information and documentation about the Khmer Rouge regime. He's had a group traveling all over the country interviewing survivors and writing stories down. He is also helping with translation.

So I'm optimistic, because Cambodian Americans and young Cambodians all over the world are wanting to learn more about themselves. They want to know more about their arts, their music, their culture, their dance, their poetry…

SM How do feel about young Cambodians—whose parents may not have talked to them much about the Khmer Rouge period—learning about it by reading your book?

LU In America, France, and other countries, there are a lot of Cambodian kids whose parents don't talk about the genocide. Many families have a language barrier, or cultural barrier, or gap between generations. I've gotten letters from kids who have recently learned that they lost siblings during the Khmer Rouge time. They had never known about it because they were too young or their parents had never talked about it. My book has given these families a way to restart the conversation.

SM You've said, "My story is a love story. It's a story of war, but it's also a story about love." When did you realize that?

LU While I was writing the book, and while I was growing up after the war, I thought it was hate that kept me alive. I thought it was hate that kept me strong, that kept my body from dying. Hate and anger. And then in America, as I met Cambodians who had suffered nervous breakdowns, who had a hard time adapting and healing from the war, I came to realize that the hate might have kept my body alive—or assisted in that—but without love, my mind would have been destroyed and my spirituality and soul would not have lived.

This is why I think my book might have such universal reach: people can't really connect to war, but they can connect to the survival of the spirit. They can connect to the love of a parent or the longing of a child for the parent, and all that love in my family, for my country—and the love my family had for me—really kept my spirit and my soul alive. And for that reason, I'm the person I am today.

Twenty years ago, if you had found me on the streets eating out of garbage cans and asked me where would I be in twenty years, I wouldn't have said I'd be a happy, healthy person. That would have been beyond my wildest dreams. But here I am. And I know that I didn't get here on my own. We are all here through the sacrifice and courage and strength of our ancestors and our communities and our allies and our friends—and even our enemies. We are all here because someone somewhere acted and gave us a chance.

Killing Fields Memorial Stupa,
Siem Reap, 2002
Photograph by Richard Murai

The Accused

Night. Seventh day of the rainless half of the month. The moon, a quarter moon between the window's bars. It shines tonight with greater intensity than on previous nights.

How I love it, this gradual moonrise! How I love the moon as it grows, gets rounder, and shines brighter! The others perhaps wait only for its fullness to begin loving it.

I have been watching you for half an hour. It's been so long. You had gotten much bigger and I hadn't realized it. Tonight, I will fill my eyes with you…

O moon! Celestial remedy! You are freshness, tied to the sweet, light breath of the wind. You are a balm on my heart. You are the smile, the duration of a long moment of forgetfulness…You are so beautiful, moon, so pure, with such a clear glow! One might say you are a gold leaf some artist has applied to the sky's ceiling! And in spite of the miasmas of our world, in spite of the impurities hurled at you by men's greed, you still shine with the same strength, beautiful, untouched, equal to yourself. You have conquered all that is sullied! You are the shadow protecting us! You are what sustains the world and are the shelter of all creatures.

You have only one fault, moon: you are too far away from me.

Lately, I've heard prayers being recited around seven at night. The voice is powerful; it almost makes my eardrums shake. It is, in all certainty, several voices. I hear them distinctly, as if they are chanting their stanzas on the other side of the wall. I see myself as a little boy at the pagoda. Each night, I would pray in order to honor Buddha and the community of monks, to receive happiness, prosperity, grace, and peace. I see myself sitting and bowing, my legs tucked to the side, next to several little boys my own age, whom I've since lost track of. Nearby are a half dozen *bonze*s, symbols of the peace of the soul, of purity, of true renunciation of personal interest; two or three candles and several incense sticks are slowly burning amid thick spirals of smoke. I prostrate from time to time, hands joined in prayer, before the smile and the serenity of the Master.

Smoke of candles and incense. Like the smoke shooting up from the crematoriums' chimneys. It rises to the sky and disintegrates little by little in the breeze. To quote a Western movie hero alone with nature: "This is the time when the living go to sleep, freed of all torment…" Touching prayers! Where do they come from? I'm digging deep into my memory. I'm trying to visualize the buildings around me: one kilometer to the east, Wat Ounalom, and a little more to the south, Wat Sarawan, the two monasteries placed far enough apart for the voices from one not to overlap with the voices from the other; at the west, Wat Kah, hidden by two hospitals and a small group of villas; finally, at the north, after Wat Phnom and I don't know how many kilometers, Wat Srah Chak.

I asked a guard. He told me it was only the prisoners praying. "Each evening," he added, "before going to sleep, they must pray in their small cells. All of them have to do it, whether they know how to pray or not, whether they are believers or not, whether they are Khmers, Chams, or Chinese." He added, "You're lucky they haven't sent you over there. Just look at them! You can find all kinds there: gamblers, outlaws, crooks, even the political kind."

I'm frightened. I lie down with my back on the mat. I'm suddenly aware of the force of these chants, of the power they have to flow inside you and seize your soul. I think about all those people. I don't know anything about them, anything about what's happening to them. But I am full of love for my poor little self! I become this light plaint, the *hmmm* full of despair that stands for the sufferings I cannot show.

I think of my wickedness as a child. I can see the nooses, the decoys with which I used to catch quail, turtledoves, blackbirds, either by their claws or their feathers, and I can see them flapping their wings and struggling to free themselves. I can see the crickets and the fighting fish I used to keep in little glass bottles, and they seem to be moaning for freedom. I can see the cane hoop nets I used to place in the ditches of paddy fields to trap *phtuek* and *roh* fish flanked by their offspring. They would sometimes stiffen like corpses or thrash in all directions, entangling themselves more as they tried to escape. All these blackbirds, all these quail, all these turtledoves, all these fish—I can see them struggling till their deaths. I see their beaks opening, I see their mouths curving with terrible pleading. They wanted to live…To go back to their mates, to raise their little ones. I wasn't aware of that. To take a life is to destroy a family.

My mother would reprimand me each time, slapping me or scolding me. I had to think, she said, of retribution for my acts. At the time, I didn't believe her. I don't know if she remembers, but since I've been in my cell, I remember everything! In my cell, I am worth nothing more than those pelicans, hens, lions, tigers, monkeys, pythons, turtles, and crocodiles that are exhibited in iron cages for the curiosity of tourists. If I am better off, it is because I, unlike them, can speak of my suffering.

But I also have several good deeds to my name: giving of alms, offerings to the ancestors, participation in Kathen ceremonies, in Flower Festival processions, in school inaugurations, contributions to the construction of sanctuaries, of monk cells, of school buildings, and of hospitals. If these good works are worth anything, if I am able to improve myself, to abstain from wrongdoing, I owe it to my mother and the virtues of Buddhism. Salvation has come to me from their tolerance: my mother's tolerance, Buddhism's tolerance...I am convinced of one thing: an ugly look is enough to engulf the world in flames and cover it with blood; and conversely, a sign of love, even a single one, is enough to spread love across the great cycles of existence.

A guard calls me. "Mister Chea Em, get dressed!"

Sudden pain in my stomach. I was starting to calm down, I was falling asleep, and here I am again, caught up in my story...

"Mister Chea Em." He calls me again, flashing the citation.

"Yes, yes, I'm coming."

I get up from the mat, my stomach tight with fear. What do they want from me now? These nighttime interrogations are done by the inspector, even at midnight. I don't mind it. I know it's an interrogation technique. They choose the moment that will yield the best results. Then why am I so frightened? Why am I incapable of staying calm? I'm angry with myself. The last time I had seen the citation order, it was right after mealtime, so I couldn't digest properly. This time, it's worse. The fear is like a ball inside my stomach. I can't do anything about it.

I get dressed in a hurry and go down with the guard, my stomach swollen with fear. I look at the guard. He seems completely normal.

The inspector slams the door behind him. I find myself in a room I don't know, buried in a deep silence. An agent of an impressive height, possessing a tough face and thick, muscular arms, stands by me. He looks at me from head to toe without blinking, without a word, waiting for orders. The inspector has told me several times that in my case they would use neither torture nor fists, but this small room and double-locked door terrify me...

Yet I am not a coward. I've never been scared by stories of the dead, of phantoms that cling to your bike, that hang by your cart, that hit you, that break your neck, or by stories of horrible, restless ghouls who stick out an enormous tongue and whose crystalline lullabies suck up your soul in a vortex. They say such encounters are terrible and the horror is such that it can make you sick, turn your hair gray, drive you mad, and even kill you. But I know that there isn't anything human in that, anything really tangible. Nor am I scared by brutes, thugs, or villains. I've always told myself that you just have to anticipate their blows, the moment when they take out a blade or draw a gun, and vanish as fast as you can. Unless, of course, you can't run. Unless you have already been tied up. In that case, everyone to his own karma...

I know it's dangerous to live among men. I've known it for more than twenty years, since I've been able to reason. And yet I've never been so afraid as now. Never. Even the day they scraped my jaw, when my head was but a vibration and the noise of the drill filled the entire room. Even the day of my surgery, when all I could hear was the rattle of the instruments and the rustle of bodies, when I saw their big needles, blood everywhere, and the sharp brightness of the lancet, when around me there were only strange faces, hidden behind masks. But now, I'm all by myself, unaware of how to react, unprepared. Here, I have no support, no recourse…

I'm curled up, my arms joined around my body, like a little wet animal. I stare silently at every corner of the room. My eyes move from the table to the floors, the walls, the door, the agent, the inspector, and come back to look at myself. I glance up, down, to the right, to the left, in front, behind.

At the north point of the room, behind the inspector's back, a photo of the Chief of State hangs on the wall. I feel as if he is looking at me. This makes me think of Sartre's play *Morts sans sépulture,* in which one of the executioners looks at Pétain's portrait and is outraged by his distance and indifference. I don't say a word to the inspector, but I focus on my comparison, hang on to it as long as I can. I'm hoping to trick my fear this way, but it resists, my fear; it encircles my thoughts, it shoves my determination down my throat.

In the west corner, by the door, is a metallic machine. It's so big it towers over me. Under the instrument's body: a space of about ten centimeters, just enough to let in an arm or a leg. A huge screw goes from one end to the other. What use could this machine have? Whom do they want to crush in it? And what if it were my bones, Lord, that they wanted to grind! There are a couple of other machines of the same kind but smaller, baring their jaws and seemingly eager to sink their fangs into my flesh.

The inspector interrogates me at great length, then suddenly gets up and rushes to open the cabinet next to me. A big cabinet, wide and solid, which has been eyeing me scornfully, casting a black, sidelong glance. What is the inspector looking for? What will he pull out of this cabinet? My heart races madly, like a locomotive in the night. I tremble all over. My chest burns with fear. My feet and hands are frozen. I try to control myself, but my nerves won't listen to the demands of my brain any longer. Suddenly an old expression comes to mind: *scare the living daylights out of you.*

Ten minutes elapse, then twenty, then half an hour, an hour, an hour and a half…In front of me, the big hand of the clock hanging on the wall seems petrified. I am exhausted, one step from passing out. I invoke the ancestors, the *tevoda,* my mother's merits, my masters' good deeds. I pray for all this to end, for the inspector to stop, to stop asking me questions in this small room where there is nothing, absolutely nothing to diminish my isolation, to ease my terror.

In the end, the inspector allows me to return to my cell.

After these interrogations, I am weakened and need almost uninterrupted sessions of coining therapy. I am wiped out for almost three days, unable to swallow anything but a little rice. Each time, I am sure, I lose several years of my life. I pray fifty, sixty times a day for my case to end. Each interrogation is like an exam I must pass in order to recover my freedom. So I prepare. It is a constant effort. I try to anticipate all possible questions. I measure the effect of my words, I ponder every possible meaning of my sentences, as I have to satisfy the inspector and try to soften him up. If I give the wrong answer, I may be sent to court—a word that alone conjures up the nightmare of the Main Headquarters or the jails of Prey Sar. Yet my grandparents have told me numerous times, "One trades in his own yard, not somewhere else!" I don't even want to imagine what would happen if the inspector punctuated his questions with a physical threat or if, between sentences, he were to grab a club or something else…What would happen to my body, so thin already, so tired? It would probably survive, but in what state and for how long?

I do have one hope left, however. A tiny one. I know I am innocent and wrongly accused. So I try to fool myself, I try to be an optimist: the inspector is a Khmer; he has dark skin and the same blood as I do.

Translation from Khmer to French by Christophe Macquet and from French to English by Daniela Hurezanu and Stephen Kessler

Ghouls, Ghosts, and Other Infernal Creatures ⸺⸺⸺

One

During 1945 and 1946, a cholera epidemic struck my village on the island of Koh Somrong, which is part of the province of Kompong Cham.

There was panic, general upheaval. At night, the villagers lit fires near their huts to ward off the dead who were coming back to take lives. These dead feared fire. That's what we as Khmers believed. As soon as the sun set, no one dared to make a noise. We were all barricaded in our homes, careful to turn off all lights and extinguish any indication of our presence.

In the beginning, a gong was struck with each new death, and people trembled like frightened little animals, especially when this happened at night. Dogs barked and moaned without stopping.

So many people died that we stopped striking the gong. Everyone kept silent. Everything was still. Some wrapped their dead in mats or towels and carried them into the forest to be buried. When a family was in mourning, people no longer came to visit, fearful of the corpse and contagion.

At night, you could hear strange whisperings all along the route.

"Let's go in this house."

"No, not right away. Tomorrow. Let's take care of the house that's on the edge of the village."

These fragments of conversation spread terror among the villagers. Dread paralyzed their tongues.

Then misfortune reached my family: my sister-in-law died. The very evening her husband was to bury her, one of my uncles died too. The following day, it was one of my older brothers.

Such tragic events! My mother was white with fear. When I fell ill two days later, she no longer had any tears left. She prayed as much as she could to all the deities and divinities. She feared that I would die too, but I just threw up a little. When evening came, only my uncle Ros dared stay in my room.

Outside, the wind swirled. The leaves of the banana trees rustled in the night with a gloomy sound. Sick and at the end of my strength, I still could not sleep. I was fully conscious of what was being said around me. My mother had lost hope: I was going to die. It was only a question of time.

At midnight, I still hadn't closed my eyes. Uncle Ros prayed at the foot of my bed. As soon as he closed his prayer book, yawning, a dog started barking furiously outside the door. Then a muffled sound was heard under the floor.

"This doesn't seem to be it."

"No."

"We must have made a wrong turn."

"Right. It's more to the south. It's not yet time for him."

"Well, let's go."

Stretched out on my bed, I heard every word. Uncle Ros must have too. As if petrified, he remained seated for a long time, then left to wake up my mother, who, thinking that I had died, rushed in to take my pulse.

"Has it happened, Older Brother?" she asked.

"No," he answered. "He's out of danger. Tomorrow he'll get better, that's for sure. I just heard the dead. They said he's not on the list."

My mother's face regained its color immediately. The next day, I got better, and two or three days later I had all of my strength back.

That year, cholera almost decimated my village, and my family, like others, lost many of its members.

Illness had struck every day, leaving behind mounds of bodies. These were usually cremated near a stand of bamboo about five hundred meters from my house. Because it was impossible to burn so many bodies in a single fire, the mounds were left in the bamboo overnight. The bodies—some only partially consumed by the flames—would be burned again the next morning.

One evening, one of my older brothers and two or three of the peasants returning from work ended up near the cremation area. My brother, who was afraid of the dead, had sweat pouring from his forehead. Suddenly, something fell heavily, and the top of a skull was thrown in front of him.

"A body!" he screamed. "Help! Help! The dead have come back to haunt us!"

Everyone stared. Sure enough, there was a body, but not a ghost or zombie, just a charcoaled cadaver, still smoking. Through the action of the tendons, the body had been propelled out of the crematorium. It wasn't the only one either. Other cadavers, partly calcified, were seated along the road, their mouths hanging open frightfully, their lipless smiles displaying all their teeth. Others had been catapulted into the bamboo and were propped on the branches in horrible ways.

The next morning, the boys returned to the spot to gather the cadavers and finish the cremation.

Translation from Khmer to French by Christophe Macquet and from French to English by Jean Toyama

Two

When I came back home for the holidays, I found my older sister lying on a mat, gravely ill. Though she breathed painfully, she was very happy to see me.

Over the next few days, her illness took a turn for the worse. It was obvious that this was no ordinary illness. She no longer recognized her brothers and sisters. As soon as night fell, she would start crawling across the house, heading for my mother's room, fighting with everyone, preventing the whole family from sleeping. A strange illness! She hadn't lost her appetite but never got up, leaving her mat only to crawl on the floor.

My mother, who observed all this with a jaundiced eye, went to fetch a master medium who would interrogate our family's protective household spirit. The spirit took possession of the medium and, through his mouth, gave this answer: "If in two weeks she isn't doing any better, the cause is Green Kantong…The powerful ghoul has come to take a life…This evil is the Evil of the Ancestors…The punishment will strike a member of the family…"

My mother understood right away what had happened. A month earlier, she had heard that, without the adults' consent, a nephew and niece of hers had made love in a clump of banana trees. The girl was now expecting, but the boy refused to ask her to marry him because of an old quarrel between the two families. My mother was very worried. In order for my sister to get well, the young couple had to perform the Giving-for-Forgiving ritual and their parents had to agree to it. She couldn't see any other way out. Finally, she decided to speak with both parties so that the lovers would make the offering to the Spirit of the Ancestors.

The ceremony took place that very evening. Rushing, we also organized the Banquet-of-Thanks ritual to the protective spirit. The medium was an old woman in her sixties.

While the preparations for the banquet were under way, we had my sister sit facing the medium. The music of the Spirits started up, and the old woman began dancing with an amazing agility.

—*I'm coming! I'm coming!* she yelled.

—*Who's there?* my mother asked.

—*It's me, Green Kantong! Green Kantong!*

—*Have mercy, Green Kantong. Give our little bird her wits back…*

—*No problem…No problem…Just pour me a small glass of wild water, and we'll snatch the little bird from death!*

The music played ceaselessly. One after another, spirits passed through the medium's body. After Green Kantong came Red Throat, the venerable Ancient who likes nibbling on *kantun bak kaa* [ripe bananas]. The old woman had drunk an incredible quantity of alcohol and was starting to sway.

When all the Spirits were finally appeased, my sister sat up suddenly, startling everyone and reaffirming our faith. The two lovers, standing on the side, seemed happy with the result. The Ancients had decided. The couple were made husband and wife. Failure of the ritual would have made union impossible.

Several days later, my sister recovered her health.

But that wasn't the last illness. Two or three days later, one of my nephews fell ill. He was feverish and trembled the way you do during the cold season.

As far as my mother was concerned, there was no question of giving him any medication whatsoever. She did for my nephew what had worked so well for my sister. All the ghouls, ghosts, and other infernal creatures of the supernatural world passed into the medium's body, and everyone assured us that my nephew would soon be on his feet.

The next day, however, his health worsened. By this time, his parents' torment was at its peak. Their eyes turned a glassy white, like that of boiled fish. With each moan, my nephew scratched the inside of his ear. Struck with curiosity, my older brother leaned over him and saw, lodged in his hearing tract, a gecko big as a thumb. Its two jaws bit into the boy's flesh.

"Poor fool!" he yelled at my sister. "It's only a gecko biting his ear!"

We took the reptile out of his ear, and he recovered completely.

Translation from Khmer to French by Christophe Macquet and from French to English by Daniela Hurezanu

Bas Relief Detail, Heaven and Hell,
South Gallery, Angkor Wat, 2002
Photograph by Richard Murai

from *Journey into Light*

II. ROOT OF AN EVIL

When the bell rang, we gathered, as usual, under the nation's flag. I noticed the older students and the teachers were talking and whispering, but I was not really concerned with what they were saying. We were all in the schoolyard of Sala Komrou (Model School), a new school just north of Siem Reap town. It was 18 March 1970.

"Get in line and be very quiet!" one of the teachers barked. We fell in line according to our grade and gender. About fifteen minutes later, everyone was in line and at attention. The chattering died down as our principal, surrounded by four soldiers in full combat gear, came out of the building. They walked slowly and stopped in front of us.

It was the first time I had seen this many soldiers up close. They held their M-16s ready, their sharp eyes scanning the area. None of them smiled. The schoolyard was absolutely quiet. It frightened me a little.

It was also a little exciting, particularly to those of us boys whose favorite subjects were guns and soldiers. Most of our parents had at least one rifle or pistol at home. My father had an assortment of weapons locked up in his room, and we children often played soldier, fighting and dying in numerous battles. I think many of us wished we were real soldiers with real guns like these young men who stood before us.

The soldier with many stripes on his uniform handed a piece of paper to our principal. We all knew the principal was in some kind of trouble. He looked very pale and was sweating profusely, which seemed strange because the morning air was still chilly. His hands trembled as he read the paper. His voice shook. I didn't quite understand everything he said.

When he stopped reading, the soldier with the stripes shoved the principal, and the other soldiers grabbed his arms. The officer said to us, "My friends, teachers, and all the good students of this fine institution, do you know why we are here today? There is a traitor among us."

He paused and then pointed at our principal. "Do you know that this man is trying to destroy our great culture and wonderful society?"

He went on for some time with his rather boring speech. I didn't pay very much attention to him. I was looking at our principal, who was starting to look like a very sick man.

The soldier ordered our principal to lower Sihanouk's Sangkum Reastr Niyum regime flag from the pole in front of the administration building. The officer rolled up the old flag, tossed it in his jeep, and gave the principal a new one. The soldiers saluted as it went up. The new flag was not much different from the old one. It had the same colors, but the Angkor Wat symbol was in the upper left corner instead of the center.

Thus was born in Siem Reap the Khmer Republic under Marshall Lon Nol. I did not know it then, but on that very day, a coup d'état was deposing the country's leader, Prince Sihanouk.

The soldiers ordered everyone to go home right away, but we stood there in shock. Three of them manhandled our principal, pushing him into their MADE IN THE USA military jeep and driving away in a trail of white dust. Some female teachers started to weep openly. A few minutes later, we heard the sounds of automatic gunfire coming from the jeep's direction. The teachers said it was nothing, school was over for the day, and we should go home.

That was the last time anyone saw our principal. The fear in his eye remains with me to this day. He was "purged," most likely for being a supporter of Sihanouk's regime—as were many of the civil servants.

A week later, I was back in school. The new flag hung from the old flagpole. The principal, also new, was very suspicious and unfriendly and probably from the big city. New teachers replaced those who had disappeared. We had to sing a new national anthem, which was a little more upbeat than the old one.

Many of us disliked the new principal. The new teachers were young, aggressive, and strict. I was not allowed to care for my vegetable garden, which had been an important part of our school's agriculture project for months. We had to study more and more, so our recess periods became fewer and shorter.

The teachers punished us for the tiniest mistakes. In Khmer tradition, it is part of school discipline for teachers to beat students, but I thought these new punishments were too harsh and often unnecessary. Many students went home with bruises. Some students began to rebel and refused to obey their new teachers. Those who skipped class to avoid the worst teachers were punished even more. Many started to skip school altogether.

III. TASTE OF HORRIFIC WAR

From miles away, column after column of monsoon clouds gradually merged into massive rain clouds. The winds died suddenly, and warm air rose to greet the cold front. The air pressure dropped, then increased. Eardrums popped. Again and again, tremendous thunder shook the sky and scattered flocks of birds. Then a massive downpour flooded Siem Reap. The monsoon season had come again, right on time.

At about ten o'clock that night, artillery explosions mixed with the thunder and lightning, shaking our house and rattling the roof tiles. Shells that were fired from miles away tore through the dense air. We listened, terrified, to the whizzing and screeching that preceded each explosion.

We should not have been surprised when the battle began that stormy night. My father, who served in the civilian militia, knew that something was about to happen. A few weeks earlier, the militia had conscripted my father and three elder brothers, who were then college students, to defend the city. They spent a few days learning how to operate surplus WWII American rifles and other war equipment. From then on, they were forced to defend the city against a well-armed and well-seasoned guerrilla force, battle-hardened Viet Cong, and fledgling Khmer Rouge fighters.

My family stored food and provisions and conducted drills almost every day. For a bomb shelter, we dug a trench in our backyard, piled sandbags around it, and roofed it with timber. "Those who prepare enough will survive," my father said to all of us before he left to defend the city. Unfortunately, no one can really prepare for war.

Our home by the forest was just outside the city's defensive line. My father said the Communists—the Khmer Rouge and their Viet Cong allies—would shell the city area, so we should stay at home. His assessment was correct. The first rainy night of the battle, while the militia hunkered down in the flooded trenches with orders to shoot anything that moved, the city was heavily shelled. We prayed that all of us would come out of the battle alive.

We ate and slept in our bomb-shelter trench. At night, a kerosene lamp gave us a little light but blackened our nostrils with its smoke. That we did not die of carbon monoxide poisoning was a wonder and a miracle. We did, however, get severe headaches from breathing in the smoke.

I longed for my warm, comfortable bed in the house. "When can we go back inside the house?" we all complained. Mother said, "Our home is not safe from the bullets. This trench is uncomfortable and dirty and wet, but it is safer." Built high off the ground to protect us from the floodwaters, our house was vulnerable to bullets and artillery fire. We stayed in the crude trench waiting for the fighting to begin and at the same time prayed that it would not come.

I missed my father and brothers. I was praying hard for them and for us as well. "Please, God, take good care of our family and I will do anything you ask of me." I would pray each morning, noon, and night and repeat my prayer the next day, week, and month.

After almost two weeks in the awful trench, my mother, who was then about three months pregnant, said, "I have had enough of living like rats in a hole. I would rather we die from bullets and rockets than by drowning!" I looked at her blackened nostrils. Then I began to laugh out loud. "What are you laughing about? What is so funny?" Mother asked. I pointed at my own blackened nostrils. Mother started to chuckle, then burst into laughter. Soon we were all laughing like a bunch of lunatics. We had not laughed so hard in a long time, especially my mother.

That first night back in the house, I felt comfortable and secure. The skies opened up with possibly the heaviest monsoon rainstorm of that season. My nice, warm bed was heaven compared to our water-filled trench. I was sound asleep when a 55-mm howitzer shell landed nearby, so close that I saw the flash of light. The entire house shook violently, and tiles on the roof broke loose. I was off the bed and on the floor in seconds.

Mother had already been awakened by small-arms fire in the distance. She roused us when the big explosion came. "Go, go, go! Move it! Let's go! Now!" Mother yelled as loud as she could.

The bullets left red and orange tracers across the night rain. I was mesmerized by the sights and sounds, but also terrified. Some bullets hit the roof and wooden walls of our house; others zipped by with a shearing noise. The shells and bullets came from the city, possibly fired by my own father and brothers and their comrades.

Helicopters and fixed-wing planes sprayed the ground with 50-mm Vulcan cannons. Occasionally, parachuted flares lit up the sky with multiple explosions. While the flares descended, the night was as bright as day.

Every now and then a bullet or a piece of shrapnel landed nearby, bounced off a wall, or penetrated the roof and hit our furniture. We stayed tight against the floor, praying that nothing would hit us. The cycle of darkness, explosions, lights, sounds, and darkness continued. My ears were ringing. Everyone screamed, terrified. Finally, Mother decided the house was not safe. We ran out into the furious monsoon rainstorm, beneath whirring bullets and exploding shells. I found the entrance to the trench and saw that it was waist-deep in muddy water. I hesitated.

"You *pret!* Get inside the trench! Now!" Mother screamed, calling me a devil. Then she kicked me. I fell in headfirst with a huge splash. When I opened my mouth to cry, I took in a big gulp of muddy water. Before Mother could kick them as well, my sister and brothers dived in, landing on top of me. I gagged on monsoon water before Mother regained her wits and pulled me out of the flooded trench. "I'm sorry. So sorry!" she pleaded with remorse.

I could not say a word. I was too busy trying to cough and vomit up the stuff I'd swallowed. Everyone else was whimpering with fear, not knowing what to do next.

Smoke and steam were everywhere. Mother was stunned. Her own foot had almost made me our family's first casualty of war.

Bullets whizzed by; artillery shells rocked the ground and lit up the sky. The trench water covered my little brothers to their chins. Mother decided we couldn't stay there. "Let's go to the neighbor's place!" she said. "Their shelter might be better than ours."

We pounded on the neighbor's door. Mom called out the neighbor's name and identified herself. We kids screamed our lungs out, hoping it would help. The door remained closed. Mother wept in utter frustration. We all began to cry.

Then the door opened slowly. A woman's voice whispered, "Who is it?"

"It's us, Sister," Mother said hopefully.

"Oh, come on in! Come in, please! You all are soaking wet," said the gentle voice. We entered the house. Since the walls and floors were concrete, it was warm and dry inside. Immediately I felt safe.

These neighbors had moved in just recently, so I had been to their home only a few times. When the small, thin woman answered the door, I didn't even know her name. We called her simply "Mother of Chhay," and her husband "Father of Chhay." That's the way people refer to each other in Khmer society: not by first or last names, but their respective titles.

All I knew about our neighbors was that, like my parents, the husband was a civil servant and the wife was a homemaker. They had three children, all of them small boys. The wife was home alone with the boys. Her husband had been conscripted into the militia, just as my dad and older brothers had been.

"We can't stay in our house because of the bullets and explosions. We nearly drowned in our trench because of the floodwaters. Can we please stay with you, just for a little while?" Mother wept out loud as she pleaded.

"Of course, of course you can. You are welcome to stay as long as you like. I know it is very bad out there. That's why we stayed inside," said the woman. She and her three little children were as frightened as we were, and they seemed pleased to have our company.

Shaking uncontrollably, we huddled in our neighbor's dry, warm house. Once in a while, a stray bullet ricocheted off a wall as though someone had thrown a rock at it. However, the bullets could not penetrate the concrete walls. Mother sang a lullaby to calm my little brothers. I leaned closer to her for comfort and warmth. I knew she was tired and scared too. I felt very sorry for her, for all of us.

Sleep was difficult with the battle raging just outside, but fatigue won over. I fell asleep, holding my mother tightly, afraid to let her go. Sleeping, everyone surrounded her. Her gentle lullaby caressed us quietly. *"Kon euy, keng tuv..."* [Go to sleep, my children...] Soon, she was the only one who was not sleeping.

The next morning, the aircraft and large artillery were gone. For about three hours, we heard only sporadic small-arms fire. *The soldiers have stopped fighting and are eating,* I thought. Against Mother's orders, I went outside and saw that the walls had bullet holes and shrapnel in them. If any artillery had hit the house directly, we would've all been dead.

I wanted to go see our house, but the fighting resumed and I ran back inside. My elder brother, Norane, had seen our home. "The south wall has a big hole, big as a midsized car. There are many holes of all sizes, but the house is not burned," he said. Naively I told myself I would have to go see it as soon as the soldiers stopped for lunch or dinner again. Later, I learned that wars do not stop for meals.

The fighting went on for five days before the next lull. Every time there was an explosion, the entire house shook and dust rained from the ceiling. I thought the concrete walls would collapse on us. We were always keeping our heads as low as possible. I remember sitting up, nervously listening to the sound of airplanes roaming the dark sky, and cursing them and God. I was afraid of the machine-gun spray, the bombs, and explosions: *tat tat tat! boom boom!* I didn't know what kind of planes they were. Were they on our side or the other side? Whose side was I on?

Like our frightened neighbors, my family and I were on no particular side. We were fighting no enemy. We were caught between the bullets of my father and brothers and those of the Communists. We were only trying to survive to see the next sunrise. "Too many are hurt and suffering. Why would anyone want to kill another person?" I asked God. No answer; absolutely nothing.

After a week, our food supply was almost gone. We survived on rice gruel and watery soup with salty dried fish.

Then we ran out of food altogether. I was desperately hungry. At first, we went out to find food whenever the fighting slowed down. Later, in desperation, we went out to scavenge even during shelling. We gathered anything edible, including pigs and chickens that had been dead for days. We were frightened and had no news to ease our anxiety. Mother tried her best to lessen our fears even though she was in tears most of the time. I tried hard to be strong, but I couldn't be strong enough. We worried that our father and brothers were hurt—or dead. We still did not know who was attacking us and who was winning. "The hell with them! They're killing each other, and for what? When will the fighting stop?" I asked God. "When will it all stop?"

Then I found myself no longer believing that God ever existed. "If He had existed to begin with, He would have heard our prayers. He would not have let us suffer like this!" I cursed.

Although I was only nine years old, I became a man of the house, and it was my responsibility to help take care of the family. I was deputy to my brother Norane, who was eleven. Though I was scared of the dark and the gunfire, I helped Norane search for food and medicine. We were often lucky enough to find dead animals and wild vegetables, but medicine was impossible to find.

One morning while gathering food during a lull in the fighting, we ran into the Viet Cong. I had heard of their brutality to Khmer women and children. Government cartoons caricatured them as vicious beasts holding AK-47s. Now, before our very eyes was a small unit: a platoon of twelve soldiers, including four Khmer Rouge fighters. They wore black cotton pajamas and the infamous Ho Chi Minh rubber-tire sandals.

They pointed new Soviet and Chinese assault rifles at us. My hands went up automatically. Immediately I wet my pants. The guerrillas laughed.

"Little Brothers, where are you going?" one Khmer Rouge fighter in his early twenties asked politely. They carried very little combat gear, I noticed, and must've been moving from place to place rapidly. Across their chests hung military pouches with three spare AK-47 magazines and Chinese-made grenades, the kind with foot-long wooden handles. On their backs hung cloth tubes about four inches around and packed with uncooked rice. Their largest weapon was a small mortar and B-40 grenade launcher. Of course, I learned the names of such weaponry years later.

"It's OK. Don't be scared, Little Brothers. We are your friends," he said.

I didn't know what to say or think. I would have revealed all state secrets to him if I had known any.

"Food, food," I said, crying.

They lowered their weapons and spoke in Vietnamese. I was no longer crying, but I was still scared. One Khmer Rouge fighter turned to us and said, "We have some rice to trade for some of your chickens. Would you like to trade?"

We had enough rice to last us awhile, so I spoke up, a bit boldly. "Big Brothers, do you have medicine for flu or fever? I'd rather trade my chickens for medicine. We really need it."

Norane kicked my butt and motioned me to shut up. He handed the man my two dead chickens and stepped back.

Scared shitless, I thought. *Some head of family you are, Norane!*

The older fighter said something, and one of his men produced some pills. "Here, a fair trade for *your chickens.*" He emphasized the last two words. "Go home and don't say anything or I'll come and find you. Go now!"

We nodded, grabbed the medicine, and slowly backed away. When the laughing guerrillas melted back into the forest, we turned and ran as fast as we could.

We collapsed in front of our neighbors' house, where everyone was waiting. My mother's face always showed great relief whenever we returned. Few of them bothered to ask where we got the food; they were only too happy to eat. We did not say anything much, fearing that the Viet Cong and Khmer Rouge fighters would come and find us. I did not know then that throughout Cambodia and Viet Nam the Communists were using the hearts-and-mind strategy to win over the local people. Sadly, after reaching the strategy's objectives, they treated the people like trash.

That night, the monsoon rains continued. Among my family and neighbors, I lay under a warm blanket and counted the ten days since the first explosion. Everything that had happened seemed surreal, like a nightmare. But this was a quiet night. There were no aircraft overhead. We prayed that my father and brothers would return soon. I prayed that things would be better tomorrow. It had been so long since I had had a good night's sleep.

Little did I know that this battle was only the beginning.

Art of faCt: An Interview with praCh _____

Called by *Asiaweek* "Cambodia's first rap star," praCh uses his music and lyrics to connect younger and older generations, Cambodia and America. Born in Cambodia in the aftermath of the Khmer Rouge regime, he and his family left when he was an infant. They eventually settled in the large Cambodian community in Long Beach, California. In 2000, when he was twenty-one, he recorded his first album in his parents' garage for the Khmer New Year celebration. Without his knowledge, the CD made its way across the Pacific to Cambodia, and a pirated version—which omitted his name—became the number-one album in the country. His work combines traditional Khmer musical forms and instrumentation with the hip-hop beat and unflinching directness of American street rap. He has been featured in *Newsweek*, *Los Angeles Times*, and *New York Post* and on *Frontline*, commercial television, and *Voice of America*. This interview was conducted by telephone in September 2003.

SM   Can you talk about the meaning of your name in Khmer?

P   The meaning of *praCh* is "advisor to the king" or "person who talks a lot." But my parents didn't name me praCh because of that. The area where I was born was called Veal Srae K'prach: farmland of K'prach. I'm from a big family. I have three brothers and four sisters—four girls, four boys—and I'm the seventh child. They didn't know what to name me when I was born at the camp place, so they just named me praCh.

SM   You were born after the Khmer Rouge period, is that right?

P   I was born in 1979, near Battambang. The Vietnamese had invaded already. It was chaotic then, the time of confusion. No one knew where they were going or where they were headed. But my mom was pregnant with me. She had me in a hut. Later, my parents went back to Cambodia and videotaped the tree I was born under, but the hut's no longer there.

SM   Do you have any memory of the border?

P   Actually, I was so young, the only thing I can remember is waterfalls. And I remember a bridge, made out of rope, but it seemed more like a dream, not even a memory. But when I asked my parents about it, they said it was an actual place. That was when we were crossing to the Thai border and I was an infant.

SM   In your song, "Welcome," you talk about arriving in the U.S.: "soon our feet hits the ground,/my mom busted in tears./words can't describe,/a moment so rare./and right by her side,/my father was there./staring at the skies,/hold'n each other./realize we survive the genocide."

P   That I remember. That is probably the first thing I remember clearly. It's strange. I remember on the plane trip they asked if we wanted peanuts. My parents and the other people were joking about the food. Oh, they're going to give us these bags of peanuts, why don't they give us *banh chhev?* And then, when the plane landed, they opened the door hatch, and I remember seeing my mom crying and my dad holding her. He said, "From this point on, it can only get better." They praised the Buddha, and they held each other.

There was hope for us. I was too young to understand what was going on, but now I do understand it. I'm glad that I remember that time.

I saw families that were kissing the ground. Because finally they made it. It seemed like we had just escaped from hell. I don't mean Cambodia is hell, but it just seemed like there was total darkness then, and finally we made it out into the light.

SM   How did you end up in Long Beach?

P   I was in Florida from 1983 until 1987, in the suburbs. Then we moved to California, to El Monte, north of Long Beach. If there's any ghetto place, this was the ghetto of all ghettos. It was bad. It was like a project—apartments on top of apartments—and the school was in the back of the apartments. In the alleyway there were drug deals, and every night we heard helicopters and shoot-outs.

We took it for two years, and then my parents decided to move to Long Beach. We had always heard about Long Beach and had a cousin down there. It was 1989.

When we moved down there, again it wasn't paradise. It was an apartment complex, on the border between Long Beach and Compton, and there were a lot of Cambodians—like a Cambodian haven. But once we went outside, to the stores or the park, no one knew who Cambodians were. We didn't really have an identity. They called us *Chinese, chinky eyes, gook.* I guess that just made me stronger. I wouldn't say anything like that to other people now because I know how it feels. You learn from stuff like that.

SM   So how did you get interested in poetry and rap?

P   Poetry, I don't remember the exact time. Some people remember I wrote my first poem on this day or that. I don't remember that. I was into art and drawing. One day my older sisters came home from school and started writing poems about flowers and nature, and I heard music on the radio, and I thought, Hey, I want to give this a try.

I watched *Sesame Street* too, maybe that got me into it. I didn't really learn my ABCs in school because I couldn't connect much with the teachers. You know, my parents didn't know English, so they couldn't teach me; I had to speak Khmer at home. But *Sesame Street* was good for me, because it kind of rhymed too. Every time they said something, it rhymed. So thanks to *Sesame Street,* thanks to Big Bird...I owe it all to them.

I was also listening to rap: Run DMC, EPMD, and NWA, with Ice Cube, Dr. Dre, DJ Yella, and MC Ren. They're here in Long Beach, in Compton, one of the biggest rap groups ever—not just here, but worldwide. So I grew up listening to rap. My parents called it jungle music because the bass was real loud.

I really liked the music. And I would go to battles—not battling people, but competing lyrically. I was the only Asian doing that. You go against each other outside in the park. Everybody's there. You know, they have their crew, I have my crew—well, basically, I didn't have any crew, I had my friend who didn't know English. You go back and forth, rap back and forth, kind of like Khmer *ayai.* The crowd declares who wins. Whoever's sharper wins. I win sometimes, I lose a lot of times, but that was a stepping stone. You learn from your mistakes, you earn your stripes. And then you go to clubs, work your way up. That's how I got started.

But during that time, it was mostly gangsta music. That was just about all there was in my area. It was a gangster environment. You saw graffiti everywhere. There were shoot-outs. Like I said, I was living in the ghetto. It was hectic and crazy and I was listening to Snoop Dogg and Dr. Dre, and everyone was looking up to them.

My turning point came when I moved back to Florida. My parents sent me to Florida to live with my older brother for almost a year and a half.

SM   So they sent you there to straighten you out.

P   Actually, yeah. With my friends and all the fights, they saw what was happening and they said, Just go stay with your brother for a while. When I was in Florida, there wasn't much to do. I was writing street music—don't get me wrong, you can't take that out of me. But I guess I was having an identity crisis. And my brother, he guided me a little bit.

SM How did you find that identity?

P Well, everybody here in Long Beach was doing the same thing. All they talked about was guns, gangs, girls—like bragging rights. Even today, you hear a lot of that B.S. on the radio. But when I went to Florida, I didn't have any connections with friends, I was isolated from society. My brother owned a car shop. I was about sixteen or seventeen years old, and he let me manage the place. He trusted me. And he started telling me stories about what had happened in Cambodia.

SM Did he just start telling you?

P Actually, I asked him. Because when I asked my parents, they would tell me some things, but I was too young to remember them. Even when we were eating dinner, they would say, You'd better finish up your plate because people in Cambodia don't have much to eat. But they never got to the point of talking about the killings. They would tell us what had happened in general about Pol Pot and the Khmer Rouge regime, but they wouldn't tell any personal stories. I think they were waiting for us to be the right age. They didn't want to tell us stories about death.

But my brother wasn't holding anything back. I told him what my parents had said and I asked him, "Is it true?" He said, "Oh yeah, it's true." And then he would go on to his own stories. He was working in the camps. They separated boys from girls, parents from children. The camps were separated by a few miles. He knew my mom and sister were starving, so at nighttime he would sneak out to find food. He would take a coconut or whatever he could steal and drop it off for my sisters and my mom and come back to his own camp. Some nights he didn't even sleep because it was hours of travel, and he had to hide at the same time. He told me if he got caught, it was an automatic death sentence.

He was saying there was a massive grave pit, where they executed people. He was describing all these horrors. And he said, I know I'm telling you stories; you don't have to believe me, but from their stories and my stories, you put it together and think about what you believe or not.

We were staying up late at night to have these conversations.

SM So you weren't even sure what they were telling you really happened?

P Yeah, because there were no documents. The only film that I remember vividly was *The Killing Fields*. Even in school books, other historical events had a chapter, but Cambodia had only a page. Two million people murdered, and there was only a page with one picture. At least give it a chapter. But now that I know, I see living documents all around me.

I started writing poetry using what my brother was telling me, my memories, and my parents'. I thought, I can't write about what I don't have. I'm not going to be fake. So I started writing my life story by crafting *Dalama*. I didn't have a title then. I was just writing on pieces of paper, throwing them in my bag. I'd write in notebooks, on napkins, whatever I had at the moment, and put it away in a pocket somewhere.

When I went back to Long Beach, I had learned a lesson.

SM   How did you record your first album?

P   When I returned to Long Beach, I formed a group with friends. I was living at my parents' house. In the garage, I gathered a karaoke machine, microphones, a tape player you could plug a mike into. That was basically the equipment I used for the first album. I didn't have any beats or instrumentals, so I bought some CDs from stores to use. I was doing it just for fun; I wasn't thinking of selling. I decided I was going to make a CD and pass it out during the Cambodian New Year—just for the fun of it.

The first album took about three months. I would stay up late at night, and I had school in the morning on top of that. My parents said I had to stop the noise by ten o'clock, so at nighttime, I put the headphones on to do my editing, sampling, cutting, adding echoes.

One night, I had an experience. I'm not really superstitious, but I remember I was doing the song "The Year Zero." I was there by myself. And when I was doing that song, I felt a sudden chill in the room. All of a sudden the room got cold. Slowly, I turned off the equipment and then I ran into my house. I don't know what it was. But it happened to me three times when I was working on that album—on the songs "The Year Zero" and "The Letter." It could have been in my head. But when I am rapping, when I'm in front of the microphone, it's just not me anymore. It's like someone else has taken over.

When I was putting the album together, I didn't know what to name it. I was thinking about the Dalai Lama. I was thinking about drama, trauma, and I made up the word "Dalama." I looked it up in the dictionary, but there was no such word. I thought, I'm going to make up my own word and turn that into the story of my life.

I also did the artwork for the cover. I did the second one too. If you look at the cover of the second CD, you can see it connects with the first one. Each symbol represents a song. It's split down the middle into mirror images: on one side Angkor Wat, on the other the White House; on one side flowers, on the other a skeleton. When the first album got to Cambodia, they substituted a picture of a kid with a rifle. I don't know how it got to Cambodia.

We passed it out at the New Year in April 2000. The adult coordinators didn't really accept rap. They said, "We're sorry, but we really can't accept rap music here." I said, "Just give me a try." They said, "No, we can't do it."

SM So you weren't able to perform.

P No, I performed. It just sort of happened. We had a booth at the event to sell our CDs and promote our record label. My friend really didn't take it seriously, but I did. I thought, I'm going to make this happen because this is what I want to do. I went to the main stage to ask about performing. They said, "No, we can't let you go up there."

At that time, they were setting up for another band. The coordinator got up to say to the crowd, "Give us a few minutes for the band to set up." And she walked away. I thought, Here's my chance. The mike's still sitting there, and it's still on, and she's walked away. I thought, Here it is now—do or die.

I just walked up there and started talking to them. I spoke Cambodian, *chumreap suo.* Not many young Cambodians know how to speak Cambodian. I remember seeing the coordinator on the side; her eyes were saying, You're going to get it for this one. I said to the crowd, "I'm going to do a song for you now. If you don't like it, just boo me off the stage and I'll leave. But this is my chance. I want to do one Cambodian song and one American song."

I sang the song "Welcome." I did the English version first. The kids liked it because they understood it. The adults didn't really understand it. Then I said, "I'm going to translate it into Khmer."

It was an experience I'll never forget.

There was no music—just me and the mike, *a cappella.* I saw in their eyes that the adults couldn't believe what I was saying. I could tell they were hanging on to every word, waiting for what I would say next. When I was done, I had a standing ovation. The adults were applauding even more than the kids.

They said, "Do another one." And I did a song called *"Ayai."* It was a rap form of a Khmer *ayai,* kind of like a ghetto *ayai.* I rapped in Cambodian about welfare and drugs and what's going on in my community. After I was done with that, I really had them. The people asked me to do more. I said, "You know I'm not even supposed to be up here. I'm sorry." The coordinator came running up to me and said, "Do another one." I said, "No, I'm done now."

When I went back to my booth, there was a line of people wanting to buy my CD. I didn't want to make money off it. I just needed to get back the money I had spent making it. After that, I started passing it out for free.

DJ Sop, a well-known deejay in Cambodia, was there. I think he must have taken a copy back to Cambodia. I don't know why they changed the cover and the name. They used two titles, actually: *Khmer Rap* and *Khmer Rouge, Khmer Rap*. The cover was gone. The artwork was gone. My name was gone. The credits were gone. Gone out the window.

About six months went by. I was starting to get noticed. People said, "Oh, you're the kid from the New Year." They encouraged me to keep going. This was from the adults. And the kids, they liked other songs. Some of them are street songs, about shootings and drugs, but that's what I was surrounded by at that time.

Then one day I got a call from a reporter for *Asiaweek* and the *Cambodia Daily*, Gina Chon. She asked, "Is this praCh?"

I said, "Yes, this is praCh." I thought I was in trouble.

She said, "I'm calling from Cambodia." I was thinking, What did I do? Why am I in trouble? She said, "I'm glad I got a hold of you. It was hard to find you."

I said, "Get a hold of me for what? I didn't do anything." But my parents sometimes go back and forth to Cambodia, so I asked, "You want to speak to my parents?"

She said, "No, I want to speak to you." And then she explained, "Did you know your album's a big hit here and everybody's listening to it? It's really hot. It's the number-one album in the country."

I said, "What album are you talking about?"

"*Khmer Rap.*"

I said I didn't make any such album. And then she started reciting my lyrics. I said those were my lyrics, but that's not my title.

All of a sudden all these magazines and newspapers picked up on it. *L.A. Times, Newsweek.* I didn't even know what *Newsweek* was. I mean, I remember reading it in school, but I never paid much attention to it. When I talked to Chris Dufford, of the Associated Press, he said, "It's selling like hot cakes here. It's not just the fact that it's selling, but they're learning something from it. Kids are asking to know more about that time and era."

A reporter from *Voice of America* called me to do a radio interview to be broadcast in Cambodia. Her name was Savan, so I called her Aunt Savan. She conducted the whole interview in Cambodian for an hour and a half. I can't really carry on a conversation that long, but somehow I did. I did other interviews for Canadian and British stations, but that one was for Cambodia, so it meant more to me. She asked me when I was going to record another album.

At that time I had no plans to record another one, and in 2002, I was somehow chosen to coordinate the Cambodian New Year. It was a privilege for me to do that, but I felt like I had a heavy load on my back. It took about five months. I didn't do any CDs because it took a lot of my time. The New Year event was very successful. When we started, we were $35,000 in debt to the city from past events. But this time—it wasn't just me, we all put it together—the event made around $60,000, plus we paid off the debt. We had about fifteen thousand attendees and two main stages. The next year, 2003, they asked me if I wanted to do it again. I said, I'm going to take a break and get back to what I do.

During this time, I was getting a lot of media attention and they were asking when I was going to do another album. I finally gave them a date: 3 March 2003, because that date was 03-03-03. I just liked the number.

SM   This was your second *Dalama* album.

P   I didn't know what I was going to write, but I knew I wanted to do a second *Dalama*. I started drawing the pictures, formulating ideas. A lot of producers approached me, but I already had my own, so I stuck with them because I believed in them. And I thought, It's not like we're doing this just for ourselves anymore. In three months, we knocked the album out. It was out for the New Year in April.

For me, personally, I think *Dalama Two* is more—I don't want to say creative, but I gave it its own life. It's not a duplication of the first album. It bears a similarity because it's an autobiography too. But at the same time, it holds its own ground. I mixed Cambodian traditional music with rap; I created a Cambodian hip-hop beat. And this time, I was really proud to say, all the beats and instrumentals were ours. We did the show for the Cambodian New Year, appearing on both stages in front of thousands of people; the crowd's reaction was phenomenal. I didn't have a chance to take it to Cambodia, but a couple of my friends did.

Right now, I'm producing a couple of other people's albums. One is for a Khmer female rap group, Universal Speakers. The other is traditional *pin peat* music. I really want to help revive that. There are only about four Cambodian master musicians left in the United States, and Mr. Chan Ho is one of them. He plays all the instruments. I was privileged to have him play interludes on traditional instruments for *Dalama Two*. There's also some traditional music with me rapping over it; his son played that.

SM   Could you talk about how you came to combine rap with traditional Cambodian musical forms, such as *ayai*?

P   Actually, when I wrote the first *ayai,* I wrote it in rhyme without any melody. But when I went to record it, the rapping didn't sound right. I needed a melody. So I came up with one, and it was an *ayai. Ayai* is sort of like rap music, but in a Cambodian way. *Ayai* is like one poetry master to another poetry master going out on stage or in front of a village and competing with their wisdom, their knowledge about certain subjects, like their land, but it has to continuously rhyme. So basically—rap. Not all rap is about streets and drugs and partying. There's every variety of rap. With

Cambodian *ayai,* it's sort of like that too. Sometimes they use bad language. I figure it's almost exactly like rap, but in Cambodian style, with Cambodian words. I got a chance to meet one of the famous Cambodian comedians, Prum Manh, when he came down to Long Beach for the New Year. He's very wise. He told me later it was not exactly *ayai.* It's called *kong kaev.*

Have you seen *Oan Ouey, Srey Oan?* It's an old Cambodian movie from before the war, with Kong Sam Oeun; he died during the time of the killing fields. In the movie, Kong Sam Oeun and Trente-Deux are selling street food, and they're singing to get the crowd's attention, competing with each other to get the people to buy their food. They're going back and forth about the prices, whose food is better. Like the rap battles I used to do in the park.

SM   Where would you like to go with your music?

P   I want to do *Dalama* in three parts, a trilogy. So far I have done two: *Dalama…the end'n' is just the beginnin'* and *Dalama…the lost chapter.* The last one will be *the beginnin' of the end.* That will be a very dark album. I will squeeze all the light out of it. It will be about political turmoil. I'll do that one when the time is right.

The music that I do is not just about me. It's a movement. We are trying to break new ground, explore new music, new sounds. On the second CD, I mixed traditional music with rap. For my next one, I'm going to try to mix old Sin Sisamouth songs. You know who he is? The great singer who was killed by the Khmer Rouge. I'll mix it so that he sings a chorus and then me. And someday I wish to write screenplays.

SM   Do you see what you're doing as unique?

P   I see a lot of people doing a lot more than me. I think we are heading in a good direction. I'm just one of many trying to do what we can to help out. There's a world out there, and everybody's got to do something, play a role. I think I found my part. Before, I was building walls—isolating myself from people. But now that I know what I can do and how people react to it, it's more like building a bridge than a wall.

SM   What do you think about the future and the role that art can play in healing people after the war?

P   I see there's hope. I see some things have survived. Like traditional music: the adults love it, because it's from before the war and it survived. What I'm doing is completely different, but at the same time, it is connecting with that.

Some people ask me what gives me the right to rap about the war because I wasn't born during the time of the killing fields. I didn't go through that. But I have that in my blood. My mother and father, my brothers and sisters went through that. I lost aunts and uncles. So how can they ask me that?

If there's anything that can help the older generation, it's giving them justice. Twenty-five years have gone by. When will justice be served? If we keep quiet about it, what they went through will be for nothing. It would be as if they lost their parents, children, brothers, sisters, aunts, uncles for nothing. I don't know how to put it in words, but my personal opinion is that they need some kind of justice. Some kind of closure. I don't believe in vengeance. I don't believe in fighting. But I do believe in justice.

Three Rap Lyrics from *Dalama* _____

WELCOME

i was welcome into this world,
nineteen seventy-nine was the year.
those was the time,
the end'n of the killing field in Kampuchea.
i love Cambodia, cuz i was born there.
but during those time,
my people was living in fear.
all cramp up in camp concentration,
millions of refugees can u hear me?
are u listening?
there just gotta be a way out of there.
so i *sah-ma sah-put-toe ta sac*
then disappear.
my country crumble'n
cuz communist is conquering
from all the brok'n promises
anonymous sponsoring.
fleeing the country, knees deep in defeat.
i can't sleep. some make it through,
the others may they rest in peace.
cuz after one thousand, three hundred,
and sixty days, struggle'n for life.
dodge'n booby traps, land mines,
travel'n day and night.
we fight for our rights,
because we refuse to lose.
flee'n for freedom use'n flip-flop for shoes.

i was welcome into the U.S.
nineteen eighty-three was the year.
soon our feet hits the ground,
my mom busted in tears.
words can't describe,

a moment so rare.
and right by her side,
my father was there.
staring at the skies,
hold'n each other.
realize we survive the genocide,
and still together.
thvay bongkum (lok yey-lok ta)
and praise to Buddha.
cuz from that point on,
"it can only get BETTER!"
bright lights, big city,
we sheltered under shadows.
a refugee community,
two family per household.
needed clothes, neighborhood thrift store.
needed food, check the fridge for leftover.
our first car was like a cart,
push it to start, and once it spark,
it's already dark.
days turn to night,
night turn to day,
something gotta change,
we couldn't live that way.
so we round up the spare changes,
from over the years we save.
then bless the rest,
and move west to the Golden State.
California, Long Beach.

ART OF FACT

beyond the killing field,
a quarter of a century after the genocide.
after 2 million people murdered,
the other 5 million survive.
the fabric of the culture,
beauty drips the texture.
i find myself in Long Beach,
the next Cambodian mecca.
beside *srok Khmer, veal srae,* Angkor Wat,
some people still struggling,
from the aftermath of Pol Pot.
for some futures so bright, looks like high beams,
for others are lost in the American Dream.

for me it seems i'm on the road to nowhere fast.
hitting speed bumps, drive'n in circles,
vehicle running out of gas.
there's a gap in our generation,
between the adults and kids.
but since i'm bilingual,
i'ma use communication as a bridge.
first i'ma knock down the walls,
between me and my parents,
listen to their stories an' all
without interference.
what they experience,
was evil in its darkest form.
their mind, body, and heart,
shattered and torn.
the trauma of the war,
affect the refugee and foreigner.
suffering from deep depression,
post-traumatic stress disorder.
it's a new world order,
new threats that we're facing.
terrorist and INS deportation.
you can try to fight it go ahead be my guest,
cuz it's one strike and you're out of the U.S.
there's an epidemic that's killing us surely,
over things we don't even own,
like blocks and territories.
so-call OG recruiting young ones.
jumping them in gangs,
giving them used guns.
not even old enuff to speak,
already hold'n heat,
walk'n a dangerous route,
talk'n about "code of the streets."

seek and you'll find,
the truth is where my heart's at.
i'm speak'n my mind
and let my rhyme design this art of faCt,
line to line from front to back,
from the heart of praCh,
comes the "art of faCt."

i've been asleep snore'n,
now i've awaken from my nap.
my brain been storming,

so i put on my think'n cap.
digging deeper into my mind,
at times i find it hard to hack.
but i'm a messenger this time,
delivering you this "art of faCt."
fast track, racers love cars,
spending every dollar and cents.
getting it all fix up, mix up in bad investments.
but that's their choice to choose,
some parents are still confuse,
the difference between
discipline and child abuse.
i use to get whip and hit,
with wire and *ta-bong.*
it use to be a family matter,
until the law got involved.
for boys hang'n out,
that's OK, unlimited minutes.
for girls; what you talk'n about,
that's prohibited.
some is scared of it,
pushing them to the edge.
some parents still believe in
fixing up marriage.
i inherited all of this,
the knowledge of the facts.
being a Khmer that i am,
i feel the weight on my back.
but look what we're building,
right here in Long Beach.
a Cambodian Town,
down Anaheim streets.
the seed has been planted,
the foundation has been laid,
all it takes is time,
and *voilà* it's all great!
i was raised not to be racist,
so my judgement is color blind fold.
to judge one by their action,
and keep that mind frame on hold!
we're gonna stick together,
like cooked rice in a bowl.
open stores, markets,
products, merchandise…sold!
Business Bureau and Agencies,
to Chamber of Commerce.

fields in teaching, medical to law,
y'all we even running for offices.
there's hope in the kids,
they're learning faster than we did,
traditional dances to classical music.
old method is still used,
you get sick, you get coined.
New Year's Celebration,
everybody in the world come and join.
i am proud to say:
"i'm a Khmer" with pride.
because i praCh,
refuse to let my culture die!
seek and you'll find,
the truth is where my heart's at.
i'm speak'n my mind
and let my rhyme design this art of faCt.
line to line, from front to back,
from the heart of praCh,
comes this "art of faCt."

THE LETTER (PRISONER OF WAR)

i'm write'n you this letter from the bottom of my heart.
behind barb wires where every day is dark.
i'm tell'n you the truth behind the lies,
because life is valuable, we must survive.

on April 17th, 1975,
the rise of the Khmer Rouge,
terrorized the countryside.
innocent cries, endless shooting,
do or die it's a revolution.
population of seven million,
everyone heard it.
within three days,
the whole country is deserted.
captured by the Khmer Rouge,
while dying from a flu a survivor wrote...

while ride'n on a moped on the way to the market.
i got the farm goods in the bag, about to go trade it.
all of a sudden, there's fire and smoke,
the Earth stood still, Hell has awoke.

now…from six in the morning till the moon begin to rise,
they yell at us, tell'n us to grow more rice.
we did but it was always take'n away,
people eat'n watery soup while work'n night and day.
families separated by sex and age,
we work for food and taught how to hate.
they put us in camp, we call it cages.
our body fall asleep, but our mind stays awake.
late at night, they come with guns and knives,
flash a lil' light, then you're beat'n and tied.
drag outside, rag blinds the eye,
not knowing what'll happen…survive or die,
it's a genocide…it's a genocide!!!

those who wore glasses or different language speak'n,
either they're executed or severely beat'n.
doctors, lawyers, teachers, bureaucrats,
and merchants was killed. they say:
"intellectual people are not needed in the fields."
books burn, schools turn into barns,
there nuth'n to do but to listen and farm.

you attend political meetings to hear them speak,
they lecture about the revolution like twice a week.
that is where you're asked to criticize each other and stuff,
they wanna know if you support the revolution enuff.
if not then you're taken away to be studied,
they carry guns, you can't run, so the outcome is bloody.
as a result we learn how to hide our thoughts,
became excellent liars, cuz it's our lives if we're caught.
the killer rouge executed people for many offense,
like when complain'n about the living condition.
mourn'n the death of a family member's the realest feeling,
i remember they shot him pointblank in front of his children.
i can't maintain, the brain turn insane,
they even abolish the use of family name.
it's hell on Earth, and it's gett'n worse…

they wrap a plastic bag around his head,
then kick the air out his chest.
while choke'n on blood,
he suffocate to death.
they had a group of people,
all in a straight line,
tell'n them to face forward,
then they fired from behind.

to save bullets you know what they'll try?
throw you in bomb hole and bury you alive.
rotten body along roadside,
death is in the air.
a bastard child cries,
but can't nobody care.
i stare into the mountain side,
see'n flame'n ashes.
know'n freedom is just miles away,
from the plane crashes.
they laugh like jackal,
these assholes dressed in black.
strip me butt naked,
then tie my hand behind my back.
told me to choose one,
the gun or the axe.
i was guilty of rebel'n against the revolution,
told me i got three seconds,
then they gonna start shoot'n.

on the count of one: i pray for my soul.
on the count of two: for my family and my people.
on the count of three: i was drench in red,
i took two to the head and was left for dead.
my body turned cold, then i started see'n lights,
then a heavenly voice told me i have to fight!
and just like that my lifeless body turn alive,
and that's when i know…i will survive!

I Hate the Word and the Letter ត [Ta] ⸻⸻

Translator's Note

       Khun Srun continues to be one of the authors most widely read and appreciated by Cambodian students of literature. The following story is an example of his innovations with form and style. It plays upon the idea—as old as Plato and as current as the French Structuralists—that there is, or should be, a correspondence between a word and the thing it names; even phonemes and the graphic shapes of letters might be parsed to reveal secret meanings inherent in words. In the Khmer language, ត [*ta*]—along with the other consonants named in this story—may be words as well as letters; the graphic signs for each consonant in Khmer always contain an implied vowel, so a monosyllabic word can be written using a single letter. For example, ត is *ta,* ភ is *pho,* គ is *ko,* and ក is *ka.*

    The word ត [*ta*] means something like "to continue," and Khun Srun suggests that the shape of the letter mirrors this meaning by coiling back on itself. Similar in appearance, the letter ភ [*pho*] is a complete homophone and partial homograph of the word *phor,* which means "to lie or deceive." The story's narrator asserts that their similarity in appearance indicates a connection in meaning. The letter គ [*ko*] is a complete homophone and homograph of the word *ko,* which means "mute." By indicting these common words and letters, the narrator criticizes a society that postpones, falsifies, and, ultimately, muzzles freedom. In contrast, the letter ក [*ka*] is graphically simple and therefore not implicated in the corrupt schemes of the others. Khun Srun asserts that the letter ក—the first of the Khmer language's thirty-three consonants and the first of its four velar occlusives—is virtuous and a model for a more admirable society.—C.M.

I like hearing radio shows broadcast live from Veal Men, the sacred plaza north of the palace. I like *chapey* concerts, Khmer operas, all these beautiful melodies and beautiful stories. But what I can't stand is hearing this statement: *We are now ending our show. Catch us next* [ត] *on this day, at this hour…*Sometimes the concerts were so beautiful, so melodic, so pleasing to the ear that I would begin to mumble in my corner, "What do I care about their nine-o'clock news? They could at least wait for the end of the show or make this dumb announcement beforehand."

    Same thing with novels: the series that are continued [ត] in newspapers from one issue to the next get on my nerves. Same at the theater: I hate operas that go on [ត] night after night.

By the same token, if I prevent my parents, my loved ones, my uncles, and my aunts from tearing each other to pieces in court over some inheritance of four, ten, or twenty square meters of land, it's not because I hate the words *misappropriation* or *bribe* or the expression "to lose one's shirt in a lawsuit." No. It's only because legal affairs drag on in endless cycles [ñ]: a single court costs you I don't know how many citations and successive [ñ] hearings, and when you're done with one, another follows [ñ].

Am I so different from everyone else? Whatever the problem, whether it concerns me or not, as soon as I hear the words *We can't do it today, it's impossible, it's not the time yet, it's not done yet, wait a minute, hold on, come back at this hour, come back at that hour, wait till tomorrow, come back on this day, come back on that day, come back another time,* and so on and so forth, my heart starts to race and my throat tightens. Sometimes I even suffer when a friend's business should, in my opinion, be resolved quickly but isn't.

My hatred for the word ñ caused my hatred for the letter ñ. It's true! I detest this sly, sinuous letter, which coils, returns, and closes back on itself without ever allowing for the possibility of being undone.

My hatred for ñ has also contaminated my rapport with ñ [*pho*]. The two letters are cousins. They differ only in the little coil, which coils back inside in one case and closes on the outside in the other. It is the way this letter coils outward that, wherever it might be, makes it difficult to discern the truth. Sometimes you have a great, beautiful story, but after two, three years of ñ and ñ, of ñ and ñ, your story gets muddled.

But ñ and ñ aren't the only offenders. I also detest the letter ñ [*ko*] because of the slightly stiff curve that distinguishes it from the other letters. In fact, I hate ñ even more than ñ because with ñ, it's quite difficult for us to understand each other, to get attention if one doesn't know how to please, if one doesn't speak the same language.

In fact, of all the letters, it's only the letter ñ [*ka*] that has some redemptive value in my eyes. I gave it a lot of thought and realized why it was the most beautiful letter: ñ is born before the others (whether in the group of four or the set of thirty-three); it hasn't been touched, hasn't been soiled, hasn't acquired the crookedness that afflicts all the other letters: the childish caprices, useless arabesques, and little schemes with loose ends.

Translation from Khmer to French by Christophe Macquet and from French to English by Daniela Hurezanu and Stephen Kessler

Love on Cowback

His parents had ordered Comrade Mok to watch over their cattle, but he had something else in mind. He turned them loose so they could wander freely in the fields while he, Comrade Mok, went off to lie down under a tamarind near the rice paddies. His eyelids half-closed, he set his mind adrift on the waves of the day's heat. Invariably, his thoughts led him back to Mademoiselle Proem, the being he loved most in all the world.

If we take a peek in the bushes opposite Comrade Mok, we glimpse a young girl. She imagines that no one sees her, so she sings, she dances, arching her back and swaying from side to side. She is petite and truly very charming, her long, black hair flowing about her shoulders and her lovely golden skin the color of soybeans. This fetching cowherd is none other than Proem, the daughter of Uncle Sek and Aunt Nom. It is she whom Comrade Mok secretly loves. He is so smitten with her that he cannot let one day pass without catching sight of her.

She has certainly changed a good deal, this little Proem, since she was maid of honor at the marriage of Nhom, daughter of the district chief. The wedding really turned her head around, made her even a little crazy. Ever since then, she sways wherever she is, even when she's seated. Ever since then, she sings and chatters like a magpie, fearless of adults' disapproving looks, shameless in front of boys.

For here's the deal: if Mademoiselle Proem seems a bit absentminded, if she takes leave of her senses from time to time, it's because she's gotten the notion to take a husband—a strange affliction with terrible symptoms, provoking spontaneous singing, rendering one now sad, now joyous, hardening one's face until the skin of it is thicker than a buffalo's hide, impervious to shame!

Thinking herself alone, Mademoiselle Proem dances the way they dance in Indian films: she takes little leaps, she moves her head sharply—left, right—like a lizard. Thinking herself alone, she sings loudly in the open air, improvising:

> *Little, little, little gecko,*
> *why do you hold your head like that?*
> *What are you looking, looking at?*

Could it be my bowl of angel hair?
Don't get your hopes up, little gecko.
I've a cleaver here—beware!

Little, little, little gecko,
with villainous face and shifty eye—
now, see he dives into your knickers
and everyone comes running on the fly
to see a gecko in his knickers
who hasn't paid the proper price—
that isn't nice!

She sings, Mademoiselle Proem, she is utterly happy singing. She sings four times, ten times, twenty times the very same verse, and without her being aware of it, her steps bring her near the spot where Comrade Mok is lying.

At this very moment, Mok, precisely our distinguished Mok, is sleeping like a baby. A woman's voice so near, so potent startles him awake. His eyes still heavy with sleep, he looks nervously about him, then sees and recognizes Proem, Mademoiselle Proem, the idol of his life. He swallows hard, coughs quietly to clear his voice, and opens wide his mouth, answering her in song:

I'm just a little farm boy
I'm just a little farm boy
No merchant's son am I
I love my folks, I drink no booze
I smoke some hash, it's true
And honk as loudly as a goose
And am as thoughtless, too.

At dawn I rise
My hair untouched by comb or brush
Out under the sun I tan my tush
Work's not worth the worry
Work'll ruin you, surely!

At midday in these woods, the girl supposed, there wouldn't be anyone else but her. And so when a man's voice replies to her right nearby, she feels opening in her an immense gulf, big as the eye of a needle, and at once she looks searchingly about her.

Comrade Mok gets up, stretches, and yawns noisily.

—Well then! he says in a joking tone. You certainly seem pretty perky this morning, little Proem. You're singing wonderfully well! You didn't happen to win the lottery by any chance?

Mademoiselle Proem plays the shy one. She shrinks, withdraws, contorts herself like an elephant trying to lie down.

—Be quiet, Mok! she says, twisting her neck and grimacing. I've won nothing. I'm ashamed. I was singing for no reason. I was just bored. Truth is, you sing much better than I.

The young man, naturally susceptible to flattery, fishes for more.

—You think? he says, opening his eyes wide.

—For sure! Mademoiselle Proem replies. You have a golden voice. All the girls in the village say so.

Delighted, our comrade breaks out laughing.

—And not only in the village…Last year, when they held the festival at Tang Krasang Pagoda, they let me get up on the platform and sing into the mike. I was a big hit! All the girls in the district cheered me! My voice, they said, was an absolute marvel. The emcee himself recorded me and is considering playing the cassette tape at the next ceremony.

—And me: do I sing well? Mademoiselle Proem asks. Tell me the truth, Big Brother, in front of all the holy *tevoda*.

Mok nods his head and looks into her eyes.

—I will be frank, he says. Those who, like me, have spent seven or eight seasons among the monks don't know how to speak falsely! Your voice, my little Proem, is as crystal clear as a cricket's. Those who hear it stand gaping or are seized with a sudden somnolence. But what indeed brings you here, Little Sister?

—I'm looking for Champa, my bull. He disappeared around midmorning. He's busy rutting. He's gone off from the herd to mount some female, and I can't find him anywhere. It was getting so hot I decided to wait until later in the afternoon to continue my search. I'd just taken refuge under that tamarind when…I bumped into you.

—What a coincidence! But then…then, well, maybe it's the work of the *tevoda!* They've caused our paths to cross! No doubt our meeting was foreordained. *Ah!* Never have I been so sleepy! My eyelids were heavy today…I had to sleep, I couldn't resist…

Mademoiselle Proem opens her eyes wide. She's still rather innocent, rather easily disarmed by the glibness of our ardent young man.

—Cross our paths? she asks as if bewildered. *For our day?* I don't understand a single word you're saying, Big Brother. Don't use those "coutured" words, please. Speak plain Khmer.

—*Cultured* words, little Proem? Mok replies, laughing. But I can't speak any other way! The problem, you see, is that old monks like me have been so studious that we speak like scholars even when we mean to be simple!

A big smile lights up the girl's face and traces two ravishing little dimples in her cheeks. She does what the great dancers do in Indian films: she looks at the young man and rolls her eyes from left to right, from right to left. The young man seems quite taken by this strange business with the eyes…

—You *do* know how to talk! she says. It's so melodious and so sugary!

Sweet as candy! Oh, if we didn't live so far from one another, I would listen to you talk all night.

Mok is in seventh heaven. Imagine! Such praise—and from the girl he loves! He beams, wracking his brain to find big, complicated words, whose meanings he might not know but that might win for him the dear girl's tributes.

—The individual immersed in the great cycle of transmigrations, such a venerable one, devoid of essence, must possess the capacity to examine profoundly, must possess sufficient ratiocinative powers to merit acquisition of the Five-Faceted Jewel, must possess that perseverance that alone promises happiness, success, and prosperity! Thus, henceforth, will he be granted a guide and attain blessed karmic fruits, good fortune, a doctoral thesis, ultimately ascending to the Unilateral Paradigm! So, Little Sister? What do you think of that?

Mademoiselle Proem, looking rather astounded, scowls.

—Very pretty, I'm sure, but I understand none of it, she says, shaking her head. What does it mean?

Mok, who would be hard pressed to translate it, assumes a superior air.

—Never mind, Little Sister. I could explain it to you, but you wouldn't understand it any better. It's enough to know that these are *cultured* words! Now, if you don't mind, I'd like us to go sit for a while over there on the shore. I have some things to say to you that you might find agreeable...

The girl's eager to cuddle up with Mok. She's been thinking of him for a long time, ever since the wedding of Nhom, the daughter of the district chief. When their eyes met that day, she had been so overcome that, without her being aware of it, the bowl she was holding slipped from her hands and shattered into a thousand pieces. She wants him very much, but being rather precious by nature, she feigns indecision.

—Just the two of us, like that...*hmm*...out of sight...*uh*...that doesn't seem quite right to me...I...don't...really...

Mok sees she's merely mouthing resistance, so he takes her in his arms and lifts her and carries her—running—to the shore. But when he tries to put her down, the girl clings to his neck, squeezing him so tightly he can scarcely breathe.

—*Argh!* Why don't you want to get down, Little Sister?

Mademoiselle Proem rejoices. She gives a little laugh and begins to nuzzle her face against his shoulder like a pet pangolin.

—Here I am and here I'll stay! Speak up if you have something to say to me.

—Fine. As you wish. But don't squeeze so hard! I'm about to throw up...

The girl loosens her grip enough to let Mok breathe a bit.

—I'll be frank, Little Sister! he says to the girl clinging firmly to his neck. I love you! I love you madly! I love you even more than I love my father and mother! If I cannot make you my wife, if we do not share pillow and mat, I will hurl myself from the top of a sugar palm. So, Little Sister? Do you agree to love me in return?

Mademoiselle Proem shivers with pleasure, too, for she has secretly loved our comrade. Nevertheless, she pretends to argue.

—Who's to say you're telling the truth? We know about you boys today, with your tight pants pinching! You talk the talk, then steal our virginity and break our hearts.

—I'm sincere, Proem! I love you! If I'm lying, let the earth open up and swallow me alive!

—That won't be necessary. It's enough to know you love me. You may instruct the elders to make the necessary arrangements with my parents.

What joy! Imagine the state our comrade's in! She says yes! She says yes! He starts running willy-nilly all about, leaping and cavorting, but Mademoiselle Proem weighs heavily on his neck. His arms weaken and his legs go wobbly. He can't quite cut the figure he means to, one that would allow him to express the full extent of his happiness.

—Proem, my sweetheart, he says, his voice trembling.

—Yes, my treasure?

—Love like this—hanging-on-to-one's-neck-without-ever-wishing-to-let-go—is not altogether really comfortable, Little Sister…I'm about to pass out!

—What a weakling you are! If you don't want a love hanging-on-to-one's-*neck*-without-ever-wishing-to-let-go, then *what* do you want a love hanging-on-to-without-ever-wishing-to-let-go?

—*Argh!* OK…What would you say…*argh*…to an open-air love, for example? A love-on-cowback? The heat…*argh*…of the sun begins to subside…It would be very pleasant, I think…

—*Hmm*…Why not…that doesn't seem so bad now…

No sooner said than done: Mademoiselle Proem leaps to the ground. Mok, whose neck is now stiff and sore, recoups his strength, then conducts the woman of his dreams to a cow grazing nearby.

Our ardent young man hoists his girl onto the cow's back and jumps on behind her, hugging her waist. He presses his heels into the animal's flanks and begins declaiming without rhyme or reason.

—In thisss ooolld!…If he cannot make you his missus, this Mister Mok, most assuredly, will spit up all his blood and pass his knife to the left! Love! Love! Our love is as sticky as caramel! Stronger than buffalo hide! It is sweet, our love, a hundred times sweeter than saccharine! Our love, it will be a perpetual song! It will remain forever young! And as much as one shall never have seen the heavens leaning on a crutch of wind—and tomorrow may not be the day before—our hobo love will go a-rambling. To infinity! To infinity! We will plait the threads of our two lives!

—Yes, yes, yes, the girl responds. Yes, yes, yes, I feel it, too! That our love has the strength of that which once bound Lady Preamkesar and the august Leaksinavong! The first of us to betray the other will have his eyes gnawed by mealy worms! I love you! I love you! With all my heart! With all my guts! If you were to split open my breast like a common pullet's, I would cut into my own gallbladder to gather the bile and marinate it in spirits so that we could drink it up together!

Mademoiselle Proem rejoices. Out of the corner of her eye, she gives Mok such a troubling look he is covered with goosebumps.

This is the moment they've dreamed of! The son of Uncle Men tightens his arms around her waist and, closing his eyes, rests his head upon her shoulder. Now *this* is as good as herding gets! Our comrade, henceforth, worries no more.

And thus youth finds love on cowback—a love entirely new, utterly up-to-date, perfectly in keeping with the spirit of the end of the twentieth century.

Translation from Khmer to French by Christophe Macquet and from French to English by Nick Bozanic

Evening, Village Cockfight,
Vicinity of Wat A Thvea, Siem Reap, 2002
Photograph by Richard Murai

Workman

Today our workman has squatted down in the shade of a kapok tree by the curb outside the store. There he waits. The morning moves along at the pace of the shade as it shrinks close to the tree trunk. Our young man stands up, stretches out his legs, and leans back against the trunk.

He is the new workman on the block, looking to hire out his labor. He first showed up yesterday, taking in the scene, occasionally chatting with another workman on break. He is back today, hoping to join a team. This is the busy season for workmen. The new crop of rice has been baled up and loaded onto trucks for sale and resale through the network of wholesalers and retailers. Adjoining the central market, this block houses a handful of wholesalers.

Our young man has just finished his lunch: a big scoop of steamy rice wrapped in lotus leaf topped with a small piece of grilled smoked fish and drizzled generously with chillied fish sauce. The lady who sold him the lunch is doing too brisk a trade to notice that she is no longer in the shade of the kapok tree.

At the commotion caused by a truck making its way decisively toward him, our fellow springs to his feet. Two workmen hanging on to the sides of the truck call out to the street vendors to make room for them. The men hop off while the truck is still moving. Swiftly, they help the vendors remove the last of their wares from the curb.

Then, combining energetic hand signals with verbal instructions, they deftly direct the driver to back onto the curb and between two cars, and then to stop. The driver shuts off the engine and walks around to the front.

The space is narrow, and the truck is parked at an angle so that a good part of its nose sticks out into the flow of traffic. Satisfied that there is adequate room to offload the cargo, the driver approaches his wholesaler.

The two have a brief exchange, and pen and papers in hand, the wholesaler starts checking off the cargo of rice. The driver turns to the workmen and assigns each a role in the offloading operation. In addition to the two he has brought with him, two men from the store help.

He pairs up one of his men with one from the wholesaler's and has them climb inside the truck. Each picks up a hook and proceeds to position the sacks so that they can be heaved onto the backs of the other men.

The driver now calls out to the wholesaler and confers with him earnestly. The wholesaler nods, and both turn to our young man, motioning with their heads toward the store. Our fellow quickly falls into step behind them. He comes back out shortly, stripped down to his boxer shorts, just like the driver and the other fellows.

Our workman now takes his turn. As he walks up to the truck, he exchanges a greeting with a boy: a quick lifting of eyebrows and a little tossing back of the head. The two had chatted briefly the afternoon before and gotten along well. Then our workman presents his bare back to his first hundred-kilogram sack of rice. It's obvious that his skin lacks the seasoning of physical labor under the sun.

Facing each other, his workmates plunge their hooks into the front corners of a rice sack and heave it onto the workman's back. They try to align the heavy load with his center of gravity. He teeters, steps forward unsteadily, and walks to the store, the rice sack balancing awkwardly on his back.

Now it is the driver's turn. He throws an empty bag over his shoulders before taking on a rice sack. Though he may be small, he carries his load with a sure step.

The driver is the shortest, stoutest, and darkest of his work team. He exudes the most authority and commands respect from the others. He has a tattoo on the front of his neck: some sacred scriptures, it is said, which add to the mystique of his being a fierce traditional Khmer boxer.

A couple of shades lighter is one of the men working with a hook. Muscles of a warm chestnut hue give his slender arms and legs a soft sculpted look, complementing a finely chiseled face and a crown of wavy ebony hair. Had he been born with broad shoulders, he probably would have been tempted to court movie stardom. Already, his smile has stood him in good stead with the lady street vendors nearby.

The other fellow working with a hook does not yet have the body of a full-grown man. And completing this cast of our Youngman, the Driver, the Goodlooking, and the Boy are the Oldman and the Familyman.

The Oldman is not much taller than the Driver. In his late forties or early fifties, he is thin and lean muscled and has a permanent frown on his face. He is definitely the oldest on the team. The Familyman, well, looks like the average husband and dad in his thirties, someone with a young family to feed.

On his second round, our Youngman is again struggling with his load. By the third round, the Oldman has caught up with him. Grabbing an empty jute bag, he covers the Youngman's shoulders with it, motions him to squat lower, and helps him balance the bulky sack of rice. After two more rounds, our Youngman falls in step with the rest of the fellows.

The team has come to its last round. Now that the fierce competition for parking spaces has ended, the Driver is straightening the truck along the curb. The flow of traffic has eased off too. The lady street vendors have packed up to head home. Other vendors, mostly men, are passing through.

One of them is a wiry man selling arrack, made from fermented sugar-palm sap, poured into containers of hollowed-out bamboo. Sensing impending demand for his drink, the man has stopped close to the truck. The Driver and the Oldman hover around the vendor, opening the bamboo tubes and inhaling the aroma of the strong drink.

They have chosen their bamboo tube and are buying the drink now. The arrack seller unties a handleless mug, also made out of hollowed-out bamboo. Into the mug he pours a little arrack and quickly swirls the liquid around the rim before draining the mug. Then, lifting the container again, he fills the mug to the brim. His two customers take turns gulping down the naturally fermented sap.

After the last gulp, the Driver orders another drink. The wholesaler's wife comes out to tell him that his team can join her family for supper and that they may go wash up now. Leaving the Oldman to finish his drink, the Driver walks to the back of the store.

The Oldman is rolling himself a dry, green tobacco leaf. He and the arrack seller compare notes on the quality of the rolled-up tobacco leaves as they suck in and puff out on them. Both relax inside a bubble of intoxicating tobacco and arrack fumes.

Out in the alleyway at the back of the store, the Driver, still wearing his boxer shorts, is soaping up near a faucet that stands at thigh level on a raised concrete slab that is also used for washing dishes. A perky little hen with reddish feathers comes up from behind to peck for water in one of the pots. With a lazy eye, a mongrel dog follows the hand movements of the cook and blinks from the occasional splatter of the tap water, a front paw tucked under its muzzle.

Fresh from his shower and standing tall in a clean pair of boxer shorts, the Goodlooking is playing with a feather shuttle, his pair of rubber thongs lying near his bare feet. Once in a while, he stops to adjust the round red discs in which the white feathers are planted, then resumes bouncing the shuttle on his knees and the sides of his feet. When he breaks into fancier moves, the Driver walks up to him and hitches up his sarong with one hand, his cigarette held firmly between his lips.

With his other hand, the Driver scoops up the shuttle, and the two of them toss it back and forth with their feet. The Oldman, the Familyman, and the Boy—also fresh from washing up—soon join in.

By now, the Driver has twisted his sarong tightly into a long tail, passed it between his legs, and tucked it in at the back. This allows his legs unhampered movement. A cigarette still smolders between his lips.

The circle of players has settled into a comfortable pace of tossing the shuttle among them when our Youngman comes out from his shower and sits himself down on his sandals by the store entrance. All around, grandmas and nannies are feeding supper to toddlers and their older siblings. The toddlers are bouncing themselves in their walkers on wheels, and their older siblings are restless too. In between spoonfuls, the children play tag, using our shuttle players as shields from their pursuers.

As our Youngman watches, the Oldman, the Goodlooking, and the Driver step up the pace of the game. The Goodlooking and the Oldman are taunting each other playfully over each and every move. The Driver squints from the smoke wafting up from his lips.

Increasingly, the Familyman misses the shuttle and lets it drop to the concrete. Our Youngman has moved up next to him, a half step outside the circle.

With a snappy toss from the top part of his right foot, the Goodlooking sends the shuttle flying towards our Youngman. Our fellow responds with half a pirouette on one foot, turning his back to all the players, and kicks the shuttle back inside the circle with the sole of his other foot.

For a second or two, the shuttle seems to hang high in the air between the Goodlooking and the Driver. The Driver pulls the cigarette butt from his lips and flicks it to the curb.

Then he steps inside the circle and intercepts the shuttle on its descent, hitting it powerfully with the top of his head and launching it toward the Oldman. The old fellow tosses back his head, sticks out his chest, and lets the shuttle alight ever so briefly. Then with brisk forward and backward jerks of his body, the Oldman lets the shuttle fall toward his feet. Swiftly he raises the sole of his right foot towards his left knee and, using the side of his foot, tosses the shuttle to the Goodlooking.

Quickly bending his right leg backwards and using the sole of his foot, the Goodlooking sends the shuttle arching towards the Driver, who is on his left. Stretching out his right arm, the Driver flips the shuttle with his hand. The shuttle spins away with its feathers tilted toward our Youngman.

Resolutely stepping into the circle, our fellow thrusts his right leg out so that his toes can tip the shuttle back into its upright position. He then bounces the shuttle a couple of times on his thigh before using his knee to gently toss it toward the Boy.

A roar of admiration sweeps through the onlookers, who have stopped what they are doing to watch this skillful display. In the fading light, the Driver quietly smiles at our Youngman. Soon, the sun will set. Soon, there will be a hush along the pavement as parents muster children inside so that the grown-ups can sit themselves down to supper. But for now, old and young alike watch the sophisticated moves gracefully executed in one complete, unbroken sequence.

The Dinner Guests

Every year, when my family finds reason to gather—for a holiday, birthday, graduation, and sometimes just because—when the coconut curry is cooked and smoke swirls heaven-bound from burning incense, the ghosts come home to feed.

Before any guests are allowed to eat, my mother prepares a tray of food, her best dishes—sticky rice, glass noodles fried with banana buds, steamed pork buns—and my father lights a handful of incense sticks. Setting these on an altar, we pray to the spirits of our dead relatives and invite them to the feast. These spirits are the ghosts of my grandfather, Khan Reang, a rice farmer; my uncle, Sao Kim Yan, a math professor; my aunt, Koh Kenor, a housewife who was married to a businessman; and so many others who died during the war in our homeland. They are the restless ones who cross oceans and continents to find my family, now safe and comfortable in America. They are the ones who did not make it while they were living.

Whether by luck or by fate, the rest of my family made it. When war tore through Cambodia in 1975, we got on a boat that carried us to freedom. A boat that brought us to America, far from the burning villages and the thunder of bombs breaking earth, but not far enough to escape a past that returns each year to haunt us.

I was too young to remember that time twenty-eight years ago when my family was forced to leave our country, and our lives changed instantly and forever.

On April 17, 1975, the Communist Khmer Rouge invaded Phnom Penh, forcing those they didn't kill to walk for days to concentration camps. In remote corners of the country, those who survived were forced to live in work camps as part of leader Pol Pot's design to create a classless, utilitarian society of peasant farmers.

That April day, my mother was at home in our village, Riem, taking care of her four children: my sister Sinaro, who was then eight; my brother, Sophea, then five; my sister Chanira, then two; and myself, the youngest, almost a year old. We were living in Kompong Som Province, in Cambodia's southern seaport, because my father worked as an accountant in the

West Corridor,
Angkor Wat, 2002
Photograph by Richard Murai

Cambodian navy. This job provided my father with a good salary, but only later, when the war erupted, did we realize its true worth.

My mother was listening to her short-wave radio when the news came crackling through the speaker: the Cambodian government had been toppled, and the regime of the Khmer Rouge, an insurgent guerrilla group made up of peasant fighters, had taken over.

The villagers immediately began evacuating. My father, who was down at the docks, rushed home to round up my family and relatives. He took us three or four at a time by motorbike to the port. There, one of three naval evacuation ships was waiting to take government personnel and their families to safety.

My father took my family to the boat first, then returned to Riem to gather others: my grandfather, my aunt and uncle, several cousins. Meanwhile, my mother huddled with her four children on the ship, flinching with each *pop! pop! pop!* of gunfire in the distance. She watched in horror as other people tried to claw their way onto the boat, only to be plucked off like crabs by crew hands worried the ship would become overloaded and sink.

Three hundred people made it onto the sitting-room-only boat. My family, allowed to board only because my father worked for the Cambodian navy, was among the lucky ones.

For three weeks, the ship drifted at sea, stopping in Thailand and Malaysia only to be shooed away by port officials who refused to accept refugees. During that time, my mother kept her children close to protect them from the waves crashing over the ship. She wondered where we were going and worried about the relatives she had left behind. She had eight siblings whom she feared had died in the bombings. But she soon realized she had a more immediate concern: the small baby lying in her sarong—her youngest child—was dying.

That baby was me.

I was dehydrated and sick. My eyes had rolled back into my head, and my chest had stopped rising and falling. At one point, my mother couldn't bear to hold my listless body and handed me to an aunt.

"You small like a mango," my mother would tell me years later, recounting the story. "You not drink milk, you not cry, you look like a dead."

The captain of the ship thought so, too. He threatened to throw me overboard, fearing a corpse would infect the other refugees crowded on the ship.

My mother wailed and clutched me tighter. She could not bear to lose another child. Seven years before I was born, she had my father bury their second daughter, Kombaleen.

She begged the captain of the ship not to take me. Even if I was already dead, my mother insisted, she and my father needed to bury me in the earth. She worried that my baby spirit would never rest in peace if I was tossed unceremoniously into the water.

The captain persisted, but my mother refused to give me up. Reluctantly, he finally agreed to let me stay on board until we stopped for food and fuel at the U.S. naval base at Subic Bay in the Philippines.

"I have a hope, just a little, you not dead," my mother would tell me years later, looking into the distance as if trying to hold on to that moment twenty-eight years ago.

When we reached land, my parents rushed me to a hospital, where nurses inserted an IV into my arm. After several hours, my mother placed a leaf in my hand, and my tiny fingers twitched. I was still alive.

Staying in the hospital, I was treated for dehydration and measles. At night, my mother slept on the floor beside the baby crib, keeping vigil over her fragile child.

Three long weeks later, news blasted over the naval-base loudspeaker. We would be sent to America. I was still sick, but we had to leave immediately. My mother once again wrapped me in a sarong, and we boarded a plane to start our new lives.

My immediate family and several relatives settled in Corvallis, Oregon, a small farming community about eighty miles south of Portland. A local Presbyterian church sponsored us and helped my parents find work and the two-bedroom apartment where all fifteen of us lived. My father washed dishes at a local restaurant and took night classes to get a certificate in accounting, and my mother worked two jobs: as a janitor at the Oregon State University health center and a cook at the campus dormitories. My siblings went to school, where they fell in love with pizza and French fries, and my cousin and I rode tight circles on Hot Wheels at our daycare center.

My family quickly became absorbed in their new lives, and I grew up protected from stories of the war. For the most part, my parents never spoke of our past. There seemed to be a door shut tight and locked. No trespassing.

Only recently, as more relatives who survived the war have immigrated and settled in Oregon near my parents, have the stories started to emerge.

At family gatherings a heavy silence surrounds my parents when we talk of Cambodia. When pressed, my aunts will tell their stories of survival as my mother prepares our holiday meals, our summer picnic food, and the funeral feasts for my grandmother and grandfather, who recently passed away here in America.

There is always a tray for them: the first sweet tastes of curry and rice.

Here is my Aunt Vuthy, whose husband was beaten to death with a shovel by Khmer Rouge soldiers for stealing a potato for his hungry wife. Here is my Aunt Nang, a schoolteacher, who was sent to a torture prison after her husband, a military official, was shot to death. Her two boys, aching with hunger, ate crab shells and chicken bones tossed in the dirt by Khmer Rouge soldiers. Here is my Grandpa Khan, my father's father, a Chinese rice farmer, who died of starvation; the single cup of watery rice soup rationed out to everyone was not enough. Here are aunts who were tied to trees and beaten to death, and cousins who were worked to death in the rice paddies. These are the stories of the ghosts we pray for. This dinner is for all of them.

Come feast. Here is the food my mother prepared; we have plenty. Here is my bed, which I have made for this occasion. Come rest with us. Come rest within us.

Bophana: A Cambodian Tragedy

Born in Phnom Penh in 1964, filmmaker Rithy Panh survived the Khmer Rouge regime, but lost his parents, sister, and many other family members as a result of the genocide. In 1979, at age fifteen, he escaped across the Thai border and traveled to France, settling there. At first, he tried to forget his past experiences, refusing to speak Khmer and rejecting all ties with Cambodia; but he found that the only way he could rebuild a life was to face what had happened to his country and himself. In 1985, he enrolled in France's national cinema school, Institut des Hautes Études Ciné-matographiques. His first documentary won the 1988 Grand Prix du Documentaire at the Festival of Amiens. Since then, he has made over half a dozen award-winning films. His most recent work is s-21, the Khmer Rouge Death Machine, *which was shown as an official selection at the 2003 Cannes Film Festival.*

The following translation of Bophana: A Cambodian Tragedy *is the first appearance in print of a documentary by Panh. Completed in 1996, the film tells the story of Hout Bophana and Ly Sitha, a young couple caught in Cambodia's political upheaval. Their forbidden letters briefly kept them in touch with one another, but eventually were used by the Khmer Rouge as evidence to justify the couple's imprisonment, torture, and execution. Credits for the film appear at the end of this volume.*

Title card reads:

> For Uncle Koeun, victim of Tuol Sleng s-21, and for Hiran, reported disappeared

Close-up of two large files containing hand-written letters, reports, and "confessions." Title card over the files and letters. Female voiceover.

> Autobiography of Hout Bophana
> Age 25, female
> Khmer nationality, married
> Born in Third District, Phnom Penh
> Former General Secretary *vi-ya-ar* humanitarian
> organization
> Arrested by Angkar

Three people are looking through the files.

ARCHIVIST   These are her letters, and over there, her husband's letters.

Camera tracks Mr. Toeuth as he scans a wall covered from floor to ceiling with small photographs. These are the photos taken by the Khmer Rouge of their victims before they were executed in Tuol Sleng, the detention center in Phnom Penh also known as S-21. The Tuol Sleng S-21 Genocide Museum is located on the grounds of the former prison. Mr. Toeuth points to a photograph of a young woman.

MR. TOEUTH

I'm not mistaken. I'm certain she's my niece. It's certainly her. People called her Mumm. It was her nickname. Her name on her birth certificate was Hout Bophana. [*Moves about the room full of photographs.*]

When she was in high school, she had a round face. When we saw each other in 1975, following the fall of Phnom Penh, she had hollow cheeks. She was worried…She had lost her family. We were rather sad. We dared not look into each other's eyes…We felt a lump in our throats. We couldn't talk to each other. Then she left and went to Phum Boeung. And I said goodbye to her. We couldn't talk to each other because the militia were spying on us. They were there next to us. I wanted to tell her to come and live with me. But I dared not ask. I was afraid of the militia. They could kill both of us. Thus, we were separated without saying a word. When I saw her photo, I felt terrified…She was in Baray and then she came here to die…I can no longer speak.

Image of sunlight through the barred windows of S-21, then an image of Vann Nath painting a large portrait of Bophana. Voiceover.

NARRATOR

In totalitarian regimes, the horror of the terror is that it rules over men and women and deprives them of their true fate. In Cambodia from 1975 to 1979, the Khmer Rouge were the incarnation of a policy that denied all reference to the humanity of those they subjugated. In Pol Pot's Democratic Kampuchea, you could look neither to the right nor to the left but only straight ahead—and even then, if you wanted to survive, you were permitted to notice nothing. Against the madness of the Khmer Rouge regime, Bophana became a heroine in the Cambodian tragedy. Her constant resistance and her striking beauty were equally unacceptable to the butchers of the Cambodian people. Bophana lived in a country where love was an outrage to the revolutionary party. [*Continuing over images of a village. A girl on a bicycle travels peacefully along the banks of the river Sen.*]

Bophana had a quiet and carefree childhood in Kompong

Thom City, the capital of the province of the same name, about a hundred kilometers north of Phnom Penh. The family house stood on the bank of the river Sen. It was a nice house. Children played in and around it. Among them was Bophana's cousin Ly Sitha. Bophana's father, Hout Cheng, was a teacher and was fond of this nephew, a poor child of the rice paddies.

Ly Sitha's mother is seated on the floor. She points to photos of Ly Sitha and Bophana.

LY SITHA'S MOTHER   Him, it's my son Sitha; her, it's Mumm, my daughter-in-law. Sitha was a monk and taught Buddhism at Wat Po. After he was defrocked, he loved Mumm, my daughter-in-law. When Sitha was four years old, Mr. Cheng, Mumm's father, brought him up like his own son. He gave him the family name and sent him to school. When Sitha was still at school, Mr. Cheng's wife died. When Mr. Cheng remarried, the family was separated. Sitha went to Phnom Penh and became a monk. He lived a quiet life. In 1969, he came to say goodbye to me. He said he was going abroad with friends. He had already bought the tickets…Then came the event. He was stuck here until 1971 or 1972. I fled the war, I lost my son. Sitha returned to Phnom Penh.

Archival footage of Cambodia at war, frightened faces of refugees. Gunfire and explosions can be heard in the background. Voiceover.

NARRATOR   On 18 March 1970, General Lon Nol staged a coup against Prince Sihanouk, the head of state. The region of Baray, where Bophana's father was born, quickly became a ferocious battleground between the forces of Lon Nol's new government and the Khmer Rouge. Caught in the middle, the peasants took refuge in temples—which were safe for the time being—or joined the Khmer Rouge at the urging of Prince Sihanouk. Cambodia quickly sank into the horrors of civil war.

At the war's beginning, Bophana suffered her first tragedy. Her father, who had become head of the district, was killed in a Khmer Rouge ambush on the road to Baray. Fighting reached the outskirts of Kompong Thom City. Bophana was forced to flee from the family home. She lost all touch with Ly Sitha.

Kompong Thom became a garrison town, and people evacuated in droves. Bophana and her two sisters lived on the second floor of an austere building overlooking the marketplace. A few months earlier, the market had been busy and active each day as peasants gathered there. But in wartime it had changed. Khmer Rouge rocket attacks on the city killed people at random…Undisciplined and brutal, the government soldiers spread terror…Young women were abducted in the streets and raped…

From her window, Bophana gazed at the soulless streets, trying to console herself and endure the trap she found herself in. She was also worried about the advances of a certain soldier, Prak Saline, a sergeant of the Eleventh Regiment. One afternoon, Bophana was in bed because of a high fever. Her sisters were playing on the ground floor…

A former Lon Nol soldier, Mr. Cheth, is seated in an empty room.

MR. CHETH   Lon Nol's soldiers rounded up people in these buildings. They caught young women and raped them. They also took people's belongings. Those things happened…They saw this pretty girl [Bophana], then they came back with guns and grenades. They accused her of being a Khmer Rouge agent. Actually, they wanted to rape her, so they planted a grenade in a corner as false evidence so that their commander would find it. They raped the girl, then reported to their superior that she was an enemy agent.

Silhouette of a young woman at a window. Voiceover.

NARRATOR   Bophana was in despair at the first signs of pregnancy. In her sorrow, she had no one to confide in. She attempted suicide by swallowing pills. But she was rushed to a hospital, where she and the baby survived. [*Image of small boats on a river.*]

In January 1971, Bophana and her sisters left Kompong Thom with the help of relatives who were living in Phnom Penh. It was time to leave her home province and birthplace. Bophana was twenty years old…[*Camera pans rooftops of Phnom Penh. Images of a crowded marketplace.*]

When Bophana arrived in Phnom Penh, she found that the war had engulfed all of Cambodia. But her main concern was the birth of her baby. She stayed indoors until it was born. It was a boy. As an unmarried mother, she was a social outcast. She began searching for a job, but had no success. The future looked bleak for her. To survive, she and her older sister sold rice and cakes in the market.

They barely scraped by amidst the city's corruption and black-market exchanges.

In early 1973, Bophana registered at a humanitarian center for war widows. The center was run by Goatana Enders, whose husband was the head of American military air operations in the region. At the center, Bophana learned how to sew in order to earn money. The Cambodian woman who was the head of the center noticed Bophana and proposed to her that she work for the organization in the refugee camps.

At this time, 300,000 Cambodians were on the roads, fleeing the fighting and American air raids. Refugees from throughout the country flooded into the shantytowns of Phnom Penh. In May 1974, at a cremation ceremony at Langkar Pagoda, Bophana suddenly happened upon Ly Sitha. [*Images of crowds, robed monks, and a cremation ceremony.*]

After years of silence and separation, Bophana was face-to-face with the man who was her childhood playmate, her cousin, her adopted brother, and her betrothed. His head was shaved, and he wore a saffron robe. He had become a monk.

Four months later, Ly Sitha suddenly vanished. He had often traveled between the Khmer Rouge region and Phnom Penh. Like his cousin Sath, who had joined the Communists because he was distressed by the bombings in Baray, had Ly Sitha become a sympathizer of the revolution?

A former monk, Oum Vann, stands looking over the grounds of a pagoda.

OUM VANN   During the war, monks came here to study; others came seeking information of other sorts. Some monks were involved in politics. I'm talking now about Saravan Pagoda. Of the many who came, some were neutral, some were not. We did not know who all these people were. They lived in the courtyard. They built small huts from palm leaves. Some were silversmiths from Koh Chen; others just sold little things to get by. I guess there were more than two thousand people living here in the pagoda.

Camera again pans rooftops of Phnom Penh. Archival propaganda footage of battles, explosions, soldiers on the attack. Revolutionary songs can be heard in the background. Voiceover.

NARRATOR   By the end of 1974, at the beginning of the dry season, the Cambodian army of Lon Nol was demoralized. Soldiers did not get paid for months; in many cases, their salaries were pocketed by their own generals. Nevertheless, some government forces continued to resist. The capital sank into chaos as the population was terrorized by falling bombs. Finally, the government collapsed.

On the morning of 17 April 1975, small men dressed in black arrived in Phnom Penh. They were peasant soldiers of the Khmer Rouge. Most of them were disciplined. They were teenagers with impassive faces. At once they began to force the entire population out of the city. "Only for three days," they said. "The Americans are going to bomb the city," they explained. "You must not take anything with you. Angkar [the invisible organization of the Khmer Rouge] will look after the people," they added. The stupefied population did as they were ordered. Soon, about two million Cambodians were on the roads, heading for the countryside.

With her grandmother, Bophana headed for Kompong Thom. Her son wasn't with her. Two days earlier, during the Cambodian New Year celebration, she had left her infant with her elder sister.

Under the leadership of Brother Number One, Pol Pot, Cambodia sank into the darkness of ignorance, into the kingdom of death. A terrible prophecy, the *Put Tumneay,* had foretold: "There shall be houses without people, streets without people...People shall fight for a grain of rice stuck to the tail of a dog." [*Archival footage of deserted city, then village where peasants are harvesting grain.*]

During this exhausting march, the people deported from urban areas—the so-called New People—were often searched and interrogated about their background. Many were summarily executed.

Bophana and her grandmother stayed in Baray with one hundred fifty other families from Phnom Penh. The two women lived under the house of peasants—the so-called Old People—who were assigned to spy on them day and night. Like millions of other Cambodians, Bophana changed her name. She took her former nickname, Mumm. The peasants called her Mumm the White, a derogatory reference to her pale skin, which they saw as evidence she had never done manual labor in the sun. She was forced to cut her hair short and dress in black. She endured forced labor from sunrise until late into the night, followed by lengthy group sessions of self-criticism.

In July 1975, Ly Sitha was defrocked and returned to Romlong, his native village. There he saw his cousin Sath, who had become a Khmer Rouge cadre. Sath secured a job for him in animal husbandry within the Ministry of Trade. In Phnom Penh, Ly Sitha—now known as Comrade Deth—learned that Bophana was living in Baray. During an assignment for the ministry, he managed to travel to see her.

Ly Sitha's mother is seated as before. She points to a photograph of Bophana.

LY SITHA'S MOTHER   Sitha and Mumm were cousins. They went to school together. When the war started, they were separated. When they met again in 1975, I reunited my daughter, Mumm, and my son, Sitha, in a common destiny. They lived like husband and wife only in 1975. They loved each other very much. At first, they loved each other as cousins. But as the situation in the country was getting worse, I had to think about their future. I was their elder, I was their mother, and so I decided to marry them so that they could live together.

Camera pans a mural depicting scenes from the Ramayana. Voiceover.

NARRATOR   Bophana tried to escape into the imaginary world of the Reamker [Cambodian Ramayana], even though there was no place for such dreams in this revolution. Angkar cast the Cambodians into Nothingness. People were forbidden to write, to move from one place to another. They were forbidden to meet, to love. All personal life was outlawed. Only total obedience to Angkar was permitted.

Revolted by this society full of sorrow, Bophana transgressed the rules. She wrote long love letters to Ly Sitha. She began signing them "Sita," the name of the heroic, faithful wife in the Reamker. In the epic, Sita is kidnapped by Ravana, a demon ruler with ten heads. Ravana imprisons her on an island, trying to persuade her to marry him. But Sita thinks always of her beloved husband, Rama, and remains true to him throughout her ordeal. Bophana embraced this tragic love story and saw in it her own suffering.

Close-up images of the love letters, then archival footage of workers at forced labor. Female voiceover begins.

FROM BOPHANA'S LETTERS

Feelings for my husband…

After ten years of separation, I saw my husband again when Cambodia moved on and started a revolution. We were cousins, then we became husband and wife.

After the sad events I went through in 1970 and other bitterness I experienced later, I felt much pain in my heart, and I said to myself, "Physically and mentally I'm already dead." Each day that went by, Sita shed thousands of tears…And as another day went by, Sita's pains got worse.

Darling, you know that ever since Sita touched the soil of Baray, friends warned her that people said that you were not really her husband. And that Sita clung to you only because she learned that you were a Party cadre. They also said that Sita had been a whore in Phnom Penh and that was the reason she caused trouble in Baray, making up the story that you were her husband.

Oh, darling! There were so many slanders that made Sita cry, that made her suffer so terribly. My friends told me that the Old People sent me to work at the dykes because they did not want to see my skin remain white. They forced me to work. My friends said that the other women were jealous of me because they had been members of the revolution for five years and yet none of them had a husband like Sita's. But what has Sita got that they haven't?

Dear husband! Please tell Sita frankly: why have you disappeared for so long? Why haven't you come to look for Sita? Sita understands that you are very busy working for Angkar. But each day living in Baray, Sita loses one year of her life. Sita feels disgust for this land of Baray.

Ly Sitha's mother is seated as before.

LY SITHA'S MOTHER   They were separated, then they met again…Every time they met, they could only stay one or two nights together, not months like they used to. Then Sitha went away… Mumm returned to Baray, her prison. People kept a close watch on her. She had no freedom. My daughter…they locked her up, they spied on her.

Every time she and Sitha met, she said to him, "Don't leave me alone, they will do harm to me"…Then my son Sitha said to her, "I cannot take you away with me. If I could, I would have done so. I would not have let you suffer like this…Let's wait until the country has peace. Then we shall see each other again and live together." I can hardly talk about them—they loved each other so much.

Peasants working in the fields. Voiceover.

NARRATOR

"To preserve you is no gain; to destroy you is no loss" was the slogan shouted by the Khmer Rouge. Sometimes, Bophana tried to escape from this hell. When Ly Sitha wanted to see her, he went to his mother's house in Romlong, seven kilometers from Baray. He would send his younger brother to tell her. Bophana would secretly leave the village to spend the night with her husband. It was a short-lived happiness.

The end of 1975 was a period of frantic collectivization. Virtually all Cambodians were working in the paddies. Nevertheless, the people were starving. Collective meals were nothing more than a bowl of clear soup and a handful of rice.

In Baray, gossip about Bophana's past began to spread. Her separation from Ly Sitha became more and more unbearable as days went by. Exhausted by work, she fell ill. The Khmer Rouge gave her an injection of medicines made by young peasant women, the untrained nurses of the revolution. The injections caused painful abscesses, and Bophana became immobile. Desperate, she attempted suicide. Pregnant by Ly Sitha, she had a miscarriage.

Archival propaganda footage of workers harvesting grain. Revolutionary songs can be heard in the background. Male voiceover begins.

FROM LY SITHA'S LETTERS

To Sita, my unhappy wife…

I want to have news from you all the time. I'm so worried about your health. Why have you taken so much medicine? Will all this medicine make it impossible for us to have children? Are you going mad? If only I could become a ghost so that you could do what you wanted! I know the sea of your tears as well as you know the mountain of fire of my life.

My adorable Sita! Trust my heart, my darling. Those in Baray who bear us ill-will owe us a debt. For the time being, they have their accomplices…I will do everything until they pay back their debt to us…Our life together is so sad. Friends who know you ask for news of you. I suffer so much that I feel like spitting blood. But we must struggle.

I would like to remind you that "Our world is changing" [written in English]. Take care of yourself and don't fall ill. I recite these verses for you from Shakespeare's *Macbeth*, act 1: "When shall we two meet again in thunder, lightning or in rain?" [written in English].

Mumm, do not wear the sarong I sent you too often because when you wear it, you are very beautiful. You must think about your own safety. I would like to give you a new first name: Virginia, my Virginia, and Mumm can call me Paul [references to a popular French story about separated lovers]. I pinch the cheeks of my little darling from far away. I like the song you wrote on the back of the envelope very much. Sing me the song "The Boat of Life"… Peace be with you.

From your long-suffering husband

Mrs. Nakry, a former deportee, sits in a chair outdoors.

MRS. NAKRY   Under Pol Pot's regime, the cruelest aspect was the distrust they created among us—and the terror. When people could no longer trust anyone around them, they couldn't do anything about their situation. They could only wait for death to come. Even at night, at home, we were afraid to speak privately for lack of trust. Moreover, there were people listening to us, hiding under the house. We no longer said anything to each other. We waited and waited…If we survived, it was one more day of life, and if they came to look for us at night, it was the end. They didn't say they were going to kill us; they said they were taking us to "study," but the word "study" meant "death." We would never return.

Even in secret we could not talk about love. If they found out, they would take us away to be killed. Where I was, there was a girl called Phalla. She happened to have sung an old song…She sang it after work, at night, while resting. It was a song from the sixties. That same night they took her away to be killed. After the execution, they brought back the pickaxe and her clothing soaked with blood. They called a meeting so that we could see the clothes. "Phalla was an imperialist who did not want to leave bad habits behind," they said. But she had only sung a song, nothing more…So, we didn't talk about love or anything…

A former general and survivor of S-21, Pha Than Chann, sits in a chair outdoors.

PHA THAN CHANN   After their victory, "Great Leap Forward" meant to the Khmer Rouge that they could destroy everything. For instance, they destroyed private property and separated people into two classes: working class in factories; and peasants. They destroyed all other classes. They said their great leap would establish socialism faster than other socialist countries did. They called that "The Extraordinary Great Leap Forward."

Propaganda footage of workers as national anthem of Democratic Kampuchea is sung in the background. Chorus of voices.

Bright red blood which covers the town and plains of
    Kampuchea, our motherland,
Sublime blood of valorous workers and peasants,
Sublime blood of revolutionary men and women fighters,
The blood changes into unrelenting hatred and resolute
    struggle,
17 April, the day the revolutionary flag was raised,
Blood liberates us from slavery.

Archival propaganda images of forced labor. Child workers carry heavy loads; others are breaking rocks. Female voiceover begins.

FROM BOPHANA'S LETTERS

To my darling whom I miss…

How many tears will a woman have to shed when they separate her from her beloved husband after spending only two nights together…I lie in wait for your return. I wait for news from you…dreadfully…It has been eighty days now and there is still no news. I know and well understand that you and our two families are worried about my problems. But what can we do? It's our karma. Our lifelines show that our lives are to be separated! I also know that in this liberated land, it's the same everywhere. But for me living here in Baray, it's like living among wolves who don't understand human speech, who despise man, who deny human values, wolves who conspire behind our backs…I know only too well…that one day I will be a victim of our enemies here. Do you know, darling, that the villagers of Baray are all afraid of me?…My close friends no longer dare speak to me. I no longer have any hope. I cannot fight against destiny in order to meet you because life has an ending, and when you reach the end, you must know how to let go of life. I'm holding you tight and kissing you from far away…with the broken heart of your wife who suffers…

Deth's Sita

Long shot of empty roads, a river, a far horizon. Male voiceover begins.

FROM LY SITHA'S LETTERS

To my beloved wife…

I'm going mad. I'm so worried about your situation I feel dizzy…As for you, you have been accused of serious crimes. On my knees I'm begging you not to give up. There are many changes at the ministry…many reversals…Angkar has stripped me of some of my responsibilities, no doubt because I'm no longer viewed as trustworthy. Victims like me, if they make a single misstep, it's the end of the line. I am lost; that's the only word I can use. I no longer have any strength.

From a man who endures this pain,
Deth

Ly Sitha's mother is seated as before.

LY SITHA'S MOTHER   I cannot understand why the Khmer Rouge separated children, husbands, and wives. I don't understand it. I cannot understand such a separation. Even small children had to live apart. I can't understand this. To this day, I still can't. Since I was born, I have had to accept many things. I'm nearly seventy years old now. I should understand things about life. I understand how a husband and a wife love each other, what a family is, love between children and their mother, how villagers and neighbors can love each other…We all know this. But I cannot understand that period. That's why I can't really talk about it.

Por Hourt, a village woman of Baray, is seated indoors.

POR HOURT   When they called them out [Bophana, her grandmother, and other Baray villagers], they told them to gather their belongings in order to go and work in a new field, a new village. They just took them away like that. They didn't know they were being taken away to be killed. They believed they were going to work in a new place. That was all they knew. Each family was taken away like that. In her case, it was three o'clock in the morning. They asked her to bring an oxcart. Her old grandmother also went with her. We went to work at three in the morning.

Yon Noung, a village man of Baray, is standing outdoors.

YON NOUNG

Many people were taken away. It wasn't just one or two oxcarts of people per village. I well remember twenty-two oxcarts were used for my village alone. And how many villages were there in Baray district? Twenty oxcarts per village, and Baray district had thirteen villages. How could I be expected to remember so many people's faces? We oxcart drivers, like the passengers, had nothing to eat. We arrived with empty stomachs. If they asked us to take people, we took them and left them, and then we returned to the village. The next day, they asked for four oxcarts from each village to return to collect clothing. They didn't tell us to collect clothing but "spoils of war" in Chamcar Andoung. Once we arrived there, they told us there was nothing left. Others had already taken everything, so we came back empty-handed.

In close-up, camera slowly pans large mound of broken human bones, fragments of skulls. Voiceover.

NARRATOR

In 1976, purges of Khmer Rouge moderates began. The Minister of Trade in charge of the Northern Region, Koy Thoun [Ly Sitha's supervisor], was among the first victims. The rice harvest that year was poor because of a drought, but the whole Ministry of Trade was accused of sabotage and collusion with the CIA.

During an investigation, Pol Pot's security agents searched Ly Sitha's belongings and discovered Bophana's letters and a false travel permit. In their paranoia, the Khmer Rouge thought they had discovered an important network of spies working for the Americans. Ly Sitha, or Comrade Deth, was arrested on 19 September 1976.

When the convoy of oxcarts transporting Bophana and others from Baray arrived at Chamcar Loeu, a massacre took place. Men, women, and children, all stripped naked, were methodically killed, one after another, and then thrown into the wells. A Khmer Rouge cadre ordered Bophana to be separated from the group. She was blindfolded, put into a van, and taken to Phnom Penh.

Bophana was incarcerated at S-21 Detention Center; "S" stands for security, 2 for second division, and 1 for Brother Number One, Pol Pot. Before the Khmer Rouge regime, the S-21 Detention Center was a high school. Bophana's imprisonment began on 12 October 1976.

Voiceover of Im Chann, a sculptor and former prisoner of S-21, as a small group arrives to tour the prison, now known as the Tuol Sleng Genocide Museum. The group is shown cells, torture devices. Then Mr. Chann sits with his back against a barred window.

IM CHANN   When the truck brought us here, they ordered us to get off, then we were blindfolded. After that, they took us in and asked us to sit on the floor for about half an hour. A photographer came to take a photo of me against the wall of the building. After that, they took me into a cell on the top floor. My feet were shackled. About ten days later, they began to interrogate me. They blindfolded me, then took me to a house outside. I did not know what house it was because I was blindfolded. I couldn't see a thing.

The interrogation went from seven in the morning till eleven; in the afternoon, from two to five; in the evening, from six to eleven. I had never met a Frenchman, an American, or a Vietnamese, and they wanted to know if I had ever met an American, if I had betrayed the revolution. I knew nothing about this treason business. If I was a traitor, I would have been an ideological accomplice of foreigners or tried to kill a Party member. But I didn't know anything about treason, so I said I hadn't done a thing. They then hit me in order to get a certain answer. They gave me the answer beforehand: "You must answer this way or that way…and I will stop hitting you." As I was afraid of suffering, though not of dying, I answered the way they wanted. They recorded my answer on a machine and gave the tape to the Party. Then they stopped torturing me.

Close-up of many letters and documents in a folder. Voiceover.

NARRATOR   Bophana was incarcerated in a building reserved for women. At night she heard heartbreaking cries and pleading. Bophana thought of Ly Sitha. She did not know that he was also there, in chains in another classroom, already bruised by torture. He was forced to write and rewrite unbelievable confessions. He was forced to say that he had been manipulated by Bophana and that he had betrayed the revolution.

For her part, Bophana was made to confess imaginary connections to the CIA. She was forced to give the names of close relatives and friends at Baray, who were then arrested. Mam Nai, formerly her teacher of literature at Kompong Thom School, was a political commissioner at the S-21 Detention Center and interrogated her.

Duch, the head of the S-21 Detention Center, was also a former schoolteacher. He underlined incriminating passages in their confessions and letters with red ink. In the margins of one of Bophana's letters he wrote, NO INTEREST. INSTRUCTIONS FOR AFTER THE INTERROGATION ALREADY GIVEN.

Vann Nath, a painter and former prisoner of S-21, walks toward the Genocide Museum with the former deputy head of security, Him Houy. The painter has his hand on Him Houy's shoulder as if to guide him. According to Vann Nath's published memoir, Him Houy was one of the prison's most brutal executioners, though he now denies it. They enter the rooms. On the walls are scenes of torture painted by Vann Nath. The two men stop occasionally before one painting or another.

VANN NATH	Come over here…This picture [*of a child being torn from its mother's arms by soldiers in black*], it's something that I imagined. I didn't actually witness this scene. But this is how I imagined it when I heard the cries of infants and their mothers. The sounds came from upstairs. Is this picture accurate?
HIM HOUY	Yes, it is.
VANN NATH	Would they struggle like that? Now, don't just answer yes all the time! You have to be certain!
HIM HOUY	It happened like that.
VANN NATH	I'm not forcing you to agree with me…
HIM HOUY	If you tried to force me and if it was not true, I wouldn't say anything. It was like that; otherwise you wouldn't have heard them killing children.
VANN NATH	This picture [*of a man being tortured*] is not something I saw…I didn't hear the screams. But someone told me

about it. I've forgotten his name; it was in 1979. He told me that he could show me the exact place upstairs. Is this picture an exaggeration?

HIM HOUY   No, it was like that.

VANN NATH   It's important that you're certain of this.

HIM HOUY   Oh yes.

VANN NATH   This picture, it's of torture [*pointing to another painting*]…I did not suffer this torture myself, but the victim recounted it to me when I was also a prisoner here. These instruments were found afterwards. He told me that they pulled out his fingernails with pliers. Then they poured alcohol on his fingertips. Did this happen?

HIM HOUY   Yes, it did.

VANN NATH   Truly? Then this picture is not a lie?

HIM HOUY   No, it's accurate.

VANN NATH   In this picture [*of a man being beaten*], I know with absolute certainty that it happened because it's my friend Meng. There were four men who took turns hitting him. Meng told me this in prison. His back had wounds. I don't know where Meng is now…And this picture [*walks to another painting of torture*], did things like this happen?

HIM HOUY   It must have happened.

VANN NATH   Nobody told me about it. I saw it myself.

HIM HOUY   I did not see that, but perhaps it happened.

VANN NATH   Don't say "perhaps"! I saw it when they brought the prisoners out. They had accidently left one door half open, over where I was painting. When I saw it, I was numb with fear. So, you think it could have happened?

HIM HOUY   Yes, it could have happened.

VANN NATH   All the paintings here—I did not make things up. I'm telling the truth. I'm not accusing or condemning anybody. I'm showing the life of the prisoners here, and I was among them. Before they asked me to go downstairs and paint for them, I suffered in the way depicted here [*points to a painting of a room full of men shackled together*]. That was the room I stayed in on the second floor. I remember it well. I was there [*pointing to a figure in the painting*], in the corner. When Peng and Thi [high-ranking guards] came to look for me, they removed the padlock here, pulled out the iron bar, and released me so they could take me downstairs. When they took me away to work, I wasn't able to walk. I didn't know when I was going to be killed.

HIM HOUY   You worked while waiting for them to—

VANN NATH   I did what I was told. In this painting, I copied what was written on the board. When I arrived, the guard banged on the board. "Turn your head over here!" he said. "Those who can read, read for others: IT IS FORBIDDEN TO SPEAK OR TO WHISPER TO EACH OTHER, WHETHER YOU KNOW EACH OTHER OR NOT. You just shut up." Did I exaggerate this painting? If you said it was not true, I would not believe you. I was there. Was it like that?

HIM HOUY   Yes, it was.

VANN NATH   All these pictures—I didn't invent what's in them, and I didn't accuse anyone. I painted the life of prisoners as human beings who once lived here. That was my only wish. This painting shows a prisoner in a cell. That certainly is accurate. I painted these pictures in 1980, fifteen years ago, after the fall of the Khmer Rouge. The desire to paint them came to me while I was a prisoner. I said to myself that when the country finds peace again, I want people to know how others died here. These are not lies, are they?

HIM HOUY   No, it's the truth.

Camera travels through the rooms where the walls are covered with photographs of victims of S-21. Stops at photograph of Bophana. Voiceover.

NARRATOR   Bophana endured this Calvary for six months. Under torture, she wrote one thousand pages of confessions.

To the Khmer Rouge, Bophana exemplified the educated people, whom they regarded as parasites to be eliminated. Of the twenty thousand prisoners who passed through S-21 Detention Center—workers, peasants, intellectuals, and, later, purged Khmer Rouge cadres—only seven survived.

In order to retain an identity of her own choosing and to demonstrate her love for Deth and her opposition to barbarism, she always signed her name Sedadet, or Deth's Sita.

On a late afternoon in March 1977, a warden went to check Bophana's identity one more time…

Him Houy walks down a corridor of cells. He stops at the last one and opens it.

HIM HOUY   Each prisoner was taken into a cell. They put iron shackles on his feet, and he slept there…Once the shackles were padlocked, Peng, the head of security, took the key to his office. The door was then closed. There was one guard per sector. He walked back and forth like this and never stopped…

When I came with the head of security and the head of recordkeeping to take a prisoner away, we first called the prisoner's name. The prisoner replied. Then we tied him with a rope or put handcuffs on him. We blindfolded him. The leg irons were removed. He was taken out of the cell. I led the prisoners and stayed near the truck to line them up. [*Continues as camera tracks down the stairs to the exit.*]

We led the prisoners by holding them by an arm, their hands tied behind their backs. They were not allowed to scream. If they screamed, we hit them. When they were put in the trucks, some said, "You are going to kill us"…I would say to them, "We are not going to do anything to you. Get in the truck and stay quiet. If you scream, we will hit you." I helped them to stand on a chair to get in the truck. Sometimes we took fifteen persons, twenty, thirty…or forty. Sometimes we needed two trucks.

[*Standing at Choeung Ek, a field on the outskirts of Phnom Penh.*] I will tell you…when we brought the prisoners here, I drove the truck. When we arrived, we asked them to get out and we put them in a hut. We kept the prisoners in the hut until the big chiefs arrived and told us it was time for their execution. I called out their names once more. Then we led these men one after another. The chief was already near the pit in order to watch…Warden Duch was already near the pits…

They brought the men over, and the executioners began to kill them. They hit the prisoners one after another…One day, Chief Duch said, "Comrade Houy…have you decided to kill?" I replied, "I'm not afraid, Older Brother." All I had to do was hit. Usually when they brought the prisoners, I stayed there with the others to take their names.

Warden Duch said to me again, "Comrade Houy, are you afraid to kill people?" I replied, "I'm not afraid…" Then I took an iron bar from somebody. I was standing up. I asked the prisoner to kneel down, and I hit him. I hit five prisoners like that, but I did not cut their throats. I only hit five persons, under orders. I did this when the warden was there; otherwise, I just took down names.

[*Standing at the edge of a shallow pit, one of many where bodies were dumped.*] When prisoners arrived, we made them squat like this. Sometimes we asked them to stand up or made them kneel down like this with their hands tied behind their backs and their eyes blindfolded. And we hit them…We hit the back of the neck—here. When they fell over, we cut their throats and threw them in the pits.

Camera tracks across a field pockmarked with dozens of pits, all dug for the same purpose. When Him Houy "defected" from the Khmer Rouge in 1995, he confessed to having killed two thousand prisoners at S-21—a claim he has since retracted.

Ly Sitha's mother is seated. She points to photos of Ly Sitha and Hout Bophana.

LY SITHA'S MOTHER   I've waited for this news for years. I've waited until I became ill, exhausted, nearly dead. I've wanted to know whether they were dead or alive. That was all I wanted to know, and now I know. Now I only have tears, but at least I know whether or not my children are dead. I haven't closed my eyes since yesterday. They loved each other so much. They said, "If we die here, Mother, bury us side by side." I miss them. They asked me to bury them side by side at Wat Po if something happened to them.

Title card with photograph of Ly Sitha reads:

> Ly Sitha, known as Comrade Deth
> Age 27
> Arrested on 19 September 1976
> Officially destroyed on 18 March 1977

Title card with photograph of Hout Bophana reads:

> Bophana, known as Mumm, as Sita
> Age 25
> Arrested on 12 October 1976
> Officially destroyed 18 March 1977

Title card with same photograph reads:

> Of the one hundred fifty families who arrived at Baray the same time as Bophana, only five survived. Nearly two million Cambodians perished under Pol Pot's regime.

Credits roll before fade to black.

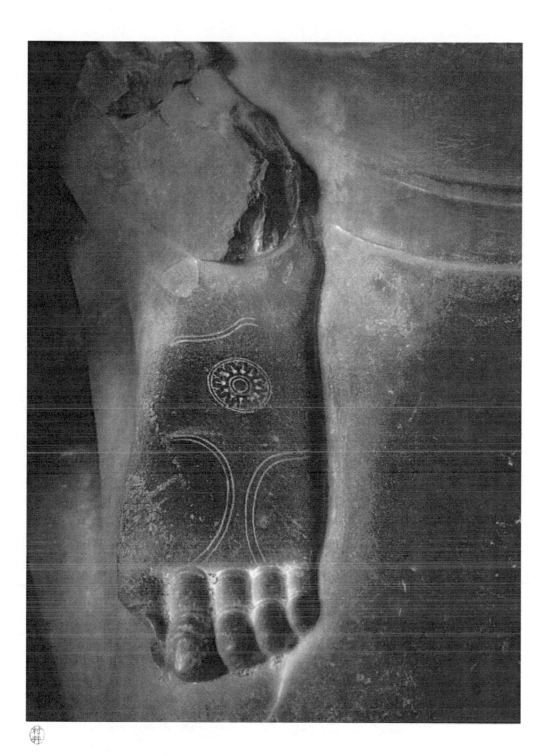

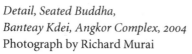

Detail, Seated Buddha,
Banteay Kdei, Angkor Complex, 2004
Photograph by Richard Murai

A Mysterious Passenger

It is late afternoon, nearly four o'clock. Returning to the capital, a Toyota Corona disappears into the shadow of Pech Nil Mountain, halfway between Phnom Penh and Kompong Som. At the wheel is a thirty-year-old man: close-cropped hair, dark skin, hatchet-faced features with slightly protruding eyes, and deeply furrowed brow, which gives him an expression of constant worry.

Next to him, a man with a light complexion but features that are typically Khmer: handsome, Eurasian, about thirty-five years old. A vague smile floats on his lips. He has an intelligent face. His large, dark eyes gaze languidly at the passing countryside. He is holding a small video camera. From time to time, he asks his driver to slow down so that he can film something in the landscape.

Abruptly, the driver turns to the man in the seat beside him and, using the deferential form of address, asks softly, "Elder Brother Veasna, when do you think you'll be going back to America?"

The handsome Veasna lowers the camera and manages a slight smile. It's evident he's not interested in chatting. "That must be the tenth time you've asked me that question, Chan! Don't you want me to stay here in Cambodia?"

"Me? You must be kidding!" the driver responds. But the furrows in his brow grow even deeper. "Before you arrived, every day was dull. But now that you're here, I'm never bored!" He sighs. "I'm sorry to insist, Elder Brother. It's just that every time I ask, you either say nothing or you change the subject."

Veasna turns slowly to his driver. The sincere melancholy in the driver's tone has surprised him.

"Well, I can see you aren't going to give up easily. OK, stop worrying about it. I'll answer your question. But while I do, be sure to concentrate on your driving. This winding road is especially dangerous, and I don't want to end up at the bottom of the ravine."

"Don't worry, Elder Brother. I'm not like other drivers. I talk a lot while I'm driving, but I always keep my eyes on the road, and both hands on the wheel."

"Your driving doesn't usually worry me," the Cambodian American says, lifting his eyebrows slightly. "But last night when you were dancing at Snake Island, you looked pretty frisky. I wouldn't be surprised if your eyesight is a little blurry today…"

Chan bursts out laughing. Easing the car expertly into a sharp curve, he smiles broadly, the ends of his mouth turned up like a gondola.

"Oh, yeah! *Ha-ha!* You've got bags under your eyes, too, Elder Brother! Last night it looked to me like you weren't feeling any pain either. Ah, yes. With all those gorgeous girls…Were you able to film some of them?"

"Film them? What for?"

"What do you mean, 'What for?' I thought that was the purpose of your trip this time: to crisscross Cambodia and film all the beautiful Khmer women! Isn't that why we borrowed your parents' car?"

"That's partly true," Veasna concedes, slowly nodding. "But I'm not here to film bargirls!"

"Well, I'll be damned!" Chan replies, not daring to take his eyes off the road. "What more do you want? Didn't you see those curves, those glowing faces? They were all as gorgeous as the celestial *apsaras* on the walls of Angkor Wat!"

The car reaches a small wooden bridge that's badly decaying and in need of repair. Veasna holds his breath until they have crossed the hazard.

"What I'm looking for," he says finally, casting a glance behind him at the bridge, "is a young country girl—a girl from the rice fields."

"A girl from the rice fields?!" squawks the driver. "You mean to tell me you're filming peasant girls? Forgive me for saying so, but they're not at all to my taste. They're far—very far—below the beauty of my little flowers at Snake Island."

The passenger's expression stiffens slightly. "Maybe so," he says, trying to smile, "but those nocturnal beauties of yours are nothing without powder, lipstick, and the pulsing of the neon lights. What I'm interested in are peasant girls—like the girls from Veal Renh or Prey Nup, for example. They have such natural grace, beauty—and without any makeup or false lighting. And then there's the exquisite reserve in their manner: a blend of sweetness and shyness…"

Chan scratches his head. He doesn't really understand, but he doesn't want to contradict his companion. All the same, with a forced smile he continues. "There can't be too many people who think like that, you know. But after all, why not? You can film such girls if you want. The most important thing, though, is that you answer my question."

Veasna once again raises his camera to his eye. "What were you asking, Chan?"

The driver lets out a groan. "As if you didn't know! Well, this time you won't get off so easily, Elder Brother! If you don't answer me right now, I am going to stop the car!"

Veasna abruptly puts down the camera, takes a breath, and says gently, "My friend, don't get so worked up. OK then, here's your answer: I'm going back to the U.S. in one month."

"Are you telling me the truth, Elder Brother?" asks the driver, a curious tone in his voice.

"That's the honest truth," Veasna responds with a faraway gaze. "It's printed in black and white on my plane ticket."

Chan sighs deeply. His despondency seems absolute.

"What's the matter?" Veasna asks, concerned now. "What's the long face for?"

"Nothing, Elder Brother," says the driver faintly. "It's just that I would have liked for you to go sooner, that's all."

Veasna's expression darkens. "But why? Are you expecting trouble to break out in Cambodia?"

"Oh no, not at all. It's something to do with me."

"To do with you? Well then, come on, Chan, tell me. Out with it!"

In answer, Chan presses the brakes and brings the car to a stop under a tree.

"Now what?" Veasna protests, dumbfounded. "What are you doing? Why are you stopping the car like this? We're in the middle of a forest, there's not a soul around, the sky is clouding over, and it's about to storm any minute. We'll never make it back on time."

Chan gets out of the car.

"This won't take long," he says, taking a deep breath. "I just need to calm down a bit before explaining this to you. Don't worry. Besides, we wouldn't have made it back before nightfall anyway."

"Then speak!" Veasna says through the open window of the car. "Why the hell must I leave Cambodia when I haven't even finished my work?"

Chan's face takes on an expression of infinite sadness. "It's because," he says in a trembling voice, "I'm in love. On top of that, the dates have been set. I only have a few days to get an engagement present, and the marriage is two weeks later. You just have to leave, Veasna, as soon as possible. Tomorrow or the day after…You really must go and tell my older sister."

Veasna is stunned. "What? That's all? But can't you just send your sister a fax?"

"A fax…but I don't have her address or her telephone number…"

At this point, Veasna begins to lose his composure. He gets out of the car and walks over to Chan. "You don't have her telephone number? Your sister has never sent her number to you in her letters?"

Above them, the sky is darkening. In the distance, storm clouds are gathering in a black, foreboding mass above the mountain peaks.

"Well, actually, I've never received any letters from her."

"Then how do you know she's in America? Give it to me straight, Chan. I can't make heads or tails of what you're telling me!"

The driver bends down, plucks a small flower out of the grass, and places it between his lips. "My sister and I," he continues, his voice fading, "were separated in 1975, when the Khmer Rouge took Phnom Penh. I thought she was lost to me forever. But just a week ago, I found out she's alive and residing in America."

Veasna covers his face with his hands. "OK. So how did you find out?"

The driver hesitates.

"Well, Chan, someone must have told you, yes?" Veasna is becoming impatient. He brings his face close to Chan's. "This someone must certainly know her address and telephone number!"

Chan spits the flower out of his mouth. "No, Elder Brother," he says, finally blurting it out. "A fortuneteller told me..."

Veasna jumps back as if suddenly bitten by an ant in a tender part of his anatomy. "A fortuneteller?!" he exclaims.

"Yes," stammers the driver, bobbing his head from side to side like an iguana. "The other day, you know...The other day when I took you for a visit to the Wat Phnom...well, I took the opportunity to consult a famous psychic...This master psychic told me everything...that my sister was still alive...that she is living in America...So now do you understand, Veasna? You simply must help me! You have to go back and find her for me!"

Veasna looks skyward as if for help. High in a tree, two or three birds take flight effortlessly on slow wings.

"Of all things...How could you, Younger Brother? You who are so practical minded, who drive heavy equipment for a living. How could you believe in the predictions of fortunetellers?!"

Chan takes Veasna's arm and tugs on it gently. "I assure you, Elder Brother, this person is amazing! Two weeks before you came to Cambodia, he told a friend of mine who had his motorbike stolen that it would reappear in three days. And guess what—unbelievable! On exactly the third day, my friend found his motorbike! Trust me, Veasna. My sister is alive. Since the fortuneteller gave me this news, I've dreamed of her almost every night."

Veasna stops looking at the sky. "I don't want to interfere with your beliefs, Chan...but come on, this is the computer age we're living in!"

"What can I say?" answers the driver. "Computer age or not, people here have absolute faith in these things. Help me, Veasna, please! Don't abandon me!"

"OK," says the Cambodian American man gravely. "Let me see if I understand what you're really saying: you want me to find your sister and tell her to send you money for your engagement present. Is that it?"

Chan joyfully circles Veasna on tiptoe. "Yes! Yes!" he cries, his eyes full of tears. "That's exactly it. Oh, you know how to heal my wounded heart, Elder Brother! It's true that I am poor and if my sister doesn't help me, I will have lost a priceless jewel for a wife."

Veasna gets in the backseat of the car and smiles magnanimously. "All right. OK, you can count on me. All right. But let's get going. It'll be dark soon."

Chan glances quickly at the road and starts the car. Behind him, he hears Veasna's resonant voice.

"I feel sorry for you, Younger Brother. There are so many Khmers in America, hundreds of thousands of them. How in the world will I be able to find your sister if you don't even have her address?"

"Ah, but my sister is special. She used to be the lead dancer in the Royal Ballet! A star!"

"A ballet star?!" exclaims Veasna, his curiosity piqued now. "What's her name?"

Chan savors his triumph. "You see," he says, brimming over with pride, "you haven't heard anything yet and you are already on the edge of your seat. How will you handle it when you know her name?! Trust me, Veasna, you will find her!"

An enormous clap of thunder interrupts the driver. The sky turns black. Explosive gusts of wind cover the narrow road with clouds of dust. Visibility is nearly zero. And then the terrifying, deafening storm strikes with full force. Sheets of angry rain crash on the car so violently that they threaten to shatter the windshield. Chan stomps on the accelerator, trying to escape this dark storm as quickly as possible.

"How strange," he mutters. "One would think the sky was angry about something…"

"Stop, Chan!" Veasna shouts. "I think I see someone waving at us. Slow down! Slow down!"

Chan takes his foot off the gas and turns on his high beams. "Where? I can't see a thing."

"There. That white figure on the side of the road, under the tamarind tree. It looks like a woman. Hey, she's trying to signal to us."

The car swerves slightly to the shoulder of the road.

"Oh, yes. Now I can see her. *Hmmm*…But what's a woman doing in such a desolate place at this hour of the night? What's going on, Elder Brother? This doesn't look good…"

"Someone is signaling for help," interrupts Veasna sternly. "We must stop! What are you afraid of? Come on, pull over quick. Hey, look. She's coming towards us!"

Chan would have preferred to drive on by, but this isn't his car. He does what Veasna tells him to do and pulls off the road to stop next to the tamarind tree. A woman dressed in black, her head covered with a white *krama*, approaches them.

By this time, Veasna has rolled down his window. In spite of the darkness and the pouring rain, he can make out a form. It is indeed a young woman. She appears to be twenty-two or twenty-three years old at most.

And suddenly her face is close enough for him to see: a face arrestingly beautiful and overpowering…Veasna feels himself stirred to the depths of his being.

I have been going around this country for almost two weeks, he thinks to himself, *and I have never seen a girl so beautiful.*

"Is anything wrong, young lady?" asks Chan.

But before the beautiful young woman can answer, Veasna takes over the conversation. "Please, get in," he says, quickly opening the back door. "You're going to be soaked. We can talk afterwards."

"Thank you, gentlemen. Thank you so very much."

Her voice…is like music, like the celestial music that comes down from Mount Kailash's fabled summit: melodious and so marvelously beautiful…with the strange power to make one's blood well up inside the heart, to transform one's heart into a volcano about to erupt. Chan dares not speak. He lets Veasna do the talking.

"What are you doing out here alone, miss?"

The young woman unties her white *krama* and pats her wet forehead. "I came to visit my aunt," she says with the smile of an innocent child. "She lives in the woods, close to here. I was on my way back home when the storm caught me by surprise."

Every word that falls from her lips is like the offering of flowers at a shrine. Veasna inhales with growing ecstasy the fateful scent of ambrosia. He cannot take his eyes from her. She appears more and more beautiful to him with each passing moment.

"I see, I see," he answers, feeling never more alive than at that instant. "And where do you live, miss?"

She lowers her eyes shyly. "At the foot of Mount Kirirom."

Chan, who until then had been content to observe the young woman in the rearview mirror, brusquely interrupts, as if he were waking from a dream. "Perfect! That's perfect! That's not far from here! Ten kilometers at the most!"

"Then it's no problem, miss," Veasna says, nodding and smiling, "to drop you off at your home. Come on, Chan, let's go!"

After a brief sidelong glance in the rearview mirror, Chan starts the car and begins driving, this time more cautiously.

The winds and rain have redoubled their violence. In an effort to dispel the malevolent atmosphere created by the storm, Veasna decides to strike up a conversation. "So…what is the name of this place?" he asks.

The beautiful young woman beside him seems to be making an effort to remember. "I think…I think that the old folks call it the Hill of the Three Skulls," she says, lifting her eyes.

Chan turns slightly towards her. Her words seem to have awakened something in him. "The Hill of the Three Skulls…Yes, I *do* remember. Something horrible happened there under Pol Pot."

"Do you know the story, Chan?"

"Vaguely," the driver answers, keeping his attention on the road. "I was deported to this region."

The eyes of the beautiful woman light up. "Then you must know the Plain of the Dead Jackal," she says in a clear voice.

Chan's lips begin to tremble. "Yes, I worked there. I was part of the mobile brigade. *Brrr*…just hearing the name gives me goose flesh! And you, miss?"

The car has begun to accelerate. In the dim glow of its interior lights, the young woman's voice seems even more beautiful.

"Yes, I worked down there, too. But I don't know much about its story."

A bolt of lightning explodes nearby with a terrifying roar. Its blue-white flash illuminates the car's interior and reflects in the eyes of the young woman, who is visibly frightened.

"And…and what if you told us a little more of the story, Chan?" Veasna says softly.

"Oh no, not now," answers the driver, who is trembling like a leaf. "I don't like to talk about ghosts when I'm driving."

Veasna holds his nose. "So are you saying that this is a story about ghosts?"

"Yes. It's about three young sisters. People say that they were murdered in a most terrible manner."

With a startled cry, Veasna interrupts. He has noticed that the young woman is on the verge of tears. "That's enough, Chan! Our passenger does not feel very well."

Chan stops speaking immediately. "Excuse me, miss. Maybe this story touches you personally?"

The beautiful young woman is making an effort not to cry. "No," she says in a barely audible voice, "it's just that I can't bear sad stories…I cry…every time…I don't know why…"

Another bolt of lightning illuminates the interior of the car.

"I understand," says Veasna, settling deeper into his seat. "Let's not talk about it anymore."

Then, after a moment of silence, he grumbles, "Damn it! Don't you smell anything? It's like the smell of something rotten…Can't you smell it, Chan?"

Holding his nose too, the driver says, "Yes, you're right. Could there be a dead buffalo on the side of the road?"

"No. I have the air conditioner turned on, and the windows are tightly closed."

"Maybe there's a dead rat in the car."

"A dead rat? In my car? Why would there be a dead rat in my car?" Veasna continues to hold his nose tightly. "Maybe you stepped in something, Chan?"

At this point, the young woman speaks up, smiling sweetly. "You're not imagining things, gentlemen," she says in her serene voice. "I helped my aunt to fill up several jars of fish paste today. The smell of the *prahoc* must still be with me. I'm very sorry that it bothers you so much."

"*Prahoc!*" Veasna exclaims, delighted. "Right! That's it! That's the smell of *prahoc!*"

Chan loudly joins in. "Veasna may have lived a long time in America, but he's not grossed out by our *prahoc!* At restaurants he always asks for more!"

The beautiful woman lifts her eyes. "Very well then," she says in her silky voice, "if we're lucky enough to see each other again, I'll offer both of you a little jar of *prahoc* as a token of gratitude."

"Thank you in advance, miss. Prepared by you, I am certain it will be delicious."

The rain has lessened slightly, but Chan, who does not feel reassured, maintains the same speed. Suddenly he yells, "Oh, no!" Looking right and left, he says, "I think we might have gone past your house. Can you look out and see if we have, miss?"

The young woman looks through the window, and now it is she who is alarmed. "A bit, yes, a little bit. But it's OK. I can jump out right here. This is fine."

Veasna sighs. "Over here? But we're deep in the woods. Where is your house?"

"Over there," she says, pointing. "Beyond the first row of trees…"

Veasna rolls down his window and squints. "But it's still raining and you don't have anything to cover yourself with…"

"Don't worry," says the young woman as she opens the door. "I'll change my clothes when I get home. Well…thank you, gentlemen. Good-bye."

"Good-bye, miss," says Veasna, slightly dispirited. "If you had not lived so far, I would have accompanied you home."

The mysterious young woman presses her palms together in a gesture of farewell. In a low voice, nearly whispering, she says, "Don't worry yourself. You have shown enough proof of the goodness of your heart…"

The sky growls again, but now the sound is deeper, occurring in long tympanic rumbles. The storm seems to be moving away, though the winds still blow and the shadows still flicker ominously.

The young woman wraps the white *krama* around her head, then slowly and delicately steps off the road and disappears into the shadows of the massive trees. Veasna's heart has stopped beating. His gaze is arrested by the beauty of her bare foot and the charm, grace, and suppleness with which she walks.

"What are you looking at now, Elder Brother?" says Chan, tapping nervously on the wheel. "She's gone, there's nothing more to see."

He starts the engine, and Veasna comes out of his trance. "She was right. The smell disappeared when she did. Chan, tell me: what do you think of this girl?"

"Not much," answers the driver with a forced air of nonchalance. "She was a peasant girl, just a peasant girl. In principle, we should have had her pay us for the ride."

"What are you talking about?" Veasna replies indignantly. "Giving her a ride didn't cost us anything." Then he adds with sudden joy, "She was beautiful! Beautiful! I think she could have asked me to take her all the way to Phnom Penh!"

Chan cannot pretend any longer. "Yes, she was indeed really beautiful. Marvelously beautiful. My eyes didn't leave the rearview mirror. It's hard to believe. A girl like her, in such a desolate place, so far away from everything…"

"I've got to tell you, Chan. Never, never have I seen such beauty. The face of an angel, framed by long hair gleaming like jade. Eyes like beautiful black diamonds under such delicately curved eyebrows. A small nose, lightly curved, lips full and velvety. The delicious dimples on her cheeks…"

"And then all the rest!" blurts out the driver, who is keen to continue this inventory. "That walk of a cat…that supernatural grace…The humble blouse and modest sarong—you can just imagine what's underneath…"

"Stop, Chan!" Veasna shouts suddenly.

Chan is so startled he nearly lets go of the wheel.

"What now, Elder Brother?"

Veasna has had the wind knocked out of him. His heart is pounding in his chest. "There, just for an instant, while you were talking, I turned around and saw her behind the glass, her eyes fixed on mine. I was about to speak to her, but she vanished into thin air. My God! My hair is standing on end!"

Chan bursts out laughing. "You are hallucinating, my friend. You're thinking too much about her."

"But just now I saw her as clearly as I see you, Chan. I saw her. She had a white rose behind her ear."

"Forget all about that, Elder Brother. We are arriving in Kompong Speu Province."

Translation from Khmer to French by Christophe Macquet and from French to English by Marie-Christine Garneau and Theo Garneau

*The Perpetrator, the Victim, and the Witness*_____

CAMBODIA'S KILLERS LIVE ON IN QUIET INFAMY the newspaper headline read. The short article, by a respected American journalist, described how the man known as Grandfather Khan continued to live unpunished among the villagers he had terrorized during the years of Democratic Kampuchea.

Khan, the article explained, had killed hundreds of people in the prison camp he commanded and in the area surrounding it. Survivors reported that some of his victims were strung up by their feet and eviscerated, internal organs left to dangle before their faces as they died. He also allegedly consumed the liver and bile of his victims in the belief that doing so would allow him to absorb their vitality.

It's difficult to write these sentences, which can never fully capture the atrocities they are supposed to describe. I have been trying to understand such horrors since early 1993, when I was a graduate student in anthropology and decided to research the Cambodian genocide. I still want to know why genocide occurs. What motivates a perpetrator to kill? How does a person like Khan bring himself to not just murder another human being but to do so in the cruelest of ways?

To seek the answers, I lived in Cambodia from 1994 to 1995. In the summer of 2000, I returned to the country to conduct follow-up research for a book, and it was then that I decided to try to find Khan and ask him, *Why did you do it?*

The Witness

At the end of my trip, I managed to track down the Cambodian reporter who had helped research the article I read on Khan. I will call her Ming. As we spoke on the phone, she told me in a mixture of English and Khmer that she had never actually interviewed Khan.

"We just talked to people who lived near the prison during that time," she explained. "But I know where he lives. We can drive right to his house and talk with him. He lives in the south, about two hours away. I can get a car. If you want, we can leave tomorrow at dawn."

Monk Boys, Looking South,
Angkor Wat, 2002
Photograph by Richard Murai

In Cambodia, everything begins at an early hour. By the time the sun edges over the horizon, most people have risen and are performing tasks that would be difficult to finish in the midday heat. By eleven o'clock, the hottest part of the day, most Cambodian farmers have already tended to their fields and returned home to eat their lunch and rest.

Ming arrived early the next morning. She wore Western clothes: a blue, button-down shirt that fell loosely over khaki pants. Her hair was pulled back into a tight ponytail, accentuating her high forehead and round face. In her early thirties, she was short and stout and had intense eyes. When I climbed into the passenger seat of her Toyota, I noticed a pair of small bells hanging from the rearview mirror. They chimed each time we hit a bump in the road.

Ming reached into the backseat. "See, I brought my camera," she said, a smile breaking over her face. "Just in case."

Just in case, I thought. *In case what?*

It was monsoon season, but we set off under a clear sky broken only by a few clouds. Ming drove slowly, threading her way through the jumble of trucks, cars, mopeds, bikes, pedicabs, and pedestrians that filled the city streets. Each time she braked hard, the bells chimed lightly.

Despite the pollution, billboards, and piles of garbage sometimes accumulating on the sidewalks, Phnom Penh is still a beautiful city: a blend of French colonial architecture, palm trees, tiered villas with balconies, bustling markets scented with spices, and majestic Buddhist temples. It's hard to believe that the entire city was evacuated during Pol Pot's regime and that twenty thousand Khmer Rouge cadres, soldiers, and workers replaced a population that had swollen to about three million during the civil war. In the countryside, the urbanites found themselves labeled "new people" and treated much worse than the "old people" who had lived in Khmer Rouge zones prior to the evacuation of Phnom Penh.

As we neared the city's outskirts, Ming turned onto the highway that would take us toward the southern provinces, a key base of Khmer Rouge support during the civil war. The traffic abated, and the urban edifices were replaced by rice fields. As the driving became less demanding, I began to ask Ming about Khan.

"Where exactly does Khan live?" I inquired. "How do we find him?"

"In a village by the mountains. He has many relatives there." She added that Khan had recently defected from the Khmer Rouge with Ta Mok, known as The Butcher because of his ruthlessness during the Khmer Rouge period and after.

I began to get nervous. We were going to meet a recent defector, a soldier who had been killing people for the last thirty years. He lived in a remote village in which we had no local contacts. Cambodia can be dangerous, particularly when one wanders into remote places to inquire about a past that many would rather forget. Guns are everywhere, kidnappings frequent, violence common. I considered turning back.

Ming continued, "I have a friend—Mum—who lives in the area. She knows where Khan lives." That reassured me slightly. Then Ming said, "I'll tell you my story, OK?" In Cambodia, people will often begin to talk about what they endured during the Khmer Rouge period. And although I have conducted countless interviews on the subject, I'm never truly prepared for what I hear. Ming's voice rose, and she began to speak quickly, often stumbling over words as she recalled her first steps on the path leading to Khan.

Ming was eight years old when the Khmer Rouge took control of Phnom Penh. Her family was well-to-do, possessing just the sort of "impure" urban background that the Khmer Rouge wanted to purge from its new revolutionary society. Ming's family paid for this immediately. Her father, an engineer in a government ministry, was loaded into a military jeep and taken away. Ming's voice shook as she told me, "I don't know what they did to him. He had a big stomach, so the Khmer Rouge thought he was a big shot."

Like everyone else in Phnom Penh, Ming's family was ordered to leave while "Angkar cleans the city." *Angkar* means "the organization." Sometimes the term referred to the higher authorities; in other situations, it signified an almost divine entity to whom unquestioning loyalty and obedience were due. Angkar had power over life and death. Those who had suspect backgrounds or who "betrayed" the new regime were taken away to "see Angkar." Most never returned.

Ming's mother told her children to gather enough clothing and food to last a few days. Then they joined the tens of thousands of people who clogged the roads out of Phnom Penh, moving inches at a time in temperatures approaching one hundred degrees. Corpses littered the streets: dead government soldiers, civilians who had died from exposure and thirst, and victims of Khmer Rouge executions. The people of Phnom Penh soon realized that the Khmer Rouge had no intention of letting them return to the capital. Ming's family headed south, toward her father's birthplace in Takeo Province, toward Khan.

Soon, Ming and I had left the outlying areas of Phnom Penh and reached the national highway. Hardly wide enough for two cars and pitted with large potholes, it passed through lush rice fields where peasant farmers bent over their land transplanting rice. Each time the car struck a pothole, bells chimed. Ming continued her story.

Her family never made it to her father's birthplace. Instead, the Khmer Rouge ordered them to live in a village near the subdistrict office where Khan was the head of the local militia. Ming's family quickly came under suspicion because of their "impure" urban background and because her mother, Sopha, was unable to perform basic manual tasks.

"My mother didn't know anything. She didn't know how to plant rice or even how to cook. My sister and I learned quickly by watching what the 'old people' did. But my mother had problems. At one point, the Khmer Rouge took her and my auntie out to the fields to watch them harvest rice. My mother had no idea how to do it. A group of people observed her, including Khan, some of his militia, and the village chief. They remarked to one another, 'So she really doesn't know how to work in the fields.' They watched us carefully after that, always checking on us."

A while later, Ming's brother got severe diarrhea. Ming's voice choked as she recalled, "He was so sick and then he died. We cried because we loved him so much. He was the baby, and we had only one boy in the family. After that, we were a family of women."

Despite these misfortunes, Ming's family did have a bit of luck. Long before, her grandfather had helped a peasant named Chum. When Chum had needed to earn money in Phnom Penh, Ming's grandfather had provided him with a pedicab and a place to stay. As fate would have it, Chum lived in the village and remembered the grandfather's good deeds. "We didn't know him," Ming said, "but he remembered us. He told us not to talk about our past lives. He said we should always be on our guard, never speak at night, and never say anything negative about the new society. We tried to follow his instructions."

Soon afterwards, an official from the subdistrict office came to research the family's background. The Khmer Rouge investigated everyone's life history, but were especially meticulous about investigating those with "impure" backgrounds. Sopha had revealed too much to them. Ming explained, "My mother is very honest. So she told them all sorts of things about our background: that we were educated and even knew French. We became very scared."

Ming and her sister were asked to attend a political-education school for children. "They told us that our parents were not our real parents, that Angkar would provide us with food. They told us to closely observe our parents and to report what they were doing. If they secretly stole food, we were supposed to tell the village chief, to tell Angkar. Like the skin of a pineapple, Angkar had many eyes. If you did something wrong, Angkar would know."

One day, their Khmer Rouge teacher, Han, took Ming and her sister aside and began questioning them. "He said to us, '*Parlez-vous français?*' We just acted stupid. I replied, 'Uh, I don't understand you. I don't know anything, not even the letters of the alphabet.' He asked, 'Why did your mother say that you know French?' We told him, 'Don't believe her. She just wanted to be proud of us.' So they tested us on basic reading skills. We could read everything, but we acted like we didn't know anything."

Ming made friends with Kasin, the daughter of the village chief and niece of a high-ranking cadre in the district office. "I was clever and saw the advantages of making friends with that girl. After we became friends, I could go visit her house and eat with her family. I didn't have to work that hard. We could go anywhere. A few times, we even went to Khan's prison and talked briefly with the prisoners. They worked continuously, until the day Angkar ordered their execution. The guards watched us from a distance, but allowed us to talk to the prisoners because we were just little kids and Kasin was related to powerful people."

This friendship probably saved Sopha's life. One day, an "old person" who disliked Ming's mother accused her of "economic sabotage," in this case disturbing some fishing nets. Around noon, several of Khan's men arrested Sopha. "I cried and cried and cried because I knew that people who were taken away like that were killed. I cried so hard I was yelling; everyone in the village knew. I was sure that we were going to lose our mother. Then we would completely be without parents." As Ming recounted this traumatic experience, she began to break down. Tears ran down her cheeks. She whispered a few words at a time. "Years later, my mother told us that Khan's men had tormented her. They had led her away into the jungle and showed her the ditch into which her dead body was to be dumped. They pointed to the tools that they were going to kill her with and asked her to say the name of each one." Ming paused. "But they let her go. They let her go. She returned home close to midnight. It was a miracle."

Ming sobbed. "We were so happy. I don't know why they let her go. Maybe Kasin knew about her and talked to her father. I cried and cried. I was so young and had almost lost my mother."

Ming had one more story to recount. In 1977, at the age of ten, she was allowed to join her sister's mobile work brigade. One morning, the group was sent to harvest rice near an old pagoda across the road from Khan's prison. "I heard the nearby screams of a person crying out, 'Ooooiii! Ooooiii!' So I asked one of my friends to come with me to see what was going on. I wanted to find out. Maybe that's why I'm a newspaper reporter now."

Ming and her friend crept up the steps of the pagoda. Most of the windows were blocked by wooden shutters. One, however, was slightly open. What they saw through it was terrifying. Several of Khan's men stood near a blindfolded prisoner strung up by the feet so that his head was a foot above the ground. "One of the Khmer Rouge took a knife and sliced open the prisoner's stomach. As his blood sprayed out, he screamed. There was blood everywhere. The man was still alive. His body was shaking. His brain was still working. Then the killer reached in and took something out of his body. It was so horrible. I was trembling all over, terrified…At that point, a couple of guards saw us from a distance, and we ran away. They couldn't find us because we mixed in with the other children. Sometimes I still dream about this horrible thing that happened in front of my eyes…So I know that Khan, he's very bad."

"Why did they reach into the prisoner's stomach?" I asked.

"Because they wanted to take out his liver or gallbladder. During that time, the Khmer Rouge ate human liver because they thought that it would make them strong. Or they used the gallbladder for medicine." In Cambodia, the liver is thought of as the seat of courage. It is also said that eating it makes the eyes turn red. Ming added, "Everyone said that Khan ate human liver because his eyes were always red, always very red."

As Ming finished this gruesome tale, she pulled to the side of the road to pick up Mum. Caught up in the force of Ming's story, I had almost forgotten we were going to interview one of the most notorious of the Khmer Rouge murderers.

Mum had short hair with bangs, and her mouth turned down slightly. She wore an orange and red shirt, as if to try to brighten her mood.

She directed us onto a fairly wide dirt road. A mountain was in the distance, and rice fields passed us on each side of the road. My initial nervousness returned. What if Khan kidnapped us? When I had arrived to do my doctoral fieldwork in 1994, three Western backpackers had just been kidnapped and taken to a Khmer Rouge stronghold in the mountains. Later, they were brutally killed.

"Do you think it's safe?" I asked Ming. "Are you scared?"

She paused and then said with a nervous smile, "Yes, a little scared." I could see that in the backseat Mum was smiling uneasily.

Ming pointed out the window. "There it is. That's the place." Looking to the left, I saw a large blue-and-gold Cambodian pagoda. Though framed by lush green trees, it was dilapidated and filled with broken stone. Two trees towered over the main hall of worship, which was surrounded by *naga*-serpent balustrades. Several of the *naga* heads were missing.

All over Cambodia, religious buildings like this one were turned into interrogation and execution centers. This was one of the ways the Khmer Rouge showed their hatred of religion, which they viewed as both a parasite and an opiate of the masses. If the Khmer Rouge didn't convert a pagoda into a prison, they might raze the building, destroy religious objects, or use the building as a storehouse.

Ming asked, "Do you want to go in?"

"Yes," I replied quickly, both out of curiosity and my desire to buy time to figure out a safe way to meet Khan. We turned onto a gravel road that took us into the temple's dirt courtyard, which had been overtaken by weeds and a few scraggly plants. Two monks sat in a shady alcove to escape the heat. Three children, probably orphans, were playing in the dirt about a hundred yards away from us. Except for them, the pagoda was deserted.

"This way." Ming set off quickly toward the pagoda's northern wall.

Mum and I followed her to a tall window with wooden shutters. "Here's where I saw them kill the man. I was little, so I had to stand on my toes to look through an opening in the window. It was horrible." Ming pointed to a nearby rice field just off the pagoda's southern wall and said, "I heard that over thirty mass graves were discovered over there."

Cambodian farmers have often led me through their fields, showing me depressions in the ground that mark the mass graves of Khmer Rouge victims. The farmers' plows still sometimes churn up grim reminders of the past: a single tooth, a tattered piece of cloth, a bone shard, a fragment of a skull. "Where else can we go?" the farmers ask me. "It's the only land we own."

Mum, who had been silent so far, exclaimed, "They killed my husband here. He was an intellectual." Although many of the Khmer Rouge leaders were themselves former teachers, intellectuals were generally distrusted and thought to have been corrupted by their contact with foreign ideas. It was much easier to transform the minds of the young and the poor, so the Khmer Rouge chose to simply kill off those whose "contaminated" minds might subvert the pure, new revolutionary society. Mum then described how the Khmer Rouge had gathered thirty-six former students and teachers from her village. "My husband had been a student before the Pol Pot period. All thirty-six of the men were tied up and led away. I followed them from a distance. None ever returned." She then began to list the relatives of hers who had died under the Democratic Kampuchea: "Phal, Neary, Duong, Chea…"

It took her a long time; only three people in her family had survived.

The Perpetrator

In silence, we walked back to the car. I was overwhelmed by Mum's tragedy, the horrible scene Ming had witnessed, and the prospect of meeting Khan, the man who was directly or indirectly involved in these events. I suggested we stop by the subdistrict office, located across the main road from the pagoda, to see if the area was secure.

A modest building with latticed windows, the subdistrict office had been constructed out of clean, bare wooden planks. Rough-hewn posts held up the roof. The current head of the subdistrict, Luong, was perhaps sixty and had close-cropped gray hair. He greeted us with a friendly smile and spoke to me in a mixture of Khmer, broken English, and French. When he heard that we were planning to see Khan, he frowned for a moment. He suggested that we send a moped taxi to see if Khan was at home and to ask if he would meet us at the subdistrict office. Ming's glance told me that she thought this was a much better and safer way to encounter Khan. We thanked Luong for his suggestion and sent the moped taxi off.

I sat down on a hard wooden bench in front of the office. It had become a hot, humid morning. I had no idea if Khan would appear. He might not be home or, if he was, might not come. Over the years, I have interviewed many perpetrators. Few admit committing the atrocities others accuse them of. Often, however, they are willing to talk in detail if asked why *other* perpetrators performed genocidal deeds. This indirect method of questioning allows them to save face and uncovers a great deal about the mind of killers. Some perpetrators downplay their involvement. Two days earlier, I had interviewed a notorious prison guard said to have executed hundreds of people. He denied this allegation but admitted he had killed "one or two." Clearly, this vague answer suggested he had killed many more.

Reflecting on Khan's serious and renowned crimes, I began to doubt he would come. Then gravel sputtered in the dirt as a moped pulled up to the office. "He's here," Luong said in a low voice. Ming shifted uneasily on the bench. We all turned to look.

The first thing I noticed were Khan's eyes, sunk into the crevice between high cheekbones and a low brow. He stared at us, which is considered rude and aggressive in Cambodia. His chin stuck out defiantly, and the skin between his eyebrows was deeply creased, giving him a fearsome look. He had likely put on his best clothing to meet us: a white shirt with only three buttons fastened at the top, a pair of black pants that didn't zip up, and a red-and-white checkered *krama* that gave his eyes a red tint.

Khan was once a poor peasant farmer, precisely the type of person the Khmer Rouge would appoint to positions of power because of his or her "pure" class background. He looked to be in his sixties and was unlike any other perpetrator I had ever met. When I stood to greet him, he responded but without any of the outward friendliness I usually encounter when meeting Cambodians, even perpetrators.

Luong offered us the use of a small "office" that contained dirty laundry, gasoline drums, dining utensils, and a desk. We sat on blue plastic chairs, Khan opposite Ming and me, perhaps three or four feet away. The only light came from an open door and the cracks between the wooden planks of the wall. Silhouetted against the light, Khan looked even more menacing.

I explained to Khan that I was a professor conducting research for a book on Democratic Kampuchea, then told him I was examining Cambodian culture and the psychology of the Khmer Rouge in particular. When I asked him if he was willing to be interviewed, he looked at me as if my question was silly and muttered, "Yes, yes."

When interviewing perpetrators, I always ask general questions first and then move toward my central concern, which is why people kill.

"Before you joined the Khmer Rouge, what did you do?"

"Farmer."

"When did you join the Khmer Rouge?"

"Nineteen seventy."

"In what capacity?"

"Soldier."

"What type of political education were you given at that time?"

"None."

Unlike Ming's story, which had begun with a cascade of words, Khan's began with monosyllables. I took a deep breath and wiped the sweat from my face.

After fifteen minutes of questioning, I managed to find out that he had served as a Khmer Rouge soldier from 1970 to 1973, fighting Lon Nol forces in Takeo Province. In 1973, he went to work at the subdistrict office. Eventually, he acknowledged that he had attended political-education meetings at which he heard about such concepts as class contradiction, building a proper revolutionary consciousness, and defeating the enemy. When I asked him if he had ever discussed Marxist-Leninist philosophy with anyone, he said no, then added that he was illiterate and didn't understand such things.

In this way, Khan indirectly touched upon a key problem of the Khmer Rouge. Impoverished peasants were often placed in positions of power, but because they lacked education and were sometimes illiterate, they had difficulty understanding Khmer Rouge ideology, much less explaining it to others. As a result, the Khmer Rouge's ideological messages were never internalized or even comprehended by the majority of Cambodians.

I began to move my line of questioning toward my goal: understanding why he had participated in the genocide.

"When did the prison open?"

"What prison?"

"The one that was located here, by the subdistrict office."

"There wasn't a prison here," he replied matter-of-factly. Ming's eyes widened.

Khan's words hung in the air. No one said anything for a long time. Uncertain of how to respond, I stared at Khan, who glared back, his face braced against the light leaking through the walls.

The enormity of what he was doing slowly began to sink in. Most perpetrators will claim that they had a lesser or different position, were just following orders, or had never actually killed anyone. But no perpetrator I had interviewed had ever tried to deny the very existence of a prison or execution center. Maybe this is why he had come to talk to me: to erase history.

Ming suddenly asked me in English, "Do you want me to tell him what I saw?"

"Only if that's what you want to do," I replied. She returned to her silence. This man linked to the suffering of so many people, including her mother, had just denied one of her most powerful memories.

I decided to question Khan from a different angle. Because I hadn't contradicted him, he seemed more at ease. His answers grew more lengthy, and he even acknowledged that he had been the head of the subdistrict militia.

When I asked him about the line of command, he offered the names of his superiors without hesitation. Grandfather Kee ran the subdistrict office while San, a relative of Ta Mok, was the district head.

When I returned to the topic of killing, however, he reverted to monosyllables.

"At the subdistrict level, how were people's backgrounds investigated?" I asked.

"In the normal manner," he replied vaguely.

Addressing Khan, Ming said, "Others have told us that people were killed in a savage manner in this area."

Immediately, he responded, speaking with a confident, self-satisfied air. "No. In this subdistrict, there wasn't any killing. They killed in neighboring subdistricts. In this subdistrict there was no killing. That is the truth. People just like to say such things."

Ming started, "But the people in the subdistrict said—"

Khan cut her off. "No, nobody was killed in this area."

Ming laughed in disbelief. In English she announced, "He's a liar."

She looked at the dirt floor, into the earth that had swallowed the bodies of Khan's victims. Maybe the sight of him had become unbearable. Without looking up, she addressed him in Khmer. "Many people have told me about the things you did."

Scowling at her, he repeated his denial. "No one was killed in this subdistrict. People say such things, but I didn't do anything. It's unjust. There isn't any evidence. Where is the prison? Where is the proof?"

At this point I broke in. "I'm a professor. I've read many books on the Pol Pot period, and I'm writing one myself. I've interviewed hundreds of people all over Cambodia, including individuals who, like yourself, were heads of the subdistrict militia. In all of these books and interviews, I never heard of a subdistrict where not a single person died. Never."

Now it was Khan's turn to pause. Our eyes locked together. Eventually he broke off his stare, perhaps uncertain of what I knew. "Not here, not here. There's no proof."

I continued, "In most subdistricts, including this one, people wrote to the government and described the horrors they witnessed, including the deaths of their family and friends."

Khan shifted in his chair. "No one was killed here. Not a single person. If we arrested people, they would later be set free. You can't believe what you hear. Nobody saw anything. If anyone was killed, it was people from the district security office who came and did it."

Ming cut in, saying, "I'm going to tell you the truth. During the Pol Pot period, I lived here also. I saw them kill a man in the pagoda—"

Khan leaned forward and gave her the full force of his scowl. His voice rising, he repeated, "No one was killed here, not even one person. There's no evidence."

"You're a liar," she said angrily.

Khan glared at her, a small bead of perspiration trickling down his forehead. Finally, he murmured, "The prison was just a holding center. None of the prisoners was killed there. The district people came and took them away. I don't know what they did with them." He said this in a matter-of-fact tone, as if trying to gloss over the fact that he had just radically altered his story.

Ming laughed and, in English, announced, "So, now he admits it."

When I asked Khan about conditions in the prison, his replies came more quickly. The area around the prison had been sealed off, he explained, and security officers from the district came to take the prisoners away. He again denied that people were executed at the prison and told us that, like everyone else, he feared for his life, particularly when people from the district security office appeared. At the end of the Pol Pot period, he said, an angry mob had chased him into the jungle, and he was later imprisoned for a year by the Vietnamese-backed government that had overthrown the Khmer Rouge regime.

When I asked why the mob had chased him, he replied, "I don't know why. They must have made a mistake."

A piece of paper slipped out of my notebook and floated to the ground beside Khan's chair. It was my list of questions and interview topics. Without hesitation, he picked up the sheet and extended it to me. When I reached out to receive it, our hands met. For an instant, I felt his skin, callused from years of labor, and the line between perpetrator and person blurred and he could have been almost any other Cambodian farmer.

"How would you respond if one of the prisoners whom you arrested and who died came back to life?" I asked.

For once, he didn't offer an immediate denial. He was perspiring a great deal now and seemed tired. "That would make me really happy. I would bow down and ask for forgiveness."

"You'd say you were sorry?"

"Yes," he replied. Was he finally acknowledging his brutal deeds? Or had he simply not understood that my question implied he was guilty?

We had been talking for well over an hour, and the interview was drawing to a close. But Ming was not ready to let Khan go. "Do you think there should be a trial?" she asked him. At the time of this meeting, the United Nations and the Cambodian government were in negotiations to bring a high-ranking Khmer Rouge cadre to trial. Many former Khmer Rouge were therefore worried about being indicted, though various officials had promised that only the top leaders would be tried.

Khan responded, "Sure, why not? I'm not afraid. Since I didn't do anything, I don't have anything to be afraid of. I just followed the orders of the leaders." Still, he looked uneasy. Maybe frightening him was Ming's way of getting back at him.

Angrily, she responded, "But you were a leader, the head of the subdistrict militia. You commanded people."

"I just followed orders."

"Everyone was afraid of you back then. I heard people say that if you stared at a person, even for a moment, that person would disappear the next day."

"No. They just say things like that about me, that I was savage. It's not true. I helped the people. If they were hungry, I would try to get food for them."

A man slipped into the room to retrieve some dishes. Khan looked at him, then back at us, indicating that it was time for him to return home.

I had saved one last set of questions for him. "How many people worked for you in the militia?" I asked.

"Forty or so."

"What were some of their names?"

"None of them is still alive," he said, spitting on the floor. He realized that I wanted to talk to other people and ask them about the prison.

"But what are their names?"

Khan named a few people who, he assured us, were dead. I pressed him. "Surely out of the forty, someone must still be alive?"

"They're either dead or moved away. I don't know where they went."

"All of them?" I asked.

Khan paused for a moment, then said, "There's one man, Samrong, who worked with me in the militia. He lives in my village."

Ming abruptly addressed Khan, "Who arrested Sopha Lim?"

"Sopha Lim." Khan repeated the name, seeming to recognize it. "She wasn't arrested."

Ming was clearly irritated. "That's my mother. My mother. She was led to a grave and told it was hers."

"No," Khan said, erasing the past with one word.

Ming raised her voice. "Stop lying to me."

"I'm not lying."

"I'm angry now because you're trying to tell me that my mother was never arrested. It's my mother you're talking about. I was there. I know."

"No," Khan repeated, adding, "it's time for me to eat. I'm supposed to meet some people."

The interview was over. We all stood up and walked outside. As we moved from darkness to light, our eyes had to adjust. Ming still looked annoyed, but gave Khan some cigarettes and two cans of soda as compensation for the work time he had lost. She then asked him if we could take his picture, and he agreed. Ming and I both photographed him. He gazed into our cameras, defiant.

We arranged for him to be driven back to his village by a moped taxi driver. The driver revved up his engine, and Khan climbed on the back. As the wheels churned up the earth where the bodies of his prisoners lay, he glanced back at us, scowling. The roar of the moped faded in the distance, becoming a hum, then silence.

The Victim

Ming and I walked back to a picnic table. It was well past noon; we were all hungry. She pulled out two large bags of peanuts, and as we talked, the piles of shells on the wooden table grew, marking the time.

I asked Luong, who had been head of the subdistrict since 1979, if Khan had ever been chased by a mob.

"The people were irate, incensed he had killed their relatives. I had just been appointed to office, and the government was promoting reconciliation, so I had to protect him. He lived here for almost two months. People kept coming around, asking if I would hand him over to them. They wanted to kill him in revenge."

"But Khan said that there wasn't a prison here," I said.

Luong laughed in disgust. "He's ignorant and a liar. He doesn't know how to read or write. He's never studied anything. That's why he didn't know any better. The Khmer Rouge just needed one person like that in each subdistrict. When I got here, there were bones everywhere. The place stank. Later, the government asked us to gather the bones and create a memorial to the victims."

"How many bones were there?"

"Hundreds, thousands, too many to count. Khan and his men killed hundreds of people, eating their livers and gallbladders. They were brutal, ruthless killers. And they did their work in secret."

"Are you scared of him?"

Luong laughed. "Not now, but I was terrified of him back then. He has the face of a killer."

Luong's assistant suggested that a man named Uncle Phan would know more about what had happened at the prison. In 1975, he was jailed for almost a year because of a moral offense with a woman. He was now a religious layman at a pagoda not too far from where we were. We sent another moped taxi off to the pagoda to see if he too would talk with us.

The sky, full of clouds, continued to darken. A light wind had kicked up. It was midafternoon during the season when monsoon rains often prepare to unleash huge raindrops that quickly turn the dirt into mud. In that area, rain waters the graves of the dead.

Everyone looked tired. Luong shook his head and said, "I doubt Phan will come. He's a religious layman now and won't talk about politics."

As I was staring at the ground, contemplating the terror Khan's victims must have felt as they were led to their graves, Phan arrived. Dressed more formally than Khan, he wore a clean, collarless white shirt and a pair of long, black pants, a blue *krama* thrown over his shoulder as a sash. His face was weathered and marked by lines from days spent in sun, rain, soil, and, perhaps, Khan's prison.

"Hello. I hope you are well," he said, smiling as he raised his hands to greet us.

After briefly explaining why I wanted to speak with him, I invited him to join me in the back room. Gesturing toward the open area, he demurred. "That's OK. I like it here, outside." I wondered if he was thinking of the months he had spent shackled inside the jail.

We sat down at the picnic table, littered with peanut shells, water bottles, soda cans, and empty wrappers. Ming and I sat opposite Phan while Luong and Mum settled into nearby chairs. Everyone treated Phan with respect. He seemed at ease, replying without hesitation. His words had a slow, measured pace, though at times he paused in contemplation or accelerated slightly for emphasis.

Before the Khmer Rouge had taken control of the area, he had been a farmer of modest means. After they had taken over, he was designated an "old person," which had probably saved his life.

"When did they arrest you?" I asked.

"In 1975. They accused me of violating their moral code, of fooling around with my sister-in-law. I used to joke and laugh with her, but that's it. Maybe jealousy was involved. Anyway, they came and arrested me. What could I do? At that time, we didn't have the right to make denials. We had to do what they said one hundred percent of the time. They put me in their prison for nine months and seven days. Then I was allowed to return to my family."

While most of the people the Khmer Rouge put in prison were accused of being class enemies or traitors, some were imprisoned for minor crimes. These prisoners were still in danger, of course, because even a minor offense could be interpreted as a traitorous act.

"Who arrested you?"

"Troung and his right-hand man, Khan. Troung was the head of the prison, and Khan was his deputy. A couple of their men came one day and asked me to help move gasoline drums at the subdistrict office. They didn't tie me up. They just brought me to the prison and then arrested me. But they didn't beat me. Still, I was terrified. I didn't know what they were going to do to me."

"What was it like in the prison?"

"Terrifying. Of all the people who were imprisoned there during those nine months and seven days, I was the only one who survived. They took people off to 'study,' but none of them ever returned. I don't know why I wasn't taken away. Maybe it was because I was older and had been accused of a more minor offense." He paused, contemplating the question more deeply, then repeated, "I don't know why."

"What was life like in the prison?"

"It was really hard. There might be fifteen or twenty of us imprisoned at once. One time, they brought in a group of teenage boys who had gotten into a fight over food. Everyone disappeared but me." He hesitated again, then continued. "The guards were brutal, really mean. They beat and kicked us if we did the slightest thing wrong. Our legs were shackled, so we couldn't escape. It was our fate. There was nowhere else we could go. And we had to call them 'Mr. Grandfather.' 'Mr. Grandfather Troung,' 'Mr. Grandfather Khan.' We even had to call the young kids who were guarding us 'Mr. Grandfather.' They guarded us closely the entire time. During the day, we were forced to perform hard labor from six in the morning until eight or nine at night. Then it was back to the shackles and hunger. We only received a little food, which we had to eat while shackled. We were like animals: barely fed, beaten on a whim, living in terror."

"How long were prisoners kept there?"

"It varied; there was no set period. Some were taken to 'study' after a month or two. Sixty or seventy people must have passed through while I was there. They'd come and then be taken away—in and out, in and out. When a prisoner heard that he was going to 'study,' his face became tight and drawn. He knew he was going to be killed. 'Study' meant death. We all knew this. But what could we do? I was lucky. I was the only one who survived. The others were all taken away and killed."

"Were they taken to the main hall of the pagoda?"

"There was another prison for the really important prisoners. I don't know what happened there. But I heard that the prisoners were killed in two places: by the temple and a little further away, in the jungle. We all knew about this, but what could we do? Nothing. We were helpless."

Ming cut in. "What about Khan and Troung: what were they like?"

"From what I saw, they were not the same. Troung had more power, but Khan was meaner." Phan pondered the question. "Khan didn't let people know what he was doing. It was always done in secret. He'd give orders to others. You know, he's illiterate but still has awesome power. People say that if you shoot him, the bullet won't enter his body. He can also break a tree with his hands. If he punches something when he's angry, it will completely shatter. Back then, people became terrified when they heard his name, even little children. Everyone was scared of him: 'old people,' 'new people,' little kids. He had incredible power. No one dared to look at his face."

"Do you think people like Khan killed?" I asked.

"It's hard to know. The Khmer Rouge took the ignorant and gave them enormous power. Before, they had nothing, so many must have been willing to kill for face and rank. Others may have had a class grudge. It's difficult to say. What I do know is that for those three years, eight months, and twenty days, we all suffered beyond belief. Now I just want to forget about it all. That's why I became a religious layperson: to live with the monks."

These words signaled that Phan was finished with the interview. Placing his hands at the end of the table as if to rise, he leaned forward and said softly, "In Buddhism, we believe that if you do something good, you'll receive something good. But those who do something bad will suffer from the consequences of this action."

I imagined these words blowing down the road toward Khan.

It was time for us to go too. Late afternoon had turned into early evening. After seeing Phan off, Ming and I thanked Luong for his help and hospitality. He gave us a broad smile and urged us to visit again. "I guess there really was a prison," he said, laughing, as we got into the car. Then, looking up at a sky dark with the promise of a thunderstorm, he added, "Be careful."

As Ming pulled the car out onto the dirt road, I looked back at the subdistrict office and the temple, trying to imprint them on my mind. Two prisons, mass graves, and a series of people who had stood in the dirt so long ago. Luong held his hand up in parting and grew smaller, fainter. The last thing I saw was the way the tops of the two trees bowed over the main temple hall, as if pushed down by the weight of memory.

Prek Tuol Floating Village,
Tonle Sap Lake, 2002
Photograph by Richard Murai

Caged Bird Will Fly

People say that rivers flow only in one direction, but in Cambodia, whether the Mekong flows into the Great Lake of the Tonle Sap or to the ocean depends on the season. During the rainy season, the water flows into the Tonle Sap, filling the lake as it rises and expands across the plain; during the dry season, the water reverses direction, draining the lake back into the sea.

Kunty stood alone in her family's small house, which had been built along a tributary of the Tonle Sap. She did not want to leave, not yet, so she packed her bag slowly as she gazed through the window at the river a few feet away. In the water, close to the bank, was the wooden pole that her father used to tie up his boat. It had been there for as long as she could remember. Her father was a fisherman and had taught her to read the seasons by watching the water rise and fall in relation to that pole. She had once spent an entire day braiding strips of cloth from an old shirt into a long thin rope her father tied to the pole to mark the water's level. Kunty knew that when the water rose above the rope, her father would soon return.

Today, she would be gone by the time he came home. It was easier to leave this way, while her father was away fishing and her mother was at the market. As Kunty packed the last of her belongings into her only bag, she wondered what would become of the pole when she was no longer around to keep it painted and retie the rope. Would her father get lost when he returned from one of his long fishing trips? Kunty had worked with her father to make the pole more visible to him in the heavy rains. Together they had painted it in two colors: green and blue. Through the years, while parts of the house were removed or added, the wooden pole had remained intact. It was the only thing about their house that had never changed.

She looked around the house one last time, zipped the bag, and placed it near the door. Still unwilling to leave, she went outside to sit on a plank that jutted out over the water. As a child, she used to sit there and watch the river flow past. "Be careful, daughter, you might fall off," her father would say when he saw her dangling her feet above the current. Kunty would smile at his concern.

"Father," she would say, "Kunty could swim to the pole and hold on to it until you came and saved her. Father, you would rescue Kunty, wouldn't you?"

She wished her father could rescue her now, but she knew that she would have to face her fate alone. How she wished she could turn back time to when she was a girl playing in the rain. She wanted to run along the levees in the rice fields when the rice was just ready for transplanting, still green and fragile. She wanted to climb a *sdaov* tree and pick the young leaves and flowers for her mother to cook, and gather lotus blossoms to sell to tourists who traveled the road to Siem Reap. She wanted to collect snails and shrimps from the river and cook them for her father to eat. More than anything else, she wanted to watch her own children doing such things as they grew up beside the river.

Kunty thought back to the first time she had left her home. If she had known that her decisions would lead her to this moment, she would have rejected the marriage proposal. She remembered clearly the day a man had passed her house in a boat, watching her from a distance. She had been sitting on the edge of this same plank, dipping a bucket into the water, and hadn't thought anything of it. But that night, she dreamed that her body was a white feather floating on the wind. When she woke up, she felt lightheaded, dizzy, and weightless. She had tried to tell her father about the dream, but he hadn't had time. And then the matchmaker had come. Her father couldn't refuse the offer of money and gifts.

She had been married less than a year when her daughter was born; the second year, she had a son. Her family's house on the river became too crowded, so she, her husband, and her children moved to her husband's village and into the house of her in-laws. That was the first time she had ever left home.

Soon after their move, her husband quit fishing and started working in the central part of the province as a motorcycle taxi driver, in order to make more money. The job took him away for weeks and sometimes for months at a time. One day, he came home sooner than expected. His face was drained of life. His eyes used to be alert and bright as stars; now they were like the dull eyes of the dead fish her father had brought home from his trips to the lake. Her husband was sick with severe diarrhea all night and into the next morning.

Kunty begged her husband to see a doctor in the village. When he returned home that afternoon, he sat in the front yard in silence. His mouth drooped at the edges and his lips sagged open. He didn't say a word to her. "Dear," Kunty finally said, "what did the doctor say?"

"It's nothing," he said. "We will be OK. Please take good care of the children when I am gone."

"Why are you talking that way? What's the matter?" She was on the verge of tears and could hardly breathe. She felt as if someone had driven a stake into her chest. "What did the doctor say?"

"Nothing," he repeated, barely loud enough for her to hear. "I'll try to go back to work soon." Then he got up and left her standing in the front yard alone.

After that day, he hardly spoke to her or anyone.

A week later, in the darkness before dawn, he drove away from the village. He did not return for a year. When he reappeared, he was wearing only a dirty pair of torn pants. Large blisters covered his left arm. He was so thin that it seemed the only thing left of his body was the skin attached to his bones. His emaciated form reminded her of a picture of a skeletal Buddha in the state of nirvana; she had seen it on an AIDS poster outside of a restaurant. At the time, she had thought the disease was caused by starvation.

Her husband was at home for six months. One night, he cried until no more sound escaped his lips. Kunty thought he had finally fallen asleep. But the next morning, he was dead.

In their grief, the parents of Kunty's husband blamed her for their son's sickness and his death. They threw her out of their house but kept her children and forbade her to see them. Kunty had no choice but to move back to her childhood home.

"The city killed him," the people in Kunty's village said. That's what her parents said too. But something had changed in the way people looked at her.

One afternoon, a stranger from the city came to her family's home, claiming that her husband owed him money. When he learned her husband was dead, the man turned on Kunty. "I have no money," Kunty pleaded. She explained that all her husband's money, along with her own meager savings, had been used to pay for his medical treatments and his funeral. "Please." Then, in front of her father and mother, the man said, "He had AIDS. You should get yourself tested to know for sure whether or not you were infected by him." She watched her mother's expression change from shock to anger. Kunty's father looked like all the blood had drained from his face. He began blinking his eyes rapidly, as if he were trying to hold back tears. He turned away and covered his face with the cotton *krama* he wore around his neck.

The man stormed out of the house to the dirt road and began yelling so that all the neighbors could hear, "She has AIDS!" He whirled around and pointed to her parents' house. "The woman who lives in this house has AIDS!"

At that moment, Kunty knew that, for the sake of her parents, especially her father, she would have to leave. Her mother had rushed outside to drive the man away. But her father held everything inside. The truth was that, if she hadn't loved her father so much, she wouldn't have cared what the neighbors thought; like her mother, she would have defied them. Kunty had always been rebellious. But she had grown up wanting to be like her father. She preferred going fishing with him to staying home with her mother. Before she married, she had thought only of fishing with her father in the Tonle Sap, watching the river overflow its banks while they glided over the flooded rice fields.

As Kunty silently said goodbye to the river, tears welled up in her eyes. Her sadness came not only from leaving the home she grew up in, but also from her fear that she would never see her children again, not in this lifetime, or in this physical form.

She turned and walked back inside. "Someday," she whispered to the empty room. "Someday when I can fly, I will come back."

She picked up her bag and closed the door behind her.

Kunty followed the dirt road in front of her house until she had reached National Highway Number 6, which connected Siem Reap to Phnom Penh. As a little girl she had watched travelers on motorcycles pass by on this road, raising clouds of red dust. It had never occurred to her that one day she would be one of those travelers. She watched several motorcycle taxis pass, then flagged one down.

"How much to the city?" she asked.

"Where are you going?"

"I have an aunt who lives on Penh Chet Boulevard." The driver smiled when he heard the name of the street. It wasn't really her aunt that Kunty was going to see, but rather a woman she had once met in the village, who had promised her work if she ever wanted to live in the city. Even then Kunty had suspected what kind of work it was. Work in the city for a woman like her, with no skills, connections, or education, could only mean one thing.

"Five thousand *riels*," the motorcycle driver said.

Kunty didn't flinch. She tried to keep her face smooth. "I'm afraid I only have twenty-five hundred *riels*," she countered, staring him straight in the eyes.

"Don't waste my time," the driver said. "You need a ride to the city and you only have twenty-five hundred *riels*?"

"Please," Kunty said. "I have more, but if I give you five thousand then I won't have anything when I get to the city. And suppose I can't find my aunt?" In fact, Kunty was telling the truth. Her parents had given her nearly all their savings and had borrowed money from their neighbors.

"All right," the driver said, his eyes narrowing. "Four thousand *riels*. And maybe your 'aunt' will pitch in the rest when we get to the city."

Kunty felt a sense of dread as she got on the backseat of his motorcycle.

She watched the passing rice fields and sugar palms for the last time. The wind stung her face, and she closed her eyes against the dust, holding the end of the *krama* over her mouth. She thought of her children as each kilometer took her further away from them. Would her in-laws comfort her son when the thunder frightened him? Would they remember to sing her daughter her favorite lullaby? Would her children even remember her?

She didn't speak to the driver until they reached the outskirts of the city. "Why are we turning here?" she asked. Even though she had never been to Phnom Penh, Kunty had heard Penh Chet Boulevard described by the villagers. The huts they passed along the dirt road seemed to fit the description, but nothing else did. It was still daylight. She saw several girls in front of a small hut eating with chopsticks instead of spoons, the way that Cambodians do. A man in an olive-green uniform sat beside them. The girls had light skin and wore their hair short. She assumed they came from Viet Nam. The motorcycle slowed as they passed over some railroad tracks. A sign read POLICE STATION. Nearby was another sign that read WOMEN'S ROOM. She wondered what the sign meant.

When they reached the end of the dirt road, the man parked the motorcycle on the corner next to a small hut, opposite an auto-repair shop.

Kunty quickly jumped off the backseat. "Don't go anywhere," the man warned. Then he laughed in a way that made Kunty anxious. "Don't worry," he said. "I'm just going to see my auntie who lives here."

"Don't be long. I need to get to Penh Chet Boulevard before nightfall," she called out after him, but he had already entered the hut. Bright purple curtains covered the two windows. Above the narrow door hung a sign: WE'RE WAITING. The driver returned shortly with an older woman who wore a bright floral sarong and a red T-shirt. Beneath her thin shirt, her breasts dangled loosely, nipples pointed in opposite directions. She wore red lipstick and a pair of red platform shoes that made her bounce up and down as she walked.

"Let me see her face," the woman said without a trace of politeness. "She'll do, but I can't pay much for that. She's too short and too skinny. She looks like she's had kids." The woman walked around Kunty, staring her up and down as if assessing livestock. "Eighty dollars," she said. "That's it."

"One hundred," the driver countered.

"All right. Ninety," said the woman. "Come with me." As the driver followed the woman inside the hut, Kunty heard her say, "She's not going to run."

Kunty just wanted to get out of there and to Penh Chet Boulevard before dark. She had to find the woman she'd met in her village who had promised her a job.

When they returned, the woman yanked Kunty's hair and dragged her into the front guest room. She pushed her into a chair opposite a dirty love seat and ordered her to sit. Kunty was so stunned she didn't have time to react when she saw the man drive away down the dirt road and disappear from sight.

"Rule number one: bargain with the men."

As she spoke, the woman paced back and forth, stopping once in a while to stare at Kunty like a mother scolding a child for doing something wrong.

"Rule number two: you take the money from them before letting them in. Do you understand?"

Kunty was staring out the front door.

"Don't think about it," the woman said. "You owe me ninety dollars. And until you work it off, you belong to this hut."

"How do I owe you money, ma'am?" Kunty asked.

"Don't be stupid," said the woman. "From now on, you will address me as 'Mother.' Understand?"

"Yes, Mother," Kunty said. "What have I done, Mother?" She asked the question again as she set her bag down on the dirty wooden floor. She stared through the holes and cracks to the ground below. She saw used condoms and a small empty box that read NUMBER ONE. She wondered what kind of men came to this little hut. The idea of having to serve them had not yet sunk in. She had the sensation that she was still on her way to somewhere else. She could not believe that her journey had ended there.

Where am I? she thought to herself as she got up and followed Mother to the back of the hut. Although it looked small from the front, the hut was long and narrow inside. As Kunty stepped from the guest room into the corridor, she saw three small rooms on each side with purple curtains instead of doors. The rooms were lit up with bright red lights and each had a small bed, barely large enough to fit one person. At the end of the corridor was a kitchen with a two-burner stove placed on top of a small table by the window. Behind the kitchen were six other small rooms—the girls' living quarters—each decorated in a different color.

Mother pointed to the last of the small bedrooms. "This is your room: room number six." Mother explained this was her sleeping room, while the front room was for men who came for a short service: payment was rendered, no name asked, and there was no need for politeness. If they paid more, they could spend the night with her in the sleeping room.

As she stepped out the door, Mother turned to add, "Listen, rule number three: don't try to run because you will not like the consequences."

"Yes, Mother," Kunty said.

"You're an easy girl," Mother said. "Just follow Mother's rules and you'll be fine."

"I thought we agreed on five thousand *riels*," Kunty said to the man after he had finished.

"You did, but I didn't," he said. "You're dark and not even pretty." He threw two thousand five hundred *riels* on the table and walked out.

It wasn't just the pain that made her first day difficult. She hadn't yet been able to adjust her mind to accept her new vocation. As she was trying to figure out how to tell Mother about the fee, a hand smacked her hard across the face. She grabbed the metal stool at the bed's edge to keep from falling.

"What did I say?" Mother asked when Kunty looked up to see who had slapped her.

"Take the money before I let him in?" Kunty whispered. She sat on the bed and looked down at the floor. Her face stung and she wondered if it would bruise.

"Why didn't you follow my rule?"

"I'm sorry, Mother," Kunty said. "I thought he was—" She stopped; there was no use in trying to explain.

"Since it's your first time, I'll spare you the pain." Mother looked straight at Kunty. At the door, she turned to add, "Oh, by the way, you owe me an extra two thousand five hundred *riels*. It will be added to your tab."

After a month of working, Kunty was used to the routine at the hut. Monday nights, only a few regulars came in, and so the six young women in the hut could talk to one another. They would close the door that separated the working rooms up front from the sleeping rooms in the back.

"So, Room Number Three," Kunty asked, trying to join the conversation, "how did you manage to steal the ten thousand *riels* from the man?" They called each other by their room numbers, instead of older sister or younger sister as they might have if they had been family. Kunty had told her real name to Room Number Three, but she only used it when the two of them were alone. None of them talked about their lives before they had come here, and none ever spoke of children or parents.

"Well, Room Number Six," Room Number Three said, bursting out laughing, so that Kunty could see the dimple on her left cheek. "Oh honey, boom, boom!"

"That easy, huh?" Room Number Two teased.

"Really," said Room Number Five. "How? Honestly, we're desperate here for a little extra cash."

"Well, you talk to them," Room Number Three explained. "But not too much, just enough to get their attention away from their wallets and then you take just a little."

"Why not all?" Kunty asked.

"If you steal just a little, they won't notice that the money is missing. Try it sometime."

Kunty was grateful for the way Room Number Three answered her questions without making fun of her inexperience. And she liked these moments in the back room, where the girls would gather away from Mother and the guard whenever they had the opportunity.

"You know," Room Number Three said, "I have a lover."

"Yeah?" said Room Number Two. "How much did he give you when you let him in?" They all laughed.

"Enough to buy new red lipstick," Room Number Three said when the giggling subsided. "He said he would come back to see me next week if he could send his wife away to the province."

"Are you sure you want to get involved with a married man?" Kunty asked shyly.

"They're all married!" said Room Number Two, bursting into laughter.

"Well," Room Number Three continued, "he gave me more money than he was supposed to. Maybe I can save that money to pay my debts to Mother, if I can keep him long enough."

One night, several months after Kunty had arrived, she started feeling sick. Constant pain and diarrhea were normal for her, but this was different. She hardly spoke to the other room numbers that night because of the headache: it felt like someone was hitting the back of her skull with a hammer over and over. The pain was so intense she vomited.

On the third day, she called out from her front room, "Room Number Three!" No one responded. "Room Number Three!" She tried again, yelling louder this time, "Help me, please!"

Exhausted, Kunty stopped calling out and gave in to the pain in her head. She passed out. As in the dream she had long ago, before the matchmaker had come, she imagined herself being lifted up and being carried away. "Oh Father!" she cried out. "Kunty misses you so much!"

She thought she heard a faraway voice faintly calling her, but she didn't want to leave the dream of her father. She wanted only to drift in the sensation of her body carried away by him. But the voice grew louder. "Please, Father," she pleaded. "Take me away now. It's too loud and I can't stand it anymore. Father, please."

"Kunty!"

Painfully, she opened her eyes and saw faces staring down at her. She recognized Room Number Three. Sitting next to her was a lady in a long white uniform.

"Are you OK?" Room Number Three asked.

"What happened?" Kunty murmured.

"You fell and lost consciousness, so we carried you here. This is Sister Cecelia."

"Where am I?" Kunty asked weakly. She tried to raise herself, but Room Number Three gently pushed her back down.

"This is the Women's Room," Sister Cecelia said. She looked almost Cambodian—short with dark skin—but she spoke with an accent. "This place is for women who work along this dirt road, to come and talk about whatever problems they have." It wasn't really a room, just a thatched roof with no walls and a wooden floor.

"What's wrong with my head?" Kunty tried to smile at Sister Cecelia as she reached out with her hand to touch the nun. "Please, tell me."

Sister Cecelia held Kunty's hand and returned her smile. "You might have a secondary infection, a type of meningitis." Kunty looked confused. "You might have fungus in your brain. It causes serious pain. The pain will come and go."

"How do I get rid of it?"

"It's not easy. You will have to move to another place where we can help you recover."

"Where, Sister? I have no money and I still owe Mother ninety dollars and two thousand five hundred *riels*."

"You need no money there," Sister Cecelia said. She explained that she had come to Cambodia from the Philippines to work with the Charity, a religious organization that provided help for AIDS patients. "I just need to know if you have any family."

"They are dead to me now," Kunty said. "Maybe someday I will ask for something from them, but not now." She thought of asking Sister Cecelia to arrange for her to see her children.

"We can admit you only if you show that you have no one to support you or care for you."

"Look at me, Sister. Do you suppose if I had anyone to care for me that I would be working here?" She pointed down the dirt road. "I lived an honest life until last year. I don't ask for your forgiveness because of my work. And I don't ask for your sympathy."

"Please forgive me," Sister Cecelia said. "When you're ready to talk, I would like to listen."

It felt strange to Kunty to be taken to the Charity. Sitting in a car for the first time in her life, Kunty wanted to vomit. Sister Cecelia sat next to her, explaining something about the Charity, but Kunty felt too sick to pay attention to what she was saying.

When they arrived, the first thing Kunty noticed as she stepped from the car were pink lotus blossoms in two ponds. She watched the petals bend in the wind as she followed Sister Cecelia down a dirt path that led between the ponds and to the high fence surrounding the Charity. The fence was so tall that only the roof of a building was visible from the road.

Sister Cecelia led her past several buildings and down a pathway lined with shrubs and flowers. The white wild daisy reminded her of the life she had led before she had married. She wanted to be that daisy so that she could dance on the wind and grow wild and be left alone. But instead she felt heavy and surrounded by her past.

The Charity's dormitory was the cleanest building Kunty had ever seen. It was sterile and new, and the garden in front was unusually healthy, even greener than the other gardens she had passed. Sister Cecelia took Kunty to a room with a dozen beds in it. Everything was white: ceiling, beds, windows, walls, even the small table placed in the far corner. The only other colors in the room were the yellows, greens, and oranges in a basket filled with jackfruit, mangos, papayas, and a few sweet potatoes.

Sister Cecelia handed Kunty a bag of clothes, towels, and a plastic box with small compartments for medicine. She explained that the ward was divided into two sections, one side for men and one for women, separated by the nurse's room. Each side had a row of toilets and showers. During the day, men and women could socialize in each other's rooms, but after dark they had to return to their own rooms. "Please, don't worry about anything. When your mind is happy, your body is healthy. Rest now."

That afternoon, Sister Cecelia introduced Kunty to the others in the ward. They were sitting in chairs in a circle. The one Kunty later remembered best was a woman in her early twenties. Her arms and legs were unbelievably thin, and her eyes were deeply sunken. She had crooked teeth and long pointy nails that she had painted bright red. She wore a pair of loose floral pants with a tight purple top. She whispered to Kunty that she had been out dancing all night and had not yet changed out of her party clothes. Kunty wondered how the woman had snuck out of the ward. In a way, Kunty admired her for living her life as if she wasn't sick. Someday, she would ask the woman how she could do it, how she could have the energy to sneak out on a date with a man, how she could go on living as if she were not sick at all.

A week later, Kunty was awakened before dawn by someone crying. It was faint but so distinct she recognized it right away. It was like the sound of a child who had wept all day long, so the only sound that came from her throat was a suffocating hiss. It was the sound of her husband's crying just before he had died.

Kunty could not lie in the dark and listen, so she bathed, dressed, and walked outside. In the early morning light, the air was still cool. The yard was lined with papaya trees planted in three rows. In the front row, most of the plants were barely knee high and the soil around them had been disturbed from recent tending. The second row was taller, with trees just starting to bear fruit. The back row had the oldest plants; some were so old they were dying. She stared at the tallest tree in the back row. More lush than the others, it was the healthiest of all the papaya plants in the yard.

"You like that one, huh?"

She turned to see a man whose face seemed too large for his shrunken body. "I planted that one myself." He smiled at her, and she gave a small smile back.

"Who planted the others?"

"Different people who lived here…" He stared at the rice field beyond the wall, barely visible from where they were standing. "Well, this first row was planted by people who still live in this ward, except for one who left to go home yesterday." As he began to walk in between the trees, Kunty followed him. "Some of those who planted the second row are still here as well, but others have gone away. This back row was planted by the people who went to live in another world. Well, most of them." He stopped at the tallest plant, the one she had admired. "This one is mine. You know why it's the healthiest plant here? Because I'm still here to take care of it." He exhaled and looked down at his own fingers.

The nun was walking toward them from the back door. "I see you met Chivit."

"Yes," Kunty said. "He was just telling me about the papaya trees."

"Chivit has been here a long time."

"He has a pretty name. Do you know what it means?" she asked teasingly because she knew the nun was still learning the Khmer language. Sister Cecelia shook her head. Kunty was surprised that Sister Cecelia, who knew so many medical terms, didn't know the meaning of this word. "Life," Kunty told her.

Kunty lived at the Charity for three months. The patients came and went, and she kept to herself. The woman who used to sneak out of the ward at night had died. Chivit was still alive, and he had helped her plant a papaya tree in the front row. The morning after planting it, she found Sister Cecelia in the garden.

"You said that when I am ready—" Kunty began. She felt nervous and didn't know whether it was the right time to bring this up. "I remember you said at the Women's Room that when I was ready to talk, you would listen."

"Yes, I remember," Sister Cecelia said. "Do you want to talk about your family?"

"No. Not about my family. It's about me." She sat down beside Sister Cecelia on the bench but didn't look at her. "First, I want you to promise me that if you ever meet my two children, you will tell them that I am sorry I was not a good mother to them."

"I promise," Sister Cecelia said.

Kunty paused. Her eyes studied the daisies near her feet as they swayed in the wind. They were the same kind she'd noticed the first day she had walked along this pathway.

"There was a short period in my life when I did things that I now wish I hadn't done," Kunty finally said. "It was during the time when my husband left me, before he came back sick." Kunty spoke slowly, staring at the ground with her hands folded. "I thought I would never see him again. I had no way to support my children. After several months, I secretly remarried. I told my parents-in-law the man was my cousin, and he moved into the house, in his own room. They didn't say anything because he helped support us all. But after a while, he started staying away on weekends, and then he left, like my first husband. I thought he was cheating on me. Actually, he was already married to someone else." Kunty turned her face away from Sister Cecelia so that she would not see that she was crying. "I have kept this secret even from my parents."

Kunty was silent for a long time. She folded and unfolded her hands in her lap. Sister Cecelia remained quiet next to her. "I didn't think my first husband would ever come back. But eventually he did come back and he was very sick."

Kunty couldn't say what she had wanted to ask next. She wanted to ask the nun if she could have caught this disease from her second husband rather than from her first—if it was her adultery that had caused her illness. All this time, she had wondered if it had been her fault.

"I've made a mistake," Kunty finally said. "I thought I wanted to talk, but it doesn't matter now. You see, I have already lost everything that is important to me." Kunty rose from the bench and looked straight at Sister Cecelia. "I just wanted to let you know that I love my children. All my life I tried to do my best to provide for them."

Kunty didn't want to eat anymore. The food had no taste to her, and she wondered why the Charity had hired such a terrible cook. But the food was not the only problem. She could no longer control the functions of her body. She seldom got out of bed.

One morning, she woke up from an unusually good night's sleep and felt slightly better. She decided to take a walk in the garden. She saw a peacock feather floating just above the lawn. On the feather's tip was a black spot surrounded by three colors: red, green, and blue. The colors reminded her of the pole back home that her father tied his boat to. She stared at the spot until she felt she could see beyond its shape, until it became an eye staring back at her. She picked the feather up off the grass and went back into the building.

She walked to her bed and pulled a blue shirt and a pair of green pants out of her bag. She put them on, then climbed into bed and under the white sheets. She had no energy left. The only sound she could hear was that of her own breathing. She closed her eyes.

"We need serum," she heard someone say. The voice seemed very distant. "Please hurry. We don't have time."

The harder Kunty tried to listen, the fainter the voice became. Behind her closed eyes, she saw the peacock feather floating just above her head. It flew near her face, then moved away. Each time she was able to fix her eyes on it, the feather suddenly moved a little farther away. She felt light and dizzy.

"Come here," she said, amazed by the power of her own voice, how strongly it resonated in her ears. She couldn't remember the last time she had heard herself speak with such force. She opened her mouth again, took a deep breath, and yelled, "Come here!" Her voice echoed off the white walls. She could feel the peacock feather brush against her nose and move away again.

"What are you trying to tell me?" The feather flew close to her cheek for a brief second and then flew off again. "Oh, now I see," she said. At first she didn't think that the air would support her, not even as weightless as she felt. But the feather lifted her up from below and took off with great speed. "I can fly!" she yelled as she willed the feather to turn left, turn right, then up and down, and around in circles. In a corner of her vision, she saw a dark bird swoop past her, and she felt even lighter than before.

"Mother," Kunty's father said, "come and look at this hawk."

"It arrived early this morning," Kunty's mother replied. "It hasn't left the pole. We have had no death in the family. I don't understand why it has to stop here."

"Maybe it needs water," he said, but he knew that the black hawk could only signify a returned spirit. When someone dies, such a bird guides the spirit to its desired destination.

The bird did not move as Kunty's father approached the edge of the platform. He stared straight into the hawk's eyes. Profound sadness overcame him. He used the *krama* from his neck to wipe his tears, chanting Buddhist precepts to himself. When he had dried his eyes, he looked up. The hawk hadn't moved.

"Please, drink some water," he said. The hawk shifted its footing on the top of the pole, and then Kunty's father added, too softly for his wife to hear, "Be careful, or you might fall off."

The bird continued to watch him. He turned away, looking down at the wooden planks. Through the spaces between the boards, he could see the current of the river flowing toward the Great Lake of Tonle Sap.

Strangler Fig Trees, East Entrance,
Preah Khan, Angkor Thom, 2002
Photograph by Richard Murai

Words from the Fire:
Three Cambodian Women Writers

■ **Pal Vannariraks**

Pal Vannariraks is a well-known writer of social and sentimental novels in Cambodia. Two of her books, *The New Horizon of Hope* and *The Waning Moon Has Already Passed,* won first and second prizes in the Seventh of January literary competition in 1989. Her novel *Unforgettable* won a Raj Sihanouk prize in 1995. With the assistance of translator Cheam Kosal, the following interview was conducted in December 2002 at her home in Phnom Penh.

SM   In the 1980s, you got your start by hand writing novels and selling them to rental shops. Can you talk about that?

PV   At the time, we didn't have publishers. There were no typewriters, no computers. We wrote in hundred-page notebooks. A novel was two or three of these, bound together. From about 1984 to 1985, I wrote thirty to forty stories like this. We wrote by hand and sold the books to shops that made copies and rented them out. Mao Somnang wrote a lot of these books too.

  At that time, most of the writing had to be about socialism. These kinds of stories—ordinary stories or love stories—were not about socialism, so the government would confiscate the books. In those days, we had to write in secret, so we never used our real names. One writer always used the pen name Rabbit: that was Mao Somnang.

SM   Are these novels still popular?

PV   No, not now. People don't read these kinds of stories so much these days. Now they rent videos. There's a lot of video watching, and that has influenced reading. Some writers have had to change from writing novels to writing video scripts to supplement their income.

Another factor that makes the situation bad is that we don't have copyright laws. Anyone can copy our work and sell it without our permission.

SM How do you get your books published?

PV Usually, a book vendor buys the book, makes photocopies, and sells them in the market. There is some support from NGOs [nongovernmental organizations] and the government.

So far, I have written ninety-two novels. But only about ten or eleven have been published.

SM Some of your books have won prizes in contests sponsored by the government or NGOs. How important are these contests to Cambodian writers?

PV It's a good chance for us to get published because we don't have money to publish the books ourselves. Many of the contests give you a topic. For *Unforgettable,* I had to write on "Peace and Reconciliation." For *If the Flower Has Water,* which won third prize in a contest sponsored by Save the Children, the topic was "The Education of Children."

SM How did you become a writer?

PV When I was in grade two in primary school and just starting to learn to read, my father gave me a very difficult book and asked me to read it, then retell the story. He gave me a series of books: the first about friends, the second about enemies, the third about war, and the fourth about peace. In the books were many stories, all educational. These books were for students getting a baccalaureate in general education, so they were very difficult. Also, my grandmother used to buy books for me and ask me to read them to her because she was old and couldn't see well. After a while, I wanted to read everything. Then while I was a student in junior high school, I started to write a book, a love story.

I think the reason I became a writer is because I loved to read. I never had any formal training in writing, but I loved our society and wanted to give back something useful.

SM Which are your favorite novels or authors?

PV It's difficult to say because there are so many. I love the *Tum Teav, Rose of Pailan, The Thief at the Border,* as well as the authors Nou Hak and Keng Vannsak. I loved the books of Soth Polin. I also liked a lot of French stories: *Les Miserables, Madame Bovary…*

SM   What do you think is the writer's role in society?

PV   Through writing, we have to give our knowledge to the reader and the community. We are like the support of our language. When our language is alive, we can nurture our culture. And when the culture is alive, the nation also survives.

   This doesn't mean that I am someone who has the best knowledge of writing or education, but I want to express what I have to give to people.

SM   What is the current situation of Cambodian writers?

PV   Oh, we have many problems. Cambodia is very poor, and not many people can read and write. Those who can don't have much time. And if they have time, they read about the subjects they are studying: medicine, law. Because they need to make a living, people with knowledge and skills do not want to become writers.

   I have a lot of work writing my books, but you can see my house is in very poor condition. Others live in places worse than mine.

SM   What can be done to help Cambodian writers?

PV   First, create an NGO whose purpose is to help writers and work with them individually. Second, I'd like to see the government pay more attention to writers.

   For women writers, it is even more difficult. We have even less time to write because we have to be housewives, take care of our children and husband. This is one reason why I got divorced. My husband wanted to stop me from writing. He burned my books.

SM   How did that happen?

PV   At that time, I wrote too much. Sometimes I didn't have enough time for my family. My sister helped look after the children and the cooking. But my husband was angry; maybe he thought I didn't take care of the household. He collected all my stories and rental books and burned them in front of the house. I didn't dare snatch the books out of the fire. I was afraid he'd become violent. At the time, I had small children. I could hold back my tears when I was hit, cursed, or blamed by my husband, but on the day he burned the books, I cried a lot.

   I knew I loved three things: my father, my books, and my children.

   One week after the burning of the books, I won the Seventh of January competition for 1989. However, even though I had won first prize, my husband still wasn't happy with me and didn't want me to write.

Burning of books happened twice in my life. The first was when I was a child. I read so much that my father thought it would disrupt my studying, so he took my books and burned them. I was about fifteen or sixteen. Later on, I was the best student in the class and received an honor certificate in the Khmer language. When I showed that to my father, he was surprised and changed his mind.

SM With so many difficulties, what keeps you going as a writer?

PV I love this work. I love it. My father said that people are born to die, so while we are living, we have to do something worthwhile. These days, writers are really poor. I don't want to be rich. I think I can find enough food to eat; three meals a day is enough. I think I have to live now to make my life useful for other people.

■ **Mao Somnang**

Mao Somnang's novels and long stories, written in the 1980s under the pen name Rabbit, have made her probably the most famous writer living in Cambodia. She was awarded a Raj Sihanouk prize in 1995 for *The Waves Wash the Shore,* and for many years she wrote for the women's magazine *Kolthida.* She is also a successful and well-known writer for TV dramas. The following interview was conducted in December 2002 in Phnom Penh at the office of the Khmer Writers' Association with the assistance of translator Cheam Kosal.

SM You began writing in the early 1980s, soon after the Pol Pot regime ended. How did you become a writer?

MS I am a writer who didn't have a teacher. When I was young, I loved reading very much, and the old stories remained in my mind. After the Pol Pot regime ended, I was thinking about how to create stories, how to write them. People were eager to read books at that time, very eager. I began to write books, and many people read them and liked them very much. Every five days, I finished a story. I was working very hard. We didn't have televisions, video. There was a very strong desire to read. Now it's different.

SM How did you decide on the pen name Rabbit?

MS The government didn't want anyone to write about anything but socialism, so I had to hide my identity. The rental shop suggested that I choose a pen name to make it easier for readers to find my books. I was thinking that in Khmer stories and folktales, the rabbit is clever, so I decided to use its name.

SM When did you start using your own name?

MS When I started to write video scripts in 1987.

SM What is the situation of Cambodian writers today?

MS Generally speaking, there are not many readers, so writers can't sell their books. As for the older writers, so many died or were killed in the war. Those who remain are very poor and can't make a living by writing.

I am one of the few who can support myself by writing because my work is well known. I started writing in 1981, and so far, I have written more than one hundred novels. From 1981 to 2002, my work was passed around in hand-written form only, except for one book that won a prize in 1995. Not until 2002 was my work published in printed book form.

SM You're very prolific. How many hours do you write a day?

MS Eight hours—sometimes up to fourteen.

SM Every day? No free time?

MS Yes, every day. I write songs too, in addition to video scripts and novels. If I don't work this hard, I can't make a living.

SM You've worked like this for twenty years?

MS Twenty years already.

SM How have you kept going?

MS I love it. I feel this work is very useful. Inside the story is something that teaches about life and society. It educates indirectly, through examples.

SM You are currently the secretary of the Khmer Writers' Association. How does this organization help Cambodian writers?

MS It helps organize contests and conducts training sessions for young writers. The training sessions last about three months. I give one lecture, not about methodology but about my experiences as a writer. I tell young writers that if they want to write a novel, they have to read many novels. If they write about a place, they have to know that place.

Pollie Bith came to writing through her research on AIDS and sexually transmitted diseases in Cambodia. Born in Battambang before the Khmer Rouge period, she lived briefly in Khao-I-Dang refugee camp, on the Thai-Cambodia border. In 1980, she moved with her family to the United States; in 1997, she returned to Cambodia to do doctoral work in medical anthropology. "Caged Bird Will Fly" is her first published story. It is based on her interviews with sex workers and health-care workers dealing with the AIDS epidemic in Cambodia. She has a novel in progress, *Stranger in My Own Skin*. This interview was conducted in Honolulu.

SM   Your story "Caged Bird Will Fly" is about a woman who has AIDS. How big a problem is AIDS in Cambodia?

PB   Well, in 1991 there were three HIV cases and no AIDS cases. Only nine years later, there were 169 HIV cases and 8,712 AIDS cases. AIDS is one of the fastest-growing killers in Cambodia.

I wrote this story because I wanted the main character's voice to be heard. I think she represents an average Cambodian woman who faces poverty and is endangered as a result. I want to express what happened to people like me who were displaced and also the people we left behind in our native country.

Modern-day Cambodia is about losing one's status as a result of one's unfortunate circumstances and spiraling downward. For example, you lose your husband or, as a result of your husband's actions, you lose your status. Say your husband is a migrant sailor or trader. He goes to Thailand to buy products and takes them back to your village to sell. Because he spends a lot of time on the road, he occasionally visits sex workers. One day, he gets himself infected and comes back to the village and infects you. He dies, and you get kicked out of your home.

SM   Your story begins with an image of a pole in a tributary of the Tonle Sap. Was this a conscious tribute to *The Waters of Tonle Sap*, one of Cambodia's early novels?

PB   I don't think I thought about that when I was writing the story. I was thinking that the Tonle Sap is very important to Cambodia: people rely on it in many ways for fishing, transportation. It provides the basis for the livelihood of the average Cambodian. I don't consider city dwellers to be typical Cambodians because over eighty percent of the population lives in rural areas. Most of the people who live and depend on the Tonle Sap are poor. The pole symbolizes stability, and the changing water level the uncertainty of life.

SM   Can you give an example of how symbols and metaphors are used in Cambodian stories?

PB   In the novel *Phka Srabon* [The Wilted Flower], the female character becomes sick after learning that there is no chance for her to marry the man of her choice. The second word of the title, *srabon,* means "to deteriorate very slowly." In the end, she loses her strength and eventually dies.

Flowers often symbolize female characters, though not all flowers symbolize goodness. In fact, some flowers suggest the opposite. Mildly scented flowers, especially those with a sweet scent, symbolize virtuous female characters. Those with a strong scent, especially the kind that gives off a sweet fragrance at night, tend to symbolize women who work at night. This extends to colors also. The color purple symbolizes suffering or sadness. A female character who is fond of purple or named after a purple flower will experience suffering and self-destruction. In the end, she will die while others live.

SM   How has your dual identity affected the writing of stories you want to tell?

PB   I like being Cambodian and American at the same time. It is what makes me me. My world is in between. It's about being human, overcoming the barriers and obstacles one encounters. Someday I hope to be able to express that more, giving voice to people like me: those who are displaced and trapped between identities.

Shared Experience,
Baphuon, Angkor Thom, 2002
Photograph by Richard Murai

Ten Gems on a Thread

For the past ten years, I have been writing plays about Cambodia. In early 2001, I went to Phnom Penh on a playwright's residency grant from the Asian Cultural Council. During the two and a half months I was there, I did two plays with Khmer actors from the National Theatre and conducted research for a new play, *Silence of God,* which would be produced at the Contemporary American Theater Festival.

Hall of Fame

These are the women I place inside my personal hall of fame. Chanthol Oung, the director of the Cambodian Women's Crisis Center, is wearing a well-pressed white blouse that highlights her dark and youthful face as she shows me upstairs to her cool office. As though uttering a mantra, she does not stop to breathe until she is done: "Confidential crisis shelter, legal representation, reintegration, vocational training, community education, monitoring violence, capacity building." She says there are men who will appear in her office, dressed in police or military uniforms, to demand she give their battered wives back. She tells me she says to them calmly, "We will let your wives know you are looking for them." There is a foreigner, she says, who raped young women, paid off the police, bribed the court, and then came to find her, yelling at her through his car window. She couldn't hear what he was saying because she was outside the center, driving away in a closed Jeep. A general in the government owns a brothel where women and girls are locked up. Two women inside the brothel throw letters out the windows, asking for help. She says that the mayor has closed down the brothel, but it is still open.

The second woman in my hall of fame, Kek Galabru, is dressed in a purple, floor-length, iridescent silk dress and a white silk scarf, which she drapes around herself in various ways. She is the founder of LICADHO, the Cambodian League for the Promotion and Defense of Human Rights. When she speaks about the Cambodian prime minister, she looks toward the city of Phnom Penh, as if he is there, hanging in thin air outside the curtained window. I can see him in her gaze. Her face moves from radiance to shadow. Information suggests that he could be involved in kidnapping, theft, bribery, and drugs. The French, who donate money to human-rights programs, don't want to know about this corruption.

I ask her about hope, and she looks at me. "Yes, you must have it," she says.

I meet Vannath Chea, the president of the Center for Social Development, on my birthday. Also gracefully dressed, she serves tea at a round table in her office. She's curious why I want to meet her. She says she is humble before the problem of "reconciliation" in Cambodia: the question of how to move on from the genocide. She bought land for a house. The house is near Tuol Sleng, the Khmer Rouge extermination center, now a genocide museum. As the construction crews were digging the foundation, they found bones of arms. The bones were tied together with electrical cord. She shows me how by putting together her own lower arms. She had the bones burned on her property, and the ashes were placed in a pagoda in Kandal Province. Every day, she prays to the bones at an altar in her house. She hopes that what she accomplishes each day will honor the spirits of those who are under her house. She gets Kleenex tissue for us as we sit together at the round table. Maybe we can go to the pagoda, she says.

She cannot read my plays, she says, because she has no time to read. She glances at the piles of paper on her desk: she doesn't even have time to read the newspaper. When I tell her I have come to Cambodia to do theater, she says that the arts are like women: the first to be degraded in poverty and war.

The fourth woman, Sochua Mu, Cambodia's Minister of Women's Affairs, comes to pick me up in her Jeep. Her driver takes us to an Italian restaurant, where we sit outside. She tells me she must dress the part of the Khmer woman and try to teach the men she works with that women are also precious gems. In Khmer culture, women are cotton and if cotton falls in the mud, it is permanently soiled. A gem, which the man is, never gets soiled. So Sochua says to the men, "Women are precious gems." Sochua has been serious in taking to court a few men who have tarnished precious gems.

Pich Tum Kravel

At the Ministry of Culture, I wait for Pich Tum Kravel and Mao Keng in Kravel's office, which has a prefab quality. Kravel's coat and tie rest on the back of his chair. The office is empty of papers and books. I make a series of calls on my cell phone, one to Kravel. I never once reach Kravel on his cell phone. My call is always answered by a group of women whom I imagine to be sitting in a circle around the cell phone, picking it up, calling out Khmer words to me, to each other, and to Kravel, who is certainly not there. After a while, a woman appears in the office where I am waiting. She's totally mystified to find me. She quickly turns on the air conditioner, returns with tea, and quietly closes the door.

Kravel and Keng arrive. The foremost living playwright in Cambodia, Kravel has taken a government post: Undersecretary of State for the Performing Arts, Fine Arts, and Libraries. An accomplished, erudite, and sophisticated man, he gracefully takes the Khmer translation of my play from me and promises to study it.

When I ask if my project is in place, Keng, the director of the National Theatre, says very simply to Kravel, in Khmer, that the actors are "waiting." Kravel translates in French, *"Les acteurs attendent."* We laugh at the simplicity of what Keng has just said and at his deadpan expression. Kravel is worried that the standard of acting has fallen: there was a time when they had actors who could do Shakespeare and Molière, he says. Before the Pol Pot era, Kravel himself was called the Romeo of Cambodia. He wrote a play based on a famous poem, *Tum Teav;* this was the Khmer *Romeo and Juliet,* and Kravel played Romeo. When I ask him to write down in Khmer the words *I am a writer* because I need to know the phrase for my new play, his handwriting is like that of all French-educated Khmer: beautiful and careful. I remember that when I learned to write French from my grandparents, the notebook had several sets of lines to make sure I got the heights of the letters right. I ask Kravel, as I ask everyone, about Pol Pot. How could it be? It is not a question, he says, that he knows the answer to. Throughout his life, he says, he has had to adapt to political regimes: Sihanouk, Lon Nol, and then the Khmer Rouge. He simply looks at me and says, "I survived as a *cultivateur.*" He says the word *cultivateur* in my native tongue matter-of-factly. *Laborer:* one more disguise in his life.

Later I hear from a Khmer friend that Kravel changed his name after the Pol Pot era. He put Tum, based on Romeo, in the middle of his name; Pich is a friend of Tum's. His chosen last name, Kravel, means "earring." The earring leaves a hole, so you can never forget, Kravel tells me later.

We are by the Mekong River, having dinner with a group of Khmer male academics. Beer girls flock around us, pleading with the host to buy their brand. I am sitting next to Kravel, with whom I have come to talk, and confess my sadness at seeing beautiful Miss Heineken and lovely Miss San Miguel with long, red promlike dresses and sashes. He simply says, "It's for money." Then he picks up his glass and looks at me seriously. "I ordered a Coke," he says. He believes my play will help younger generations remember and understand. It creates a memory, he says, for Khmer people who will see it, enabling them to remember their own experiences. Some young people don't even know about Pol Pot or believe their parents when they talk about the period from 1975 to 1979. It is a strange amnesia—a kind of anti-amnesia, I think to myself, because as much as some people want to erase the memory, it is there, perhaps even stronger because it is being resisted.

Even in his name, Pich Tum Kravel resists. He has become a new person and, as such, survives.

Why Did He Correct My Memory?

On the first day we meet in the red-curtained theater of the French Cultural Center, the actors slip off their shoes at the bottom of the stairs and we sit in a circle on the gray-carpeted stage. We go around the circle, saying our names. My interpreter, a visual artist who graduated from the Royal University of Fine Arts (RUFA), translates for me as I tell the actors that I've been writing about Cambodia for ten years. My plays and oral-history work are passed around the circle, and the actors look at my writing.

Eleven of the actors and actresses are from Mao Keng's National Theatre, the only professional troupe of modern-theater actors in Cambodia, a country in which there are virtually no contemporary plays produced. One actress is from RUFA, which before the war was a prestigious training center for Khmer performing arts but now lacks funds. Joining the project as an actor is Arn Chorn-Pond, a Khmer survivor, artist, and activist who divides his time between the large Cambodian community in Lowell, Massachusetts, and Cambodia. As we sit in the circle, I say to the actors that I have found, through the years, that I like to write what's close to my heart. "If you were going to die tomorrow, what would you write?" I ask. Trying to convey my meaning through gestures as well as words, I say that it would be better if they act out their responses to my question rather than narrate them in the third person.

We break from the circle, and the actors take some time to have lunch and think about their responses. Around two, they come back, holding papers: some are folded into squares, some attached in notebooks, some have words all the way to the very edge, as if to save and not waste precious space. There is a kind of nervous hush. I sit next to my interpreter, Dom Nang Pin, whose mouth is very close to my ear. He feeds me the words in English in a furtive whisper as the first actor, Bunron, runs onstage, ducking, hiding behind a bush, calling, gesturing downward with his hands, urging his friend to hide. He unwraps some food from his *krama*, his scarf, then fearfully scans the area, stuffing his mouth, his being, his life. What is the food? I ask Dom.

Potatoes.

Bunron pounds his chest, gasping for air. His invisible friend tells him he will steal more potatoes that night. They look out at us, the audience. We are now armed guards with scythes, swords, knives, sickles. We sink down in our seats. Bunron tells his friend, "No, don't go tonight. You stole today, they'll kill you this time." The invisible friend beside him says, "What does it matter? To die of starvation or by their blade?" Bunron makes a strong case for him not to go: he asks his friend, "Who will take care of your old mother?"

The friend goes to the field anyway. Bunron watches him. We watch Bunron. After the scene is over, he bows to us and makes his way down the stairs. At the bottom, he puts his shoes back on. I get up from my seat and hug him. In Khmer culture, it is not customary for a woman like me to hug him, but he is gracious and accepts it. I tell him that I love him for what he has done with such beauty and courage. Dom translates. Bunron nods. He responds with the same gesture and expression he always will: one of accepting the inevitable—as if to say, "It had to be done. We had to do this play." But I can see that it has cost him to recreate the story. Later that week, I ask him about it, and he says yes, it can give him a headache and bad dreams, but he wants to do it. He assures me and the others that he wants to do it.

Bunron chooses another National Theatre actor, his friend Kry Onn, to play the friend in the piece he has written. At a press conference for Khmer journalists twenty-seven days later, they perform the piece, "Because of Hunger," as a preview of our performance. The press immediately asks, with a camera pointed at me, "Why the Khmer Rouge? Is this about the tribunal?" "It's a play," I say. "Theater." The actors say the same.

After Bunron and Kry Onn perform, we take questions. One of the journalists in the audience says, "The Khmer Rouge did not have swords, they had bayonets." Later in our circle, Bunron asks, puzzled, "Why did he correct my memory?" Bunron knows what he remembers. I say apologetically, "He probably wants to share his own story." Bunron is an artist, a survivor of a regime that tried to annihilate artists, and now he can tell his story as an actor. The journalist does not seem to have had that opportunity.

Lamentation of a Widow

When she does her piece, it is as if I am watching a silent film, except that Prak Vanny whispers to herself. Later when we stage what she has written, she moves the actors around to match her memory of things; she directs them. She takes Chhouep Tang, the young man she has chosen to play her husband, by the shoulders and moves him to the place onstage where she wants him to be. What she does is recreate her piece—in rehearsals, in run-throughs—each and every time and with the same amount of dignity. It is a short piece, maybe two minutes, but by repeating it, she gives it the impact it clearly has for her: the moments leading up to the last time she saw her husband. She was wrapping rice in banana leaves, and there was a knock on the door; it was a Khmer Rouge officer. She is the oldest in the group, and it is eerie to see handsome Chhouep Tang play her husband; he is as young as her husband would have been at the time. Fitting that she chose him. I learn that she was once a playwright herself.

One actor is unsatisfied when Prak Vanny has finished performing her piece. He asks, "Shouldn't you tell us onstage what happened to your husband?" I am surprised by his question because every movement she makes—from the moment she starts to wrap the rice in the banana leaves to the moment she leaves for work, miming putting the hoe over her shoulder—tells us what happened to her husband. There was never any doubt for most of us who watched Prak Vanny's piece.

Coming Home

After the first day of watching the actors, I go home exhausted and get in bed. On TV is the film *Coming Home,* in Khmer with English subtitles. As I watch, I cry for what happened on this first day and for the actors' bravery. I wait for the scene in which Jon Voight's character makes love to Jane Fonda's, but it has been cut. The movie rolls along, and I can hardly tell where the scene had appeared in the uncut version.

Photographs

Rithy Panh, the French-Khmer filmmaker, has chosen Than Nandoeun (Doeun), one of the National Theatre actors, to direct my short play, *Photographs from S-21,* and has cast the actress Ly as the Young Woman and Roeun Narith as the Young Man. Narith was the lead in one of Rithy's recent films.

Doeun, Narith, and Ly make up their own group and decide to rehearse in the mornings in the French Cultural Center's cinema theater, where we will have our performances. There are tensions surrounding how much they are getting paid, and they ask that I come up with more money for the four performances. The director at the Center agrees to raise the money, and we are able to pay the actors a better fee.

Photographs will be done in tandem with the actor-written pieces, collectively titled *Night Please Go Faster,* after Monika Yin's piece. She has written about the flooding of her squatter hut and a prayer she makes to her missing parents.

In humid sunshine, the Khmer photographer Remissa Mak photographs Ly and Roeun Narith at Tuol Sleng, or S-21, the extermination center. He puts them in the poses of the two victims in my play. In one photograph, there is supposed to be a child's hand reaching up to the Young Woman. I offer my hand for this purpose and lie on the ground as Remissa tells me how to clutch the bottom of Ly's black skirt the way a child would. Doeun, the director, wants to blow up Remissa's photos and use them as the set, explaining that the souls of the images will walk out of their frames as Ly and Narith.

There is almost no barrier for me when I listen to my script being read in Khmer. During rehearsals, I give my notes to Doeun through Dom, my interpreter. To me, the pace seems slow and the tone sometimes monotonous. My comments don't seem to have much effect.

For my play, Doeun has created impressionistic light and sound that surprise and intrigue me. In retrospect, I see that they created a kind of theater that was more poetic and nonlinear than what I was used to in the

U.S. An actor himself, Doeun does the sound for the play by breathing into a microphone in a booth in the back of the theater. During the performances, the theater is quiet, and by the end of the play, it is completely silent except for sniffling. And when the lights come up, no one moves from his seat.

On the Saturday that *Photographs* and *Night* are to open in Phnom Penh, Vannath Chea, the woman whose house was built near Tuol Sleng, takes me to the pagoda where the ashes of the bones are kept. She and the other women in the Jeep tease me that I won't make it back in time for the performance because the Jeep will break down and a lady walking on the side of the road, carrying four packages, a baby on her back, and a bundle balanced on her head, will have to take me in tow as well. Along the way, we see schools named after the prime minister; the one road that is paved leads to his private home. I see a helicopter in the distance, landing at his compound.

Along the road, pork is drying in the sun and a man pulls a cart piled high with cucumbers. There is a lushness to the green along the river. The older women wear skirts and walk barefoot—so fit, so graceful, their hair so naturally swept. People brush the dirt outside their homes with thatch brooms.

In Kandal Province, about an hour from Phnom Penh, the Jeep turns in to the pagoda, and after a few minutes, we find the monk who takes us to the altar where the ashes are kept in a marble urn. We pray to the urn. The monk says that when the bones were cremated, the flames sparked many colors and that the bones are special. He had a dream the night of the cremation that a doctor was giving him a shot. I ask if he thinks the bones had been those of a doctor, and he says yes, he thinks so. He tells us that he takes special care of the urn, making offerings every holy day, Saturday, and that he will not leave the pagoda because he does not want to leave the bones. I make an offering for the ashes in the urn and for the souls of those portrayed in the plays to be performed that night. Every night before their performance, Narith and Ly burn incense and pray to the two nameless victims they are playing.

When Rithy, the filmmaker, read *Photographs*, he asked me if I'd be interested in writing a play about Bophana, a female Tuol Sleng victim about whom he had made a documentary. Bophana was first written about by Elizabeth Becker, who devoted a chapter to her in her definitive book about Cambodia, *When the War Was Over*. I go to the archives at Tuol Sleng and find the dusty old box in which Bophana's confessions are kept. I look at the absurd confessions she was forced to write in careful lettering and at the attentive archivist.

Yes, I say to Rithy, I want to write about Bophana. I discover she is almost a national heroine. So many know her strong face. She fought to her death, defying the Khmer Rouge leaders by writing love letters to her husband, who was also killed at Tuol Sleng. When I meet Elizabeth Becker, she generously offers to let me see her translations of the documents.

A Khmer friend used the word *unnecessary* to describe the Pol Pot era. When he speaks of that time, of its perpetrators, he starts to laugh: it's a kind of helpless snicker, which I interpret to mean he associates Pol Pot with insanity and perhaps shame. He says he has never been to Tuol Sleng. Tourist buses unload at the gate, right in the middle of the city, and tourists flock in. At the entrance are photos of Pol Pot's so-called clique, most of whom have escaped punishment. White flowers that drop from the trees cover the white tombs of victims who were found when Viet Nam invaded in 1979. A man selling tickets near the souvenir shop eats white turnips, which he dips in salt. Beggars wait at the gate for the tourists. When I go there, I ask my moto driver, Saly, to come in with me. He points out the photo of Sin Sisamouth, the famous singer who was killed then. He tells me what a great singer he was and takes me to buy one of Sin's CDs.

Directing and Producing
Before each performance of *Photographs* and *Night,* I pull the stage's red-velvet curtains so that they're the same width on each side. I hang a black sheet over the backstage door that is ajar, and I turn on the air conditioner. I commiserate with the young Khmer man who keeps telling me the French-subtitle machine is broken and there is no one to fix it because it is the weekend. I am delighted when the machine is fixed by someone who happens to be standing nearby. I listen to audiotapes of frogs that sound like ducks; I persuade an actor that he should not play his melodramatic, audiotaped music during another actor's piece. I remember Rithy being sensitive to the actors' melodramatic style when he watched a rehearsal. I get someone to take down a banner welcoming lawyers to a convention being held in the theater during the day and someone else to re-hang the photographs for the set of my play. I make sure the door is open in the back of the theater so that Kry Onn won't be locked out when he runs offstage during Bunron's piece. I try to air out the theater a little so the smell of incense, which lingers after the actors have prayed, won't be so strong. I repeat that we want Khmer music, not Charles Aznavour, before the show starts. I send the stage manager, Pok Dirama, to buy new batteries for Doeun's microphone. I pay Ly for her wig. I smile at Ros Navy's daughter, who plays herself in Ros's piece about the time her daughter became very ill and a traditional Kru Khmer wanted to burn incense and pray rather than take her to the hospital. I pick up the trash in the theater and bathroom. I get the tickets from the French Cultural Center office, I take the money from the audience, I give out programs printed in Khmer, French, and English, and if the program is in English, I give the person a flashlight, enabling him or her to read the translated text in the dark. I try to encourage mothers with babies to take them outside if they start crying.

My favorite thing to do is watch the actors carry in plates of fruit when they arrive for performances two or three hours early, and to see them laugh at me because I am working so hard and seem so busy.

Saly

We arrive at Saly's house at night, driving on his moto through a maze of squatter huts and over planked pathways built above a large sewer system. Most of the huts are open in the front and lit with candles, though occasionally one has electricity and a few have televisions. In the dark, the TV looms larger than life. As Saly parks and honks his horn, I realize that I have no way to know where we are or how we got there. At the doorway, we step over a board that blocks the entrance and keeps the baby from going outside. Saly's one-room house is made of cardboard and planks. As I glance at some pictures of women singers, cut out of magazines and hung on the wall, he says, "We are very poor." My heart is beating fast, and I am trying to smile as I nod. His wife, laughing, shows me their baby. I touch the baby's cheek and he giggles; he looks like Saly, who is in his thirties but looks younger. The baby has a bandage on his navel, and I remember Saly telling me that he was at the hospital recently. Saly's wife has a dazzling smile. In the glow of a kerosene lamp, we sit down on the floor. There is a mosquito coil nearby and some noodles Saly's wife has prepared. Saly quickly shows me an English tape he has been using to learn the language. The baby is enjoying playing with the cassette tape, then Saly takes it away. I thank his wife for letting me have Saly as my driver every day. Saly translates, and she laughs and thanks me. I keep my eyes fixed on her beautiful, glowing face.

When he drives, Saly and I speak English and he asks me questions. He wonders if he can use the word "gentlewoman" the way he uses "gentleman." I think about it, then say people usually don't use the word "gentlewoman," but I don't see why he can't. He says that I am a gentlewoman and that Laura, the woman who introduced us, is also a gentlewoman. Saly tells me in English that sometimes he is "not clever" and that he dreams with his eyes open. At night, he says shaking his head, he dreams and his eyes are open. He wants to talk to me about the Pol Pot era, but his English is not good enough. I assure him that it's normal he dreams with his eyes open; he survived a bad war, and for the same reason, he may not always be able to think cleverly. And anyway, I say, "No one is clever all the time." He thinks about this as he drives.

Laura and I help Saly buy a new house. This one is not above the sewer water of the squatters' village. It's made of wood and thatch and has some running water, electricity, and primitive toilet facilities. It is better, Saly agrees. I see that he has pinned up a poster I gave him of an Angkor art exhibit. He goes to all the rehearsals of my play and works putting up posters, buying water and bread for the actors, and sharing any comments he has about the show. When it rains, he hangs some of the wet posters on the theater seats to dry. Near the end of the rehearsal period, he shows up with three circles on his forehead from cupping: he says his wife has given him a treatment because he hasn't been feeling well. On opening night, we rush to the change shop to get change for the bills I will pay the actors with. He is happy when the shopkeeper charges no fee for giving us change. In the glass case below the woman are bills from many different countries, placed in small stacks and bound with rubber bands.

On the moto going to the theater, Saly says he won't be going to opening night. Since I had invited him long ago, I ask him why, and he says he must go home, that the air conditioning makes him sick. I take a deep breath. I touch his shoulder and say, "Saly, I want you to be there tonight. You should come." He nods and says he will. After the performance, when he sees that all went well and the audience was pleased, he admits he is relieved. As we drive home, he tells me that he wasn't sure if the performance would be good. He was afraid some actors wouldn't be good, he admits, and he didn't know if the audience would like the show. Now, he says, he knows it is good and he is very happy.

The Dump

As the path narrows, Saly and I start to smell smoke, see more trash, a naked person walking in a daze, and some scrawny dogs. He lets me off to walk into the dump on foot. To the horizon in every direction is trash, with smoke from burning waste rising in the haze of dawn. Before they go scavenging through the trash to make money for their families, children line up to get breakfast from a French nongovernmental organization (NGO). A nurse treats a man who has lifted up his pant leg to show her the bloody side of his calf and ankle, lacerated by metal in the dump. A little girl holds a baby and scrutinizes me. Also scrutinizing me are Saly and two other moto drivers, Heng and Kim. They have accompanied Laura and me; Laura runs her own NGO, Global Children. Some kids joke with each other as they wait in line for their food. In the dump itself are older women who have *krama*s wrapped around their heads and search through trash with a pick, just steps behind a bulldozer rotating the trash. The scavengers look for anything they can melt, recycle, collect to get a few pennies. People live in makeshift huts on top of the trash. It's morning time, and a mother is cooking soup for her family; I can see the steam rising from the rice. As if on their way to school, children with backpacks make their way through the dump. They have an air of simple necessity, like the ones I usually notice playing badminton on the side of the road.

Kim drives me away from the dump. He says he thought his life was bad, but seeing this makes it seem better. As we wend our way through clusters of huts, my cell phone rings and we stop so that I can answer it. When I finish talking, I see two young boys running towards me, holding a plastic, pink toy phone and saying into the receiver in English, "Hello? Hello?" They laugh with glee.

Never Again

Shortly after I return to the United States from Cambodia, I am introduced to a Khmer man who has received a human-rights fellowship from Columbia University and works for LICADHO. He and I sit on a couch in the beautiful, plush lobby of Columbia International House. He keeps returning to the Pol Pot era, saying, "But you want to know what happened to me…" The first few times he says it, I kindly reply, "No, that's all right. I don't need to hear…" When he continues to say, "*You* want to know what happened," I finally nod and listen to the story of how he survived Pol Pot. We talk about the fact that the prime minister has the ultimate and only power in the country. And I remember what a Vietnamese artist told me: "Cambodians want peace at any price." I say goodbye to the man, and he gives me his e-mail address. He says he will be starting a program protesting torture. As I walk home, I renew my commitment.

Youk Chhang, the young director of the Documentation Center of Cambodia, says a human soul cannot be destroyed. He is neither scholar nor lawyer, merely a collector of pieces of paper, he says. At the end of all his e-mail messages, he has SEARCHING FOR THE TRUTH! below his name.

Before my trip, my father had sent me a poem by José-Maria de Heredia about travelers who

> Watch in unknown skies, rising from the deep:
> Stars they'd never seen before.

There *are* stars. Precious gems to chart the way. Searching for the truth.

River of a Thousand Lingas,
Kbal Spean, 2002
Photograph by Richard Murai

Ambassador of the Silent World:
An Interview with U Sam Oeur ⎯⎯⎯⎯⎯⎯⎯⎯⎯⎯⎯⎯⎯⎯

U Sam Oeur was born in Svay Rieng Province in 1936. In 1962, he was selected to attend California State University at Los Angeles to study the teaching of industrial arts. From there he went to the University of Iowa Writers' Workshop and received a master-of-fine-arts degree in poetry. He returned to Cambodia and was elected to Parliament, then served in the military until the Khmer Rouge victory in 1975; he survived the Pol Pot regime by feigning illiteracy. In 1992, he returned to the U.S. and in 1996 published a book of poetry, *Sacred Vows,* translated into English with American poet Ken McCullough. The following interview was conducted by telephone and e-mail in September 2003.

SM What inspired you to begin writing poetry, first in Cambodia and now in the United States?

USO The aspiration to be the Ambassador of the Silent World was so profound that I could not sleep without expressing my emotions and feelings of loss, sorrow, pain, and agony on behalf of Nature, the souls slaughtered by the Khmer Rouge, and those who could not express their views for fear of persecution by the Indochinese Communists. I have this special privilege to express the cry of anguish of the Silent World⎯the world which cannot speak for itself—and the plight of my people and country, balanced by an unflagging belief in our imminent return to freedom and stability.

SM What was the role of poetry in Cambodia, before and after the war?

USO The world changes the poetry, and the poetry changes the world. Before the war, life was peaceful, so our poets wrote pastoral poems about contemplation, admiration, adoration, the female form, blossoms...beautiful things. But when the war broke out, the atmosphere changed, so our poetry became about suffering, loss, pain, grief. We couldn't get the peace back, only pain. We wrote about sorrow, about wailing, using desperate vocabulary terms like *o sen sranoh srok Khmer,* which means something like "pity for Cambodia."

SM   Do you think poetry or writing can help in healing?

USO   In one way, when you sing a happy song, people never feel happy, but when you sing a sad song—like separation from a loved one—people smile, people say this sad song is so beautiful. Poetry is the same way. When we write about loss and wailing, we can heal people's hearts—the people who cannot write, cannot express their pain. When they listen to my poems, they shed tears. So many ladies, several times…after they see my opera, *The Krasang Tree,* they say, "Thank you, sir; thank you very much." The performance helps them to remember, to cry, to release the pain they experienced. Then they can heal. They don't worry anymore about expressing because I have expressed on their behalf.

Once I performed a reading at the Minneapolis Center for Victims of Torture, I think in 1998. They invited me there to perform just a short, fifteen-minute reading, so I performed my poem "The Loss of My Twins." After the reading, a female doctor, a professor at University of Minnesota, said, "I thought only medicine can heal the sick. But now I know poetry can also heal the sick people, in a way that heals the emotions, the psychological trauma."

SM   You studied in Iowa from 1966 to 1968 and got your MFA there. What was it like going back to Cambodia in 1968?

USO   I was so ignorant at that time, I didn't understand the world situation. I was a peasant, a farm boy. I wasn't thinking about the war or the future. I only thought about writing. I had a poem in mind—"The Cursed Land," like T.S. Eliot's "The Wasteland." Cambodia is the cursed land. After the ruins of Angkor, the decadence, the decline of the Khmer Empire, the leaders stopped listening to the educated ones and shunned God. So I try to explain in my poetry about the loss of common sense. Each king was so egocentric; each leader thought he was God—higher than God—and he could do anything. But in my view, they acted more like beasts. I tried to write about that. That was my poetry book at that time.

But I still did not understand, even after I left the U.S. In my province, Svay Rieng, I saw the Viet Cong, but I did not pay any attention. I did not ask, What are you doing here? It was like I was dreaming or watching a movie. I could look at it and see it, but I couldn't interact with what was going on around me. My brother was a deputy governor of the province and knew a lot, but I never asked him about it.

SM   How were you chosen to come to the U.S. in 1962?

USO I did not understand that either because at that time I was at the Technical High School, built by the U.S. in Phnom Penh. They had to train about four hundred teachers in every field: industrial arts, general shop, drafting, electricity, woodworking, automobiles, carpentry…everything. So AID recruited us, forty students at first, to come to the U.S. and train in general shop and drafting. Then we'd go back home and teach. At that time, I was so eager to teach.

But when I returned to Cambodia to teach, I got into trouble. They assigned me to teach English. The students kept asking me about democracy and freedom, so the secret police followed me all the time. I was so scared. Then my guardian angel told me he wouldn't allow me to stay in Phnom Penh because the secret police were everywhere and I might get arrested. Sihanouk didn't like people talking about democracy. So my guardian spirit sent me to Koh Kong. Every night I heard in my skull, *Koh Kong, Koh Kong.* I wondered where it was. I didn't know Koh Kong was in Cambodia. One day I walked to the new market and saw a sign in an office window recruiting an engineer to work in Koh Kong. I applied right away and immediately got the job.

We call it *veasna.* Fate. My relatives asked me to work in Chamkar Mon, in Phnom Penh. But my fate and my spirit sent me away from there, floating like the wind.

SM How did you get selected for the MFA program?

USO At that time, Dr. Mary Gray, the director of the Asia Foundation, wanted to recruit two artists: one in poetry, the other in music. She was teaching intensive English in Cambodia and she loved Cambodia very much—like you—working for nothing, no money. At the time, I was at Cal State University at Los Angeles, just writing for fun. I wanted to transfer my credits to philosophy, but the department of industrial arts told me I couldn't because I had already graduated. I did not understand that, so I wrote poems.

For a graphic arts project, I printed nine of my poems. Someone sent them to the Asia Foundation. Dr. Mary Gray read them and came to Cal State University. On that day I saw her walking in front of my class. I just peeked at her for a few minutes and then thought, *Who is that, so beautiful?* In industrial arts, there were no women, no girls. Only boys. So when a girl passed by, we thought, *Wow.*

She came just to look at me, but I did not know. She didn't talk to me.

A month later, she sent an air ticket. The postman came to my door, but at that time postmen wore uniforms and I could not differentiate between the police and the mailman. He knocked past midnight. Who would knock at my door at one in the morning? He said, Here, airfare. Tomorrow morning at eight o'clock you have to go to the airport and fly.

Well, I thought, *What's wrong? What have I done wrong? Why were they arresting me and sending me to prison?* I did not pack anything. Not a thing. I just left what I had. I put on my clothes and asked my friend to pack my books and send them to Phnom Penh. And I went to the airport and then the plane took off. The hostess could not even serve me because from Los Angeles to Iowa my tears came down. Crying, crying. I felt so sad. *Why are they sending me to prison?*

SM So you really didn't know?

USO I didn't know. No one told me. When the plane landed in the middle of the cornfields, I thought, This is not prison. When I got off, a beautiful woman picked me up and took me from the airport to the apartment, on the University of Iowa campus. I'm thinking, *This is not prison.* She just said, Stay here; Dr. Engles is going to bring you a sack of rice. In the apartment there was nothing, no food, nothing. So later on Dr. Engles came and took me to lunch. He didn't explain very much to me.

SM When did they finally tell you?

USO When we went to class. By that time, everybody from every country—India, Singapore, Taiwan, Iran—was there. They were happy, laughing. They knew they were there as poets, so they were enjoying themselves. I did not understand. I wrote poems, but I did not understand. I thought poetry was just writing for fun, not for a certificate for graduate studies.

I had never heard of that. Studying trades like welding, general shop, drafting, architecture, engineering—those were classes. But poetry class, well, was like something made of air; there was no such thing in the world. How could anyone make a living out of poetry?

Poetry in Cambodia: they sing only, like *ayai.* They sing and women answer—question and answer. Or sing with a long guitar, a *chapey dang veng,* like Prach Chhuon. Prach Chhuon is an old blind poet who can record every word instantly. He was a great poet of the day. When I was in Cambodia, we sat side by side, but he didn't know me. He whispered into my ears, all in poems, so beautiful that I'd never neither read or heard. I'd like to return home to listen to him again about prophecy. But I'm cursed. Prach Chhuon is a great poet. But he is illiterate.

These poets don't need a degree. There's a degree for poetry? After graduation, I understood. It took two years to understand.

SM Do you think it was your fate to become a poet?

USO I think so. I resisted being a poet—because a poet's life is dangerous in Cambodia. But I cannot win against fate.

SM You're the first prominent Cambodian poet to write in free verse, and have been called the Walt Whitman of Cambodia. You've also translated Whitman's "Song of Myself" into Khmer. How did that come about?

USO I was writing a composition in Georgetown University in the fall of 1961 [before entering the MFA program], and my teacher wrote on my paper that I was influenced by Walt Whitman and to please write again. I asked myself, *Who is Walt Whitman?* I didn't know. So I tried to translate his work, but it was very hard to translate into Khmer language. When I went back to Cambodia in 1992, I had to translate "Song of Myself" to show that his free verse was considered poetry, so why not mine?

I loved *Leaves of Grass*. Just loved it. I felt I was liberated by Walt Whitman. There are many poets, but few are as simple and at the same time as hard to understand as Walt Whitman. He wrote mostly about nature, and since I was a farm boy and lived in nature, he captured my soul. I felt free to write. I didn't worry about rhyme or monotonous things just to fill up the syllables. I had to introduce free verse into Cambodian society.

SM Can you talk about the traditional forms of Cambodian poetry?

USO There are about fifty, but most people use four or five forms. Some examples are hopping crow, which has four syllables in a line, seven lines in a stanza. The eight-syllable form has eight syllables in a line, and four lines in a stanza. The seven-syllable form is similar, but the rhyme scheme is different. It sounds beautiful, but we don't put anything meaningful in it; we just make the sounds rhyme. It does not express the real thing.

So I use Walt Whitman's free-verse form. I know and understand the richness of our traditional forms—and even employ these forms in some of my poems—and it is my conviction that, given Cambodia's recent history, we must preserve our culture. But at the same time, we must evolve. Culture is not static; art is not static. We cannot express the atrocities of the Pol Pot experience in tight traditional forms; it is just not appropriate. To express those experiences, we must expand our means of expression, to admit new voices, new forms. We must liberate ourselves from the parts of our culture impeding our spiritual evolution, our evolution as members of the human race. What has so far remained inexpressible in our Cambodian experience—the sorrows hidden in the hearts of Cambodian poets—must now be sung by the full choir of voices.

SM Your memoir, *Crossing Three Wildernesses*, is coming out from Coffee House Press. What do you hope people will get from it?

USO I hope the world will understand my writing. I wrote my memoir to explain to the world that the war…that there is a larger war against the dharma. I hope the dharma wins, that evil is defeated by good deeds. During my time, I saw some terrible things. It shook my whole body. I was so scared, I could not speak. Even though people asked, Are you deaf? Are you mute? I always shook my head. There were no words. Just work and work. No talking. No looking at anyone. No looking at the sky, nothing. We could only look at the sky if we were away from the Khmer Rouge.

SM The last line in the last poem of your book *Sacred Vows* is about the relationship between positive and negative: "the positive and negative— every strand is precious/in the web of life."

USO In Cambodia, we have very bitter *sleng* seeds. They are poisonous. But when you use the seed as medicine, you halve or quarter it, and you chew it one piece at a time. The seed can heal malaria. It has quinine. But if you eat the whole thing, it will kill you; the effect is negative, not positive. On the positive side, the wise man helps a lot of people. Professors, doctors, philosophers, mathematicians—that's the positive side. But the negative side—the outlaws—can also be useful if you take care. If we love them, take care of them, then they become educated and that reduces the danger to society. In Cambodia, if the government and society take care of children, orphans, and the like, then something positive can happen.

SM Did you know when you were young that you'd become a poet?

USO I loved to sing on the back of the water buffalo when I was young: call-and-response songs; a song about myself; a love song.
 When we were herding the water buffalo, there was nothing to do, so we'd sing. Just pretend we were geniuses on water buffalo. We felt like giants, but when people looked at us, we were small birds on the water buffalo's back. People hear only the songs, but can't see us. Small as a bird, loud as a giant.

SM So is that where your poetry career started? Did you ever think when you were singing on the back of the water buffalo that you would end up being the first major Cambodian poet in the West?

USO I never thought about it till I talked to you.

SM Do you have hopes for the next generation of Cambodian writers?

USO Oh, yes. They will be born poets and playwrights. It cannot be otherwise. Those born to be killers, they'll be killers. You cannot change them. Very, very hard. Who can you change?

Four Poems _____

ONLY MOTHERS WILL EMBRACE SORROWS

I wade through solitude
to the cottage where we used to
gather to drink rice wine,
enjoying false peace.

I sit under the same palm-leaf roof,
gaze at your chairs
but see no one,
hear only your laughs.

Here, it's like everywhere else—
deserted,
villages of black roofless houses;
I don't see even one dog.

The explosions of mines,
the roaring of heavy artillery
from frontier to frontier, shake every
grain of pollen from the champa flowers.

No places to hide, no skies under which to rest;
and the moaning of children
and the cries of mothers
out of blazing fire across the land,

And your bodies, brothers, shielding us
from the bullets, and your blood
splashing over our Mother, induce my soul
to ever worship jasmine and lotus blossoms.

Apsaras (Celestial Dancers),
Banteay Samre Temple,
Angkor Complex, 2002
Photograph by Richard Murai

WATER BUFFALO COBRA AND THE PRISONER OF WAR

for Gregory Ann Smith

Work, work—hacking at trees, uprooting them, clearing bushes,
transplanting rice, no time to rest.
At noon, alone, as I cleared the canebrake,
a beautiful black cobra

opened his hood before me, displaying his power.
He thought I was his foe.
"He's beautiful, just like in the Indian movies!"
I exclaimed to myself while my knees knocked.

"O cobra! Your flesh and blood are truly
Buddha's flesh and blood.
I am just a prisoner of war,
but I am not your food.

You, cobra, are free,
and if my flesh is truly your blood,
plead my case with the spirits of this swamp
to lead me to Buddham, Dhammam, and Sangham."

The cobra stared at me with loving kindness
then lowered his head.
He slithered into the swamp to the south,
and I went back to my work of surviving.

THE LOSS OF MY TWINS

Deep one night in October '76
when the moon had fully waxed,
it was cold to the bone;
that's when my wife's labor pains began.

I searched for a bed, but that was wishful thinking;
I felt so helpless. Two midwives materialized—
one squatted above her abdomen and pushed,
the other reached up into my wife's womb and ripped the babies out.

What a lowing my wife put up
when she gave birth to the first twin.
"Very pretty, just as I'd wished, but those fiends
choked them and wrapped them in black plastic.

Two pretty girls…
Buddho! I couldn't do a thing to save them!"
murmured my mother.
"Here, Ta!" the midwives handed me the bundles.

Cringing as if I'd entered Hell,
I took the babies in my arms
and carried them to the banks of the Mekong River.
Staring at the moon, I howled:

"O babies, you never had the chance to ripen into life—
only your souls look down at me now.
Dad hasn't seen you alive at all, girls…
forgive me, daughters; I have to leave you here.

Even though I'll bury your bodies here,
may your souls guide me and watch over your mother.
Lead us across this wilderness
and light our way to the Triple Gem."

MAD SCENE

In those days of despair, in 1991,
at dusk, at dawn, we drank rice wine.
Pedicab drivers and I would gather
at our mentor's shack, the rice wine merchant.

After one or two belts, we began to smile at each other,
but inside we bore agonies; we'd been rich but now were poor.
Illiterates were in power; the eyes of the educated were white
    with fear—
they'd lost their jobs and become drunkards.

While still sober, we didn't dare squawk.
But when afternoon came, I sang for the Khmers—
"Americans shall return, return to Cambodia!

And Yuon shall vanish, vanish like red ants at the smell of petroleum,
like red ants at the smell of petroleum."

And "out from the gloomy past"
all Khmers shall be removed from
misery, disdain, and at last we will
stand "where the white gem of our bright star will cast."

I declare that, yes, I'm afraid of you Three:
O Ho Chi Minh! O Len-in! O Grandpa Marx!
You should know that before the illiterate came to power
we never worried about food.

Since you came to liberate us,
there is not even aquatic grass to eat.
Oh, yes, we don't worry about eating
for you say, "no work, no eat."

How can we work
for you trample our human rights,
look down on Khmers as the neo-minority
while the land becomes your minefield.

Now I bow in the four directions,
and I solemnly pronounce:
"I'm really afraid of you THREE!
And I swear I will never dream of you forever, ever!"

First, cackles would burst out everywhere,
then the audience would wink at each other, furtively,
and retreat into the night, one by one.
Yet I crooned on, on the road to freedom.

Translations by Ken McCullough and the author

Entrance, Mid-day,
Bakong Pagoda, Siem Reap, 2002
Photograph by Richard Murai

Crossing the Killing Fields _____

In the temple of Balath, through the dim light of a lamp, I sat in my sickbed looking at other workers who lay in their sickbeds. Some were tossing and turning, for the bedbugs and mosquitoes had been pestering them. Some were moaning painfully, some lay unconscious, and some were dying. It grieved me to see this peaceful temple turned into a makeshift clinic without medicine or proper treatment for patients, but I knew that my children and I would be leaving soon.

Next to me, a teenage girl lay dying in her bed, and her moans were fading with each breath. I walked over to her, sat on the edge of her bed, and prayed for her life. As I whispered the Buddhist last rites into her ear, she breathed her last. I lifted her arms, put her palms together, and rested them on her chest. Then I tore off a small part of my *krama*, covered her face with it, and wept silently. *Young Sister*, I said in my thoughts, *rest in peace. Do you remember that a few days ago I promised to try my best to convey your last words to your mother? Now I don't think that will be possible, for tomorrow my children and I will be taken away. You have just faced death by disease, but can you imagine what it feels like to face death knowing that you will be killed in some horrible way? I am now facing just that. It is better to die as you have: by an act of God. Good-bye, Sister.*

Broken-hearted, I went back to my bed. I pulled a small piece of paper from my pocket and reread it for the hundredth time. My teardrops had smeared the words, but I had no trouble reading them. It was a letter from my husband that had been handed to me secretly six months ago.

To Min,

Sweetheart, I am doing OK. Please take good care of our children for me, and tell them that I miss them terribly.

> Your husband,
> Sophat

My husband's face lingered in my mind. I wondered if he was still alive. It had been seven months since his arrest. Next to me, my children, aged five and three, were sound asleep. With my *krama* in one hand, I shooed the mosquitoes away from them. With pity, I looked at their innocent faces and bent down to kiss them through my tears. *Children, please forgive me,* I thought to myself, *for Mommy can't protect you. I would do anything for your sakes, but it is impossible for me to save our lives. God, why did it have to happen this way?* I lay down next to my kids, put my arms around them, and tried to get some sleep.

When it was near dawn, I raised myself slowly and wiped the tears from my face. Heavy-hearted, I woke my children and watched them wash their faces. I was lost in thought when a voice calling my name startled me. A lady in her early thirties approached. She was a Khmer Rouge collaborator who had been appointed leader of my work group. She told me that an oxcart was waiting for my family in front of the temple.

Before we left, the lady told us she was sending us to live with my husband in Konpong Koar Village, located about twenty miles from the temple. "Go to live with your husband," "Let's move to a better place"—these were ploys by which the Khmer Rouge made their captives and workers go where they wanted. Though the Khmer Rouge never said what they did with their captives, the rumor heard throughout the villages was that the victims were tortured to death. No one ever again saw the victims or heard of their whereabouts. When someone was arrested, his family members and friends would not dare cry or show their sorrow, for they were afraid they themselves would be accused of treachery—the charge the Khmer Rouge made against people they considered their enemies.

Unseen by the Khmer Rouge, I and other workers had accidentally witnessed many of the savage acts they had committed. If they had found out what we had seen, we would have been targeted next. Not daring to speak of those acts to anyone, we swallowed the truth like a bitter, frightening pill.

I looked at the temple for the last time, hung a bag of clothes on my back, held each child's hand in one of mine, and departed feeling light-headed. I felt as though I were leading my beloved children and myself to torture and execution. I could no longer bear the thought of moving toward my own grave and was about to burst out crying when I tripped and injured my foot. Even though I was cut and bleeding, I did not feel much pain. However, my injury gave me an excuse to release the pressure of hiding the truth from my children, so I went ahead and cried like a baby.

When I got to the cart, I saw it was being driven by Phin, a man who had always been friendly to me and my children. Today, however, I noticed that he tried to avoid eye contact with me and did his best to say nothing. Over the course of two hours, I asked him four times to tell me our destination, but I got no answer. Understanding his fear, I gave up. When someone has been captured, no one dares talk to her. Phin must have been afraid that the Khmer Rouge would think he told me something he shouldn't have. Our destination was obviously a secret, but I was afraid I had already figured out where we were going.

For hours we rode in the oxcart. All along the way, my children kept asking questions: "Where are we going? Will Daddy really be there? When will we see Daddy? What is Daddy doing there? I don't want to go to Balath again. Can we stay with Daddy where he is now? Will we have enough food in our new place?" I did not know how to answer them, so I tried to change the subject, but they had no interest at all in what I said. They turned to talk to each other, saying how much they were missing their father and how happy they would be to see him again. I never saw them happier. Surely my terror was written all over my face, but they were too young to realize anything was wrong.

About ten o'clock that morning, we arrived in Chinik, a small village that looked more like a ghost town. On the side of the road was a dilapidated cabin covered with dirt, vines, and trees. Some people had stolen the planks from the cabin, and only the frame and half of the roof were intact. The cabin reminded me of a hut I had seen in Tuol Ampil Bei Daem four months before: inside had been the bodies of a woman and three little children; the woman's head had been cut off and placed on her chest, and the stomachs of two of the children had been slashed open. Black-headed flies covered their bodies. This cabin in Chinik reminded me of that horrible place, the image of which had haunted my memory for months.

The driver stopped the cart next to the cabin and directed us to get off, his voice stern but husky with emotion. We had just gotten off when he drove away as fast as the oxen could go. As soon as we put our feet on the ground, we saw hordes of mice running in and out of the cabin. With my hair standing on end, I pulled my terrified children to my chest to comfort them. Trembling with fear, they wouldn't leave my arms, and they cried their hearts out. It took me a while to calm them down. Children believe that ghosts live in ruined cabins in quiet towns and like to scare, kidnap, and hurt kids.

I sat down and leaned against a big mango tree near a corner of the cabin, one child on each side of my lap. They were whimpering about how frightened they were, how much they wanted to see their father, and how hungry they were. I told them fairy tales, one after the other, until they fell asleep and couldn't ask me any more questions about their father's whereabouts. I couldn't bear to hear their questions, for I had no answers. My lap was wet with their teardrops, and their hair was wet with mine. I ran my fingers through their hair while they slept.

I was lost in thought when two other families and a young woman were dropped off. The first family consisted of a couple in their midthirties and two children about five and three years old. The second family consisted of a mother and four children about eleven, nine, seven, and five years old. The woman who was by herself was about twenty-three, five years younger than I. We all sat on the ground, shaded by mango and tamarind trees. The young woman sat next to my family and me. Though we were all sitting close together, we were quiet and just looked at each other with pained expressions. The children stayed near their mothers as if there was not enough room for everyone. The older ones seemed to know what was going to happen, and they wept and shook like leaves. Their mothers' faces were pale, like dead bodies.

For hours we said nothing to each other, but through our body language, we conveyed how frightened we were. It was about one o'clock in the afternoon when the waking of my children broke the silence. Their questions started again: "Mommy, where is Daddy? What is taking him so long to get here? Where is food?" I put their arms around my neck, took a long, deep breath, and said in a broken, tear-filled voice, "Food is on the way, darlings. Please, be patient." My daughter asked me, "Is Daddy going to bring the food to us?" Before I had a chance to make another excuse, my son turned to his sister and said, "I am sure that Daddy is the one who is bringing food to us." I bit my tongue hard to hold back my tears, and then I got up. I stretched my body and paced back and forth while the sobs of the other families got louder and louder. We had guessed that by sunset we would all be dead.

My innocent children ran to the road to wait for the arrival of their father and the food. They were less scared, for there were now a lot people with us. The young mother who was by herself had been quietly weeping. She raised her head slowly from her knees and asked me how long I had been there. I told her that I had been there long enough. The silence fell again.

About half an hour later, one of my children came back, pointed east, and said, "Mommy, I saw a house there. Maybe Daddy is there. Let's go look." I gazed in the direction they pointed and could barely see a small white house beneath tall trees. I wondered if anybody was living in that isolated place beside the road. My children pulled my hands and begged me to go with them. They were so eager that I agreed. I turned to take a look at the other families. They seemed amazed by my courage. And then off we went.

As we got close to the house, I realized that it was not a house but a brick cottage that had been used as a checkpoint station in the Lon Nol era, before the Khmer Rouge had taken control of Cambodia. Two Khmer Rouge soldiers stood chatting in front of it. When they saw us, they approached. I pulled my children to my chest and fell to the ground. My hands turned cold as ice, but my blood boiled and surged through my body. My children thought that I had tripped and fallen, and they tried to help me get up. At the same time, one of the soldiers grasped my hair, pulled me up, and dragged me along the road. They ordered my children to follow us. My children ran after me and cried, "Please let Mommy walk by herself. She can walk. Mommy, you can walk, can't you?" Before I could answer them, I was in the front yard of the cottage. The soldier let go of my hair and ordered us to go to the side and wait for his next order. Ten more soldiers were inside the cottage. They all came out and glared at us as if we were their worst enemy.

After a little while, one of the soldiers interrogated me. "Why are you here without a pass—against the rules?"

I answered, pointing to the place we had just left, "We were dropped off there in the morning. My leader told me that she was sending me here to meet my husband."

The soldier said, "What is your husband's name?"

"Sophat Or."

The interrogator turned to his comrades, who stood listening to us. They made a signal to each other that I couldn't figure out. He turned back to us and ordered us to stay put, then he left with the other soldiers. Some went back into the cottage; others walked away. My children, who had been hiding behind me the whole time, came out and sat on my lap. Their faces were pale with hunger. We sat down under the banana trees at one corner of the cottage and waited.

A few minutes later, one of the soldiers returned to ask me how many people were in the place I had just left. I counted my fingers and told him that there were nine. I made a mistake, for there were actually ten. He ordered me to cook rice for my family and the others. I almost could not believe what I heard. Greatly relieved, I made a fire in a stove at the side of the cottage. The stove was made of three large pieces of stone set in a triangle, just big enough to support a kettle of rice. I told my children to watch the fire, then I put on my shoulders a yoke with a bucket suspended at each end and left to get water from a pond behind the cottage.

Crossing the rice fields and small orchards, I carried water back and forth, filling up three jars that were kept behind the cottage. The pond was about half a mile away. The path was very slippery because of a light rain the night before. I knew God was giving me the strength to do what I was doing. I put the rice on the fire, and by the time I had filled up the last jar with water, the rice was cooked. My children looked at the rice, their stomachs growling. The soldiers were impressed with my work, as I had hoped they would be. They told us to eat our fill, and we did so thankfully.

Carrying the kettle of rice on my head and a small bowl of salt in one of my hands, I told my children to wait for me. The soldiers had ordered them to stay while I took the rice back to the other families. My children agreed, knowing they could not refuse. Staggering under the weight of the rice, I headed back. My children called after me, "Mommy, please come back soon. Mommy, don't go away too long. I don't want to be here without you." I yelled back, "Mommy will be right back—don't worry! Everything will be OK!" I didn't believe my own words, for it was almost twilight.

I walked back to the other families and offered them the food. At first, they refused to eat, for they believed their time had come to an end and were overcome with grief. I knew what they were thinking, but forced them to eat. I told them, "What good will it do you if you don't eat?" Finally, they tried to eat, and then they looked at me as if to ask what was going to happen to us all. I told them nothing, for I knew nothing. After they finished eating, I took the kettle and hurried back to my beloved children.

I set the kettle next to the stove and looked around for my children. They were nowhere to be seen. I flew into a panic. That was the great shock of my life, second only to the sudden death of my father eleven years before. I ran around, nervous and frightened, wanting to scream, but my tongue was shrinking back into my dry throat. My eyesight blurry, I leaned against the wall of the cottage to keep myself from falling. I then noticed a small window above my head, and without thinking, I stood on tiptoe and peered through it. What a dreadful sight! About ten naked prisoners were bound together by a long, wooden leg cuff. Their skinny bodies were black and blue and covered with wounds. They lifted their hands to me, begging for food. Quickly I stepped back, hitting my foot on a rock of the stove and losing my balance. I was fortunate that I fell away from the fire, which was still burning. Several times I tried to get up, but I was weak in the knees. Finally I was able to stand, and bewildered, I wandered as though sleepwalking.

It was about dusk when I realized that I lay crying at the edge of the pond. I got up slowly and sat leaning against a small *sangkae* tree, my mind numb. I felt an emptiness I had never felt before. Still I couldn't resist crying, so I went ahead and let my tears flow. Suddenly I heard footsteps and saw three soldiers coming to bathe at the pond. Once again I was frightened and shook like a rabbit. The soldiers were surprised to see me weeping there. All three of them asked me at the same time in a normal voice, "Comrade, what's wrong?" I grabbed one of the *sangkae*'s branches and pulled myself up, then stammered, "My children! Where are they?! They are mine!" The soldiers looked at each other, then one of them said, "They were here just a while ago." Another soldier said, "They might have gone over there with Comrade Hoeun." He pointed south to a small orchard in the distance. I was about to run there to look for my children when a scolding voice stopped me: "Just go back to the house! Wait for your children there, and no more tears—I mean it!" I dared not look at the soldiers any longer. Despite thinking that I couldn't care less about my own life, I tottered back to the cottage as ordered.

About halfway there, I saw the cottage window and remembered what I had just seen. Frozen with fear, I hesitated to go on, but I also hesitated to go back, for I could still hear the soldier's order. While I was walking and trying to decide what to do, I began to hallucinate: *I see both of my children in the cottage with the prisoners. I run to the back and try to break the lock of the back door to get in. My children hear me trying to break the lock, and they scream, "Mommy, hurry up!" Finally I am able to make my way in. As soon as they see me, they run into my open arms, hug me, and say, "I don't want to stay in this room. I am scared. Please, let's escape from here. Where is Daddy?"*

While I was lost in thought, a familiar voice startled me. I stopped walking, held my breath, and listened. When I was certain I knew the voice, I burst out laughing and shed tears of happiness. It was the voice of my beloved children. Then I remembered the order of the soldier who had forbidden me to cry. I hurried to dry my tears, and I opened my arms wide to receive my children, who joyfully stumbled into them. They competed to feed me the mango they had gotten from the orchard and put the pieces in my mouth, saying, "Mommy, mine is sweeter—eat it! It is delicious. We haven't had it for a long time." Cheerfully, we ate, teased, and chitchatted. My children strove to tell me about their trip to the orchard with Comrade Hoeun. I was not paying much attention to their chatter or the mango because I was listening closely to their sweet voices and watching their gestures, feeling a deep gratitude to God, who had given me such wonderful gifts of life.

Lightning, Banteay Kdei Temple,
Angkor Complex, 2002
Photograph by Richard Murai

To Rule the Universe

In the beginning, the gods and goddesses held an election to determine who would be best suited to rule the universe. The first candidate was Agnidevaputra, the God of Fire. "I am the strongest," he said, "so I should rule. Witness my power." Then, as he began to chant in a loud voice, a huge fire rose up from the center of the universe and began to burn everywhere. The other gods and goddesses trembled with fear, and they all raised their hands to elect Agnidevaputra. All the deities, that is, except Valahakedeputra, the God of Water.

Valahakedeputra said, "I can control fire." And immediately, he created a huge deluge to extinguish the fire. As the floodwaters rose higher and higher, all the deities raised their hands to vote for him, except Saradadevi, the Goddess of Art and Wisdom.

Saradadevi said, "Dear friends, fire and water can frighten and kill people, but I give birth to beauty. When I begin to dance, you will relax and completely forget about fire and water." Saradadevi then danced and sang, and all the gods and goddesses became entranced. Instead of drinking water through their mouths, they began pouring wine into their ears, eyes, and noses. Awed by Saradadevi's power, all the deities raised their hands, except Gandharva, the God of Celestial Music.

Gandharva said, "Woman can overcome man, but man can also overcome woman." Then he began to play his heavenly guitar and sing, and all the deities swooned as the music flowed through the hall. As if in a stupor, they all raised their hands, except Santidevaputra, the God of Peace, Mindfulness, and Clear Comprehension.

Santidevaputra said, "I am the God of Peace. I always practice mindfulness and clear comprehension. Whether you vote for me or not, I rule myself. To rule the universe, you must first rule yourself. To rule yourself, you must be able to rule your own mind. To rule your mind, you must practice mindfulness and clear comprehension."

All of the gods and goddesses recognized Santidevaputra's strength and elected him unanimously. They understood that peace is the strongest force in the world.

Interior, Wat Bo,
Siem Reap, 2002
Photograph by Richard Murai

About the Contributors

Pollie Bith was born in the province of Battambang during the Pol Pot era and moved to the United States in 1980. She lives and works in Honolulu.

Nick Bozanic lives in Honolulu with his wife and two sons. His most recent book is *This Once: Poems 1976–1996;* selections from his work-in-progress, *Devotion,* are forthcoming in an anthology celebrating the thirtieth anniversary of Anhinga Press.

David Chandler was a U.S. foreign service officer in Cambodia in the early 1960s, then took up an academic career. From 1972 to 1997, he taught history at Monash University in Melbourne, Australia. His books include *A History of Cambodia, Brother Number One: A Political Biography of Pol Pot,* and *Voices from S-21: Terror and History in Pol Pot's Secret Prison.* His books of translation include *Favorite Stories from Cambodia.* He lives in Melbourne.

Chuth Khay was born in 1940 in Koh Somrong, an island on the Mekong about one hundred kilometers north of the capital. The youngest son, he was the only one in a family with ten children to attend a Western school. He pursued primary and secondary studies in Kompong Cham. While working as a teacher of French, he attended classes at the University of Phnom Penh, and in 1968, he received his law degree. Opposed to the monarchy, he became a legal advisor to the ministry of defense after Sihanouk's removal from power in 1970. From 1973 to 1974, he served as interim dean of the law school. In 1973, he published two successful collections of short stories: *Ghouls, Ghosts, and Other Infernal Creatures* and *Widow of Five Husbands.* He also wrote for Soth Polin's newspaper, *Nokor Thom,* and published his books and translations through its publishing house. Forced into the country-side by the Khmer Rouge, he miraculously escaped death. Granted refuge in France in 1980 and French citizenship, he took the name Chuth Chance, for receiving a second chance in life. He worked for several years as a taxi driver, and is now retired and lives near Paris. He has never returned to Cambodia.

Jeremy Colvin recently moved to Hawai'i from England, where he received a graduate degree from Oxford University. A researcher and editor, he lives with his wife in Honolulu.

Catherine Filloux is the author of numerous plays, the holder of various distinctions—including Fulbright senior specialist and James Thurber playwright-in-residence—and the recipient of new-play commissions from Contemporary American

Theater and Theatreworks/USA. From the Asian Cultural Council, she received an artist's residency fellowship, which allowed her to go to Cambodia. Her essay in this issue of *Mānoa* first appeared in the winter 2002 issue of *@and...New Dramatists Publication.*

Marie-Christine Garneau is an associate professor of French language and literature at the University of Hawai'i at Mānoa.

Theo Garneau has a master's degree in French literature from the University of Hawai'i at Mānoa and is a master's-degree candidate in English.

Maha Ghosananda was elected Somteja (Supreme Patriarch) of Cambodian Buddhism in 1988 and has been nominated four times for the Nobel Peace Prize. He is also a scholar and translator of fifteen languages.

Hak Chhay Hok was born in 1944 in the province of Battambang. Between 1965 and 1975, he wrote thirty novels, collaborated with a number of journals, and occasionally worked for the cinema. His best-known works include *O Smoke of Death, Drifting with Karma, The Lightning of the Magic Sword, In the Shadow of Angkor,* and *Oh! Sorry, Dad!* The story in this issue of *Mānoa* is from the last book; in this piece, he adapted the structure of *ayai*, a traditional Khmer verse form, to prose. A few months after the fall of Phnom Penh, he published *Little Manual for the Dissipation of Misery.* He was disappeared by the Khmer Rouge.

Alex Hinton is the author of three scholarly books on genocide: *Annihilating Difference: The Anthropology of Genocide, Genocide: An Anthropological Reader,* and *Why Did They Kill? Cambodia in the Shadow of Genocide.* His essays on genocide have appeared in such journals as *Anthropology Today, American Anthropologist, Journal of Asian Studies,* and *Ethos.*

Daniela Hurezanu is a lecturer in French at Arizona State University and a specialist in translation. She has published several translations, most recently *Phrase,* a collection of poetry by Philippe Lacoue-Labarthe, and a book of literary criticism, *Maurice Blanchot et la fin du mythe.*

Keir Saramak was born shortly after Cambodia reclaimed its sovereignty from France. She left Phnom Penh in 1973, the year she finished high school. Since then, she has studied, worked, and lived in English-speaking societies. She resides in Toronto, Canada.

Stephen Kessler is a well-known translator of Spanish and Latin American writers. His latest book is a translation of Luis Cernuda's *Written in Water: The Collected Prose Poems.* He has also published six books of original poetry, including *After Modigliani* (2000). He lives in Northern California, where he is an editor for *The Redwood Coast Review.*

Khun Srun was born in 1945 in the province of Takeo. When he was eight, his father died, and he and his siblings were raised by his mother. A brilliant student, he studied Khmer literature and psychology at the university in Phnom Penh, becoming widely read in the sciences, mathematics, and European literature.

Amid the turmoil of the 1960s, he worked as a professor of mathematics and a journalist while writing novels and poetry. In less than four years, he published three collections of poems, short tales, and philosophical anecdotes; two collections of autobiographical short stories, *The Last Residence* and *The Accused;* and a final volume of poems, *For a Woman*. He was imprisoned twice by the right-wing Lon Nol government for refusing to collaborate, but refused to align himself with the extreme left. After 1973, he joined the revolution; but in 1978, he and his wife were assassinated by the Khmer Rouge. "The Accused," in this issue of *Mānoa,* was influenced by both existentialism and Cambodian Buddhism; it was written in 1971, after his first imprisonment by the Lon Nol regime.

Kong Bunchhoeun was born in 1939 in the province of Battambang and grew up during the French Occupation, the Japanese Occupation, and the fratricidal struggles following independence. "In my crib, my lullabies were the sounds of bullets and the cries of suffering families," he wrote much later. After the death of his mother in 1957, he moved to Phnom Penh and published *The River of Death,* the first of many books in a long career as a popular novelist. His works often combine the romantic and the supernatural, and his satiric novels attack corruption, exploitation of the weak, and social injustice. In 1963 he was imprisoned for six months for writing a novel criticizing a high official in the royal government. During the Pol Pot regime, he escaped execution thanks to a Khmer Rouge cadre who had read his novels and testified that he was a writer with a "profound sense of social justice." After the Khmer Rouge regime ended, he returned to Phnom Penh in 1981 and worked in the Ministry of Culture. In 2000, however, he was forced to flee the country as a result of publishing *The Destiny of Marina,* a diatribe against what he called "the culture of arrogance" in high places. With the exception of the period when the Khmer Rouge regime was in power, he has never ceased writing and publishing. His body of work includes plays, poetry collections, a hundred novels, and more than two hundred songs, of which a great number were composed in honor of the celebrated poet-singer Sin Sisamouth. His story in this issue of *Mānoa* is an excerpt from *Tomb of Satya,* written after he witnessed the murder by the Khmer Rouge of a former member of Cambodia's Royal Ballet. The main character, a Cambodian American named Veasna (Khmer for "destiny"), falls under the spell of the beautiful Satya (Khmer for "truth"), who is the supernatural synthesis of three murdered women.

Lavonne Leong received her doctorate from Oxford University in 2002. She is an award-winning writer and editor living in Honolulu.

Christophe Macquet is a translator, teacher, and researcher. He was born in 1968 in Boulogne-sur-Mer, France. After receiving a master's degree in literature, he taught French for two years in the Philippines. Since 1994, he has taught literature and translation at the Royal University of Phnom Penh, where he is the head of the French Translation Program. He has translated numerous books from French to Khmer, including Herge's *Le lotus bleu,* St-Exupery's *Le petit prince,* and Maupassant's *Le Horla.* From Khmer to French, he has translated a Bassac opera, poems by Kram Ngoy, and fiction by Khun Srun, Kong Bunchhoeun, Soth Polin, and others. He has also published numerous articles on Khmer culture and language. In 2003, he published, in the French literary review *Europe*, a portfolio of Cambodian writing.

John Marston has been involved in research related to Cambodia since 1982; from 1992 to 1993, he worked for the United Nations Transitional Authority in Cambodia. After completing a doctorate in anthropology, he began teaching at the Center for Asian and African Studies of El Colegio de México in Mexico City. He is the coeditor of *History, Buddhism, and New Religious Movements in Cambodia.*

Sharon May researched the Khmer Rouge for the Columbia University Center for the Study of Human Rights. Her stories and photographs have appeared in previous issues of *Mānoa*, as well as *International Quarterly, Alaska Quarterly Review, Other Voices,* and the books *Seeking Shelter: Cambodians in Thailand* and *The Saving Rain.* She is completing a collection of short stories.

Ken McCullough has received numerous awards for his poetry, including a National Endowment for the Arts fellowship and grants from the Witter Bynner Foundation for Poetry, the Iowa Arts Council, and the Jerome Foundation. With the poet, he translated *Sacred Vows,* a bilingual edition of U Sam Oeur's poetry published in 1998. McCullough lives in Winona, Minnesota, with his wife and son.

Richard Murai was born, raised, and educated in the San Francisco Bay Area and now teaches creative photography in the Central Valley of Northern California. His fascination with sacred sites of the world has taken him to India, Peru, Turkey, Egypt, Russia, Asia, and Western Europe. The photographs in this issue of *Mānoa* are selections from a continuing project on the ruins of Angkor Wat. He plans to produce a book of his Khmer and Angkor images.

Min Keth Or resides in Falls Church, Virginia, and is a language instructor in the U.S. State Department's Foreign Service Institute. She was born in Cambodia, where she and her husband were schoolteachers until the Khmer Rouge takeover. They escaped to Thailand with their two children in 1979 and immigrated to the United States in 1981. She thanks David Gustafson for his help in preparing the essay published in this issue of *Mānoa*.

Rithy Panh is a highly acclaimed Cambodian filmmaker living in France. His films include *Site 11, Rice People, Bophana: A Cambodian Tragedy, One Evening after the War, Land of Wandering Souls, Que la barque se brise que la jonque s'entrouve,* and *s-21, the Khmer Rouge Death Machine.*

praCh was born in the farmlands of Cambodia but raised in America. He received international attention with his first album, *Dalama…the end'n' is just the beginnin',* and his follow-up album, *Dalama…the lost chapter.* He is the CEO of Mujestic Records and in 2002 became the youngest coordinator of the Cambodian New Year. He lives in Long Beach, California.

Putsata Reang is a reporter for the *Mercury News.* Her book, *Deadly Secrets: From High School to High Crime—The True Story of Two Teen Killers,* was published by Avon Books in 2001.

Darina Siv was born in 1957 in Pursat Province, the daughter of a schoolteacher. When she was twelve, a story she had written was chosen for broadcast on Cambodian radio. During the Khmer Rouge regime, she worked on youth agricultural teams. Soon after the regime ended, she and her remaining family members fled as refugees and were resettled in the United States in 1981. Her story in this issue of *Mānoa* was written the same year. Her Khmer-language novel was published in 1991; her English-language autobiography, *Never Come Back: A Cambodian Woman's Journey,* appeared in 2000. In 1999, she became the director of the United Cambodian Association of Minnesota. She died of cancer in 2001.

Soth Polin was born in 1943 in Kompong Cham Province to a middle-class, intellectual family that spoke French and Khmer. He wrote numerous novels, including *A Meaningless Life,* and founded the newspaper and publishing house of Nokor Thom. In 1974, he left Cambodia and took refuge in France, where he continued to write. He later reestablished himself and his two sons on the U.S. West Coast, where he now resides.

Jean Toyama is the interim associate dean of the College of Languages, Linguistics, and Literature of the University of Hawai'i at Mānoa. She is also a professor of French.

U Sam Oeur was born in Svay Rieng Province in 1936. In 1968, he received his master-of-fine-arts degree from the Iowa Writers' Workshop. Upon returning to Cambodia, he served in the army. In 1972, he was elected to the National Assembly, and in 1973, he was appointed secretary general of the Khmer League for Freedom. After the fall of the Khmer Rouge regime, he worked in various governmental positions, but he was asked to resign because of his pro-democracy leanings. In 1992, he returned to the United States as a fellow of the International Writing Program at the University of Iowa. He now lives in Dallas with his wife, their son, and his son's family. U's book of poetry, *Sacred Vows,* was translated with Ken McCullough and published by Coffee House Press. His autobiography, *Crossing Three Wildernesses,* was written with McCullough and is forthcoming.

Ranachith Ronnie Yimsut was born in Siem Reap City and came to the United States at the age of fifteen, after having lost almost all his family in a Khmer Rouge massacre in Cambodia. In an effort to help rebuild his homeland, he has returned to Cambodia each year as a volunteer. He has worked with the USAID funded Cambodian American National Development Organization and other nongovernmental organizations in Cambodia. He is a cofounder of the Big Brother, Big Sister program in Cambodia, which supports orphans in the country, and serves as an environmental consultant to the World Monuments Fund on conservation projects at Angkor World Heritage Site in Siem Reap Angkor Province. His work has been published in the book *Children of Cambodia's Killing Fields,* compiled by Dith Pran, and at various internet websites.

Permissions and Acknowledgments _____

■ **PERMISSIONS**

"To Rule the Universe" by Maha Ghosananda from *Step by Step* by Maha Ghosananda, edited by Jane Sharada Mahoney and Philip Edmonds. Berkeley: Parallax Press, 1992. Reprinted by permission of the publisher.

"Communicate, They Say" by Soth Polin, "Love on Cowback" by Hak Chhay Hok, "Ghouls, Ghosts, and Other Infernal Creatures" by Chuth Khay, "A Mysterious Passenger" by Kong Bunchhoeun, and "I Hate the Word and the Letter t [Ta]" and "The Accused" by Khun Srun were originally published in French in *Europe* (Paris), May 2003, in the feature *"Littératures d'Asie du Sud-est"*; translations from Khmer to French by Christophe Macquet. Reprinted by permission.

"Crossing the Killing Fields" © 2004 Min Keth Or. Printed by permission.

Bophana: A Cambodian Tragedy by Rithy Panh, © 1996 by CDP-INA-France3; a coproduction of CDP Productions, France3 Documentary Programs Unite, INA. Executive producers, Center for Audiovisual Production (Cambodia), Claude Guisard and Catherine Dussart, CDP (France). Produced with the support of the French National Center for Cinematography, the Ministry of Foreign Affairs, the Ministry of Culture–International Affairs Department, PROCIREP, and the Center for Cambodian Cinema. English translation printed by permission of CDP Productions.

"The Diabolic Sweetness of Pol Pot" by Soth Polin, from *Le Monde* 18 May 1980. Reprinted by permission of The New York Times Syndicate, Paris.

"Welcome" and "The Letter (Prisoner of War)" by praCh from the CD *Dalama…the end'n' is just the beginnin'* © 1999 Mujestic Records, and "art of faCt" by praCh from the CD *Dalama…the lost chapter* © 2003 Mujestic Records. Printed by permission of the artist.

"Only Mothers Will Embrace Sorrows," "Water Buffalo Cobra and the Prisoner of War," "The Loss of My Twins," and "Mad Scene" by U Sam Oeur from *Sacred Vows* by U Sam Oeur, translated by Ken McCullough and the author. Minneapolis: Coffee House Press, 1998. Reprinted by permission of the publisher.

■ ACKNOWLEDGMENTS

Special thanks to the following individuals for their help: Klairung Amratisha, David Chandler, Cheam Kosal, Youk Chhang, George Chigas, Catherine Dussart, Hongly Khuy, Christophe Macquet, Mao Somnang, Mey Son Sotheary, Tomoko Okada, Bruce Sharp, Soth Polin, Dith Pran, U Sam Oeur, Loung Ung, Bhavia Carol Wagner, and Teri Shaffer Yamada.

We would also like to thank the following organizations for their assistance to the people of Cambodia, and we urge readers to contact and support them:

The Dith Pran Holocaust Awareness Project, Inc., P.O. Box 1616, Woodbridge, NJ 07095, http://www.dithpran.org.

The Documentation Center of Cambodia (DC–Cam), Youk Chhang, Director, P.O. Box 1110, Phnom Penh, Cambodia, http://welcome.to/dccam, http://www.dccam.org.

Center for Khmer Studies, 210 East 86th St., Ste. 204, New York, NY 10028. center@khmerstudies.org.

Association of Khmer Writers Abroad, Association des Écrivains Khmers a l'Étranger, B.P. 78, 95370 Montigny-les-Cormeilles, France, aeke@ifrance.com.

Khmer Writers' Association, Wat Botum, Phnom Penh, Cambodia.

Readings

The Gate by Francois Bizot. New York: Alfred A. Knopf, 2003.

Soul Survivors: Stories of Women and Children in Cambodia by Carol Wagner. Photography by Valentina Du Basky and foreward by Jack Kornfield. Berkeley: Creative Arts Book Company, 2003.

Leaving the House of Ghosts: Cambodian Refugees in the American Midwest by Sarah Streed. Jefferson, NC: McFarland & Company, 2002.

When Broken Glass Floats: Growing Up under the Khmer Rouge by Chanrithy Him. New York: W. W. Norton, 2001.

A Blessing over Ashes: The Remarkable Odyssey of My Unlikely Brother by Adam Fifield. New York: Perennial Books, 2001.

Killing Fields, Living Fields by Don Cormack and Peter Lewis. Grand Rapids, MI: Kregel Publications, 2001.

Heaven Becomes Hell: A Survivor's Story of Life under the Khmer Rouge by Ly Y. Edited by John S. Driscoll. New Haven: Yale University Southeast Asia Studies, 2000.

Never Come Back: A Cambodian Woman's Journey by Darina Siv. St. Paul, MN: The Writer Press, 2000.

First They Killed My Father: A Daughter of Cambodia Remembers by Loung Ung. New York: HarperCollins, 2000.

Stay Alive, My Son by Pin Yathay with John Man. Foreword by David Chandler. Ithaca, NY: Cornell University Press, 2000.

Music through the Dark: A Tale of Survival in Cambodia by Bree Lafreniere. Honolulu: University of Hawai'i Press, 2000.

Children of Cambodia's Killing Fields: Memoirs by Survivors compiled by Dith Pran. New Haven: Yale University Press, 1999.

The Stones Cry Out: A Cambodian Childhood, 1975–1980 by Molyda Szymusiak. Translated by Linda Coverdale. Bloomington: Indiana University Press, 1999.

Dancing in Cambodia, At Large in Burma by Amitav Ghosh. Delhi: Ravi Dayal, 1998.

The Murderous Revolution by Bunhaeng Ung and Stuart Fox-Martin. Bangkok: Orchid Press, 1998.

Sacred Vows: Poetry by U Sam Oeur. Translated from Khmer with Ken Mcullough. Minneapolis: Coffee House Press, 1998.

A Cambodian Prison Portrait: One Year in the Khmer Rouge's s-21 by Vann Nath. Bangkok: White Lotus, 1998.

River of Time by Jon Swain. New York: St. Martin's Press, 1997.

The Traditional Literature of Cambodia by Judith Jacob. Oxford: Oxford University Press, 1996.

Resolute Heart: Selected Writing from Lowell's Cambodian Community. Edited and translated by George Chigas. Lowell, MA: Loom Press, 1994.

Cambodian Folk Stories: From the Gatiloke. Retold by Muriel Paskin Carrison from a translation by Kong Chhean. Boston: Charles E. Tuttle, 1993.

Step by Step by Maha Ghosananda. Berkeley: Parallax Press, 1992.

The Clay Marble by Mingfong Ho. New York: Farrar Straus & Giroux, 1991.

Imagining America: Paul Thai's Journey from the Killing Fields of Cambodia to Freedom in the u.s.a. by Sharon Sloan Fiffer. New York: Paragon House, 1991.

Cambodia's Lament: A Selection of Cambodian Poetry. Edited and translated by George Chigas. Lowell, MA: Loom Press, 1991.

Children of the River by Linda Crew. New York: Bantam Doubleday Dell, 1991.

To Destroy You Is No Loss: The Odyssey of a Cambodian Family by Joan D. Criddle and Thida Butt Mam. New York: Anchor Books, 1989.

Beyond the Horizon: Five Years with the Khmer Rouge by Laurence Picq. New York: St. Martin's Press, 1989.

A Cambodian Odyssey by Haing S. Ngor with Roger Warner. New York: MacMillan, 1987.

Cambodian Witness: The Autobiography of Someth May by Someth May and James Fenton. London: Faber and Faber, 1986.

Swimming to Cambodia by Spalding Gray. New York: Theatre Communications Group, 1985.

The Death and Life of Dith Pran by Sidney Schanberg. New York: Viking Press, 1985.

About Mānoa

In the Shadow of Angkor is a production of *Mānoa: A Pacific Journal of International Writing,* a nonprofit publication of the University of Hawai'i Press. *Mānoa's* mission is to foster understanding among peoples and cultures of Asia, the Pacific, and the Americas; to encourage tolerance and respect by creating transnational communities and conversations; and to make Americans aware that our shared heritage includes significant contributions from peoples whose origins are in Asia and the Pacific.

Mānoa is particularly concerned with issues of free expression, censorship, and human rights, and with the ways expressive writing reflects, advances, and sustains democracy, in America as well as abroad.

Twice a year, *Mānoa* presents outstanding contemporary writing—often in translations commissioned by the journal—from throughout the region. Past volumes have featured new work from such places as the People's Republic of China, Tibet, Nepal, Taiwan, Japan, Korea, Viet Nam, Indonesia, Malaysia, Papua New Guinea, New Zealand, Australia, and the Pacific Islands, as well as Canada, Mexico, and South America. Works in *Mānoa* have been cited for excellence and reprinted in such anthologies as *Best American Short Stories, Best American Poetry, Best American Essays, Prize Stories: The O. Henry Awards,* and the *Pushcart Prize. Mānoa* has also received national awards for its design and editorial excellence.

In addition, *Mānoa* sponsors readings, conferences, exhibitions, and performances; creates curricular materials for secondary schools in order to promote teaching and learning about Asia and the Pacific; and is developing programming for public radio and television.

We welcome your support of *Mānoa's* many initiatives. You may become a *Mānoa* Partner through a tax-deductible gift to the University of Hawai'i Foundation, *Mānoa Journal* Account 121-6060-4, 2444 Dole Street, Honolulu, Hawai'i 96822. Or you may subscribe and receive volumes of *Mānoa* at substantial discounts. Subscriptions to *Mānoa* for individuals in the U.S. and Canada are $22 for one year and $40 for two years. For individuals in other countries, subscriptions are $25 for one year and $45 for two years.

For more information, write to us at *Mānoa Journal,* University of Hawai'i English Department, 1733 Donaghho Street, Honolulu, Hawai'i 96822; e-mail us at mjournal-l@hawaii.edu; or visit us on the Web at http://manoajournal.hawaii.edu.